Kenneth J. Thumber

Praise for BIG WAVE SURFING

"Dr. Thurber's surfing metaphor is a very apt one for today's Information Age economy. There are more honors students in India than total students in the USA and there are more honors students in China than students in India, but we are only 27th world-wide in educational performance. So, where does our future lie? Dr. Thurber's philosophy for dealing with rapid technology change is not just the hope for maintaining our economy and our way of life, it is the only hope."

"We must simply turn the crank of our genius for innovative technology faster than India and China can copy us. Ken Thurber tells us how to do it in this very well-written book. I have known and worked with Ken for nearly 40 years and have seen him apply what he teaches in this fascinating book many, many times. It works, and as a Pragmatist I assert that if it works it is true, and if it is true it must work!"

—Peter C. Patton, Ph.D. Professor of Engineering and Philosophy, Oklahoma Christian University (Formerly) Chief Technology Officer Lawson Software

"A fascinating and thought provoking analogy of big waves and the technology innovation ecosystem. Every technology entrepreneur must know where they are on the wave and then paddle like hell!"

—Pat Dillon (Formerly) Executive Director Minnesota Project Innovation

"Readable! Unique! Practical! I am able to read the book in convenient bits and pieces that fit into my time constrained hectic lifestyle. Ken puts the reader on the face of a technology big wave and insures that they are able to ride the wave by providing insightful and easily understood examples. A must read for everyone interested in the future of our economy and wanting to better understand the dynamics of the technology industry. I wish everyone big waves and long rides!"

—Luana Metil Author of the best-selling book *The Story of Karate: From Buddhism to Bruce Lee*

"As an investment professional for more than 30 years, I have met my share of bright and successful entrepreneurs. However, in the world of technology, I have come across no one with a background as diverse and thorough as Ken Thurber's. Innovation, business development and investing, when it comes to technology, Ken has done it all and then some!"

"When Ken asked me if I would read his book and share my thoughts, my first impulse was, oh no, a technology book that will put me to sleep in minutes! I was sure relieved to find that reading *Big Wave Surfing* was like going to dinner with Ken. In a conversational manner, Ken is able to impart to the reader a lifetime of experience. Whether you dream to create the next must-have technology, or could gain from insights in transitioning that idea to a successful business or, like me, are looking to surf that next big wave as an investor, there is something in *Big Wave Surfing* for you."

—**Stephen Gierl, CFP Gierl Augustine Investment Management, Inc.**

"Ken takes you on the ride of your life and teaches you how to become a successful big wave surfer. He shares his stories on how to recognize disruptions, payoffs and tradeoffs and that every wave will be different depending on the structure and timing of the marketplace. He makes you laugh as he leads you to think strategically."

—**Betsy Lulfs, Executive Director, Minnesota Science and Technology Authority**

"Unconventional, like no other, Smart, beyond anyone's imagination. And, when all of us dreamed of having a 55-57 Chevy, Dr. Thurber was driving an unconventional 1929 Model A in a lovely bright lime green primer with a Dearborn balanced and blueprinted Ford flathead sporting twin Stromberg 97s. This treatise of unconventional and necessary wisdom comes from an exceptional engineer who speaks from his 40 plus years of success in the high tech world of computers. Well written with a dash of humor and unbridled optimism, Big Wave Surfing is a must-read for anyone who is concerned about the economic future of our country."

—**Earl F. Griffith, President, Griffith Environmental Consulting, Inc.**

Big Wave Surfing is definitely a prerequisite before you paddle like crazy to make your next wave. Creating, riding and capitalizing on the big wave can be a daunting adventure, but Ken's insightful approach may just be what it takes to get you out of the beach chair and enjoy the ride of your life. Keep Surfing.

—**Jeff Martin, CEO, Carollo Systems, LLC**

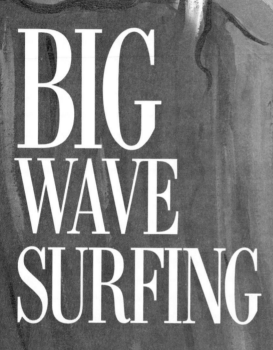

BIG
WAVE
SURFING

**Extreme
Technology
Development,
Management,
Marketing & Investing**

KENNETH J. THURBER Ph.D.

ISBN 10: 1-59298-380-4
ISBN 13: 978-1-59298-380-3

Library of Congress Catalog Number: 2011920744

Printed in the United States of America

First Printing: 2011

15 14 13 12 11 5 4 3 2 1

Cover illustration by Shawn McCann

Cover and interior design by James Monroe Design, LLC.

Beaver's Pond Press, Inc.
7104 Ohms Lane, Suite 101
Edina, MN 55439–2129
(952) 829-8818
www.BeaversPondPress.com

To order, visit www.BeaversPondBooks.com
or call (800) 901-3480. Reseller discounts available.

To my wife

Contents

Preface

Over the years, I have read a lot of books. Many of the books have interesting premises about how to be a better person, be a better salesperson, or be happy in your job.

These books contained interesting and engaging strategies and assumptions. They build and develop principles that let you model and expand on issues that can help you improve yourself and your life. In fact, if you follow their examples, you will usually be a better person. I have no doubt that the copy of *The Power of Positive Thinking* that my mother kept in her house was a great comfort to her. My personal friend Steve (Big Tuna) Lundin's *Fish* has been quite helpful to a number of my relatives and other people in the global workforce, allowing them to approach their jobs with a more positive attitude.

Over the years, I found such books interesting, helpful, amusing, and entertaining. Eventually, I saw my daughter reading these books. What caused me to pause was that these books tended to deal with issues that did not reflect the dynamics that I personally felt in the workplace and in the world.

Many of my favorite news show hosts seemed to get mired in what I felt was a pessimistic one-issue view of the world and what could be done to change it. I had difficulties understanding their views. They seem surprised at goings on in the financial world. They had difficulties explaining how companies work. They had bizarre views of the interrelationship of financial mechanisms. Their view was that the middle class was doomed. I agree that as a class of people, the middle class is under constant financial pressure. But the pressure was due to changes that could be overcome. The people who made buggy whips for a living eventually ended up without jobs due to technology changes. But could they have evolved to a different type of work? Can you make a thirty- to forty-year career plan when the whole world changes at a rapid rate?

This process of technology change is ongoing. There is constant change in the world as well as in our economy. Fortunately, I have always had the luck to work at the bleeding edge of technology and, thus, see progress in a different way. In many ways, I felt that trying to capture the potential of technology was like trying to catch a wave to go surfing.

This book tries to capture that view. I see a world in constant change. It will cause economic dislocation and disruption, and there will be another day. Big waves appear! I am optimistic! Change is good, and it is inevitable! Clearly, tolerance of change biases my view of the world. Many people cannot deal with large amounts of change. I embrace it. Change creates challenges and opportunities.

The purpose of this book is to discuss techniques, attitudes, reasons, and ways to balance extreme optimism and risk in the technology business.

This is a book about technology and innovation. Technology is important to a healthy and prosperous economy. Innovation drives technology. Innovation creates waves of opportunity. Economic development in the United States is driven by technology. Technology creates jobs and wealth. It may also destroy existing processes, infrastructure, jobs, and wealth. Technology and innovation create risks for the people and investors involved in technology development. But technology changes, and its attendant risks create massive amounts of opportunity and the potential for success and wealth. This is a book about controlling and understanding the risks involved in this constantly evolving process.

Today the technology business is driven by small firms that can adapt and maneuver rapidly. These firms create the high-paying, high-tech jobs of today. They also create the new products that drive our economy. Innovation in new technology creates new products and jobs, but it may kill other jobs and products as well as cause entire companies to disappear.

In the 1960s and 1970s, large firms created the jobs and innovation. By the early 1980s, our economy was in a mess, but a set of tax cuts changed the risk–reward ratio and set off a small high-tech industry that brought us unprecedented prosperity. Today, small companies are where high-tech jobs exist. High-tech jobs create the new breed of manufacturing jobs.

In the 1960s and 1970s, the measure of a company was its assets. Today, those measured assets are intellectual property (IP). IP measures innovation. Small, agile firms create IP. Whether it was railroads, cars, computers, or the Internet, economic development equals high tech at any particular time in history. What constitutes high tech at one time is obsolete at another time! Change is a constant. You must adjust. This book will take you through that adventure. In this book, we will zip through many aspects of the high-tech industry, and I hope that you will find it an interesting trip.

Small businesses are the engine of the innovation economy. Many of the Fortune 500 companies that are in the technology business today were launched in a recession or bear market. There are always technology opportunities available, regardless of the state of the economy.

This book may not help you be a better person, but it will certainly let you see a different style of life and attitudes. And it will clearly let you see techniques that can be adapted to give you a more entertaining view of what's happening in the world.

In my experience, it is important that you have a good self-image and self-worth. Part of the issue in achieving that status is to be satisfied in your daily endeavors. You would not want to go to a job every day if it were a burden.

I am not a shrink. I have no formal training on how to tell you how to have a better life, feel more satisfied in your job, or how to look forward to going to your job. All I can tell you is that you should seek tasks in your daily life that are fulfilling. I can show you how various people in the technology business get into position to develop and sell innovative products. In a majority of these cases, developing such products is the way these people achieve satisfaction. In my case, I gained satisfaction by having and working at exciting technology jobs and dealing with the interesting characters, problems, and technologies that come along with such jobs. There is a real thrill in getting a technical breakthrough to work for the first time.

My friend, a Harvard MBA graduate, looked at this book and told me this is not the stuff he was taught in school. My response was that I was not educated on this material through formal schooling. If you want formal business methods and feel-good strategies that involve a lot of analysis, there are a lot of good books to read and schools to attend. But this is not a theoretical book about how to analyze a business. It is a book about getting it done. The ideas in this book have proven effective. However, the typical business professor will have problems with numerous strategies in this book. The strategies are unconventional and extreme, but you should expect that because the book is about dealing on the extreme edges of technology.

This book is a street fighter's guide to technology change and how to manage risk and profit from that change. It is a book about controlling the risk associated with high-technology innovation. It assumes that because of economics, we are going for the brass ring each and every day. We want to win, and that will require us to have a widely varied set of skills. In the small start-up company, there are very few people to lean on and every action (successful or not) has a huge effect.

I have lived the lifestyle described in this book. I worked for and consulted with large companies for a number of years, but more importantly, over the years I have cofounded several successful small companies. I have designed large-scale systems as well as conceived of and sold products of various sorts in the software arena. The products and systems that I worked on when I was with large companies ended up being worth billions of dollars. The products that I helped end-user companies purchase for their systems were worth tens of billions of dollars. In various incarnations of my life, I have been fortunate to be quite successful at a variety of corporate and investment opportunities that I sought out over the years.

This book will have a distinct computer bias. There are a number of reasons for this bias. Computers are my business. My education, experience, and interests lie in the area of computer technology. The computer industry is ripe with a lot of technology, product examples, failed companies, successful companies, and interesting stories and anecdotes. There is nothing unique to the computer industry that does not appear in other technology fields.

In the medical device field, for example, there are devices that are essentially computers classified as medical devices. There are special robots, for example, that now assist in surgery. However, there is at least one difference in the medical field: The devices must undergo more extensive testing than standard computer devices. There is a problem the first time the regulatory agencies see a completely new device: They may not know what to do with the device. Because it's in the medical field, the device will go through a more rigorous testing process and should provide a more robust device that has fewer failures and more reliability. Even simple medical devices may, however, be subject to the rapid adoption of technology and its attendant price cutting. Take, for example, the pricing structures and companies involved in the Lasik eye surgery business as a proxy for a big wave technology in the medical field.

If you start a small company, you stand the chance to be rewarded in several ways. That includes contentment and money. You need to understand your motives and make sure that you move toward your own view of success. Just like surfing a big wave, there is only you out on the face of that giant wave, and the experience is both scary and exhilarating. Having started several small companies, I always try to tell my partners how lonely it will be out on the face of the wave. Typically, they underestimate both the rewards and the fear that they will face. To spot a technology big wave is to get the opportunity to create value for yourself and associates. To ride a technology big wave requires a varied set of skills. Both propositions are enumerated in this book.

Optimism and risk-management strategies are what you will need in a start-up and rapidly growing company. Those strategies are what you will find in this book. Even if you don't decide to ride the big wave, I hope you find this book interesting, insightful, and amusing. But my personal advice is to give it a shot. You will never know if you can succeed unless you try. I recommend that you seek the big waves both as a lifestyle and a vocation.

Acknowledgements

In the adventures prior to developing this book, there were many influences and people that I encountered that are too numerous to mention. But I have appreciated all of the relationships and friends who I have known, studied with, noodled with, competed against, and worked with over the years. If you recognize our adventures in this book, I hope you remember them as fondly as I do. I thank all of you, particularly the people who I competed against, for sharpening my skills. Thanks go to the following people for helping shape the concepts and content of this book: Julie Baker, Noel Schmidt, Gene Proctor, and John Metil. Special thanks go to Paul O'Neill for his invaluable editorial assistance with all aspects of the book, including detailed shaping of chapters 9 through 12.

About This Book

This book is organized into two parts: "Spotting Big Waves" and "Riding Big Waves." Each part consists of several chapters that provide a summary associated with that part. Each of these chapters is broken into sections that contain detailed discussions.

This book contains no introduction and no conclusion. There is no way to introduce technology because even before there was recorded history there has been technology and its resultant change. So it would be presumptuous of me to introduce technology. It is only lately that the rate of change has become fast and furious, causing technology big waves about which I have some knowledge. There is no conclusion because as time goes by, technology will just keep advancing. It's a set of waves we won't get off.

The focus of "Spotting Big Waves" is to introduce you to the idea of technology big waves and examine the relationship between big-wave surfing and being an entrepreneur. The focus of the chapters in this part is to examine the development of big waves and how you may be able to spot them.

The second part of the book, "Riding Big Waves," focuses on lessons and techniques that are useful if you are trying to ride a big wave. In the technology field, there are four major disciplines that are involved with the technology big wave surfer. Usually these functions are performed by different people, but at various stages of a company, they can be performed by one or more persons. In this part, I describe a variety of techniques that have served both my friends and me in the development of technology businesses. These chapters contain strategies and techniques that are highly unconventional and are not the type of reading that the faint of heart will find comforting. Thus, I have labeled them extreme techniques.

Generally, the book's chapters should be read in order. However, the chapters on "Extreme Technology Development," "Extreme Technology Management," "Extreme Technology Marketing," and "Extreme Technology Investing" can be read in any order. There is some redundancy built into these four chapters so that if you are not interested in one of them, you can skip it.

I find it difficult to read books due to my schedule and distractions that occur in my life. I often find myself having to go back and review extensive portions of a book to remember what was said. To make this book easier to read, each section in a chapter is organized as a vignette that is self-contained and easily compartmentalized based upon the section title. If you do put the book down, it is my goal that you will be able to get back to your position in the book with minimal effort.

Surf's up!

PART ONE

Spotting Big Waves

PART ONE: SPOTTING BIG WAVES

In this part, we will talk about the issues of spotting big waves; however, there is no tried-and-true method of spotting a big wave. The wave may take years or decades to form before it crashes on the shore and forms the big waves we are seeking.

There is a key to spotting trends that could form a big wave: disruption!

No matter what, there is always disruption in the fabric of life. If you want to spot a big wave, then you need to look for disruption.

Disruption can take many forms: political, economic, legislative, and technological. What you want to do is to think about the effects of disruption on possible future products and systems. You need to develop unconventional scenarios that look at the possible effects of disruption.

You need not be the person who causes disruption, but you can be the person who uses disruption to your advantage. In the *Minneapolis Star Tribune* on January 5, 2010, the chief executive officer of Loffler, in discussing his technology business integration company with annual sales of about $50 million, stated, "You watch for the next big wave, then you start paddling like crazy."

You can participate in the technology big wave surfing environment in a variety of ways! You can be an entrepreneur, developer of technology, integrator of technology, salesperson, investor in technology stocks, and reporter in the trade press. However, you will need to be on a constant lookout for large-scale disruption to become one of the few big wave surfers. You will need to have the vision and skill to not only spot the disruption, but also be able to capitalize on the effects of the disruption.

Spotting a big wave allows you to begin the creation process for new products or sales opportunities.

In this part, we will create a big wave model and learn to spot big waves.

Chapter 1

Big Wave Surfing Metaphor
How we get to this point–riding big waves– it's really a simple story.

Big Wave Surfing

In describing my experiences over the years to associates, the big wave surfing analogy eventually developed during the early 1980s. New technology does not result in a monolithic growth pattern, but instead comes in waves. The people developing new technology and products take similar risks as big wave surfers as they try to achieve a rapid ascent on the wave of new technology. Big wave surfing is conceptually the same as technology development and marketing because of the risks and rewards involved and the need to have skills unique to deal with a particularly disruptive environment. There are lots of surfers (developers), but there are only a few big wave surfers (superstar product developers).

In the past, big wave surfing has been a uniquely American technology experience. That may be changing. And if it's changing, profound structural changes will occur in American society. A major part of our standard of living is based on having, conceiving, exploiting, and developing the best and most advanced technologies. The idea that Americans will be a manufacturing power house with our labor rates is simply an unrealistic dream. We have evolved into an innovation society. Fortunately, most other countries do not have the economic incentives that are present in our society. That may be the only reason that the technology big wave riders predominantly come from America. The world does not present an equal opportunity to all technologists. In the United States, there is an institutional bias toward education, economics, and risk profiles that causes big wave surfers to appear. Just like you will not find big wave surfers riding the waves in a municipal kiddy pool, you will probably not find big wave surfers developing technologies in third-world countries.

Technology big wave surfers have very opinionated views of good and bad technology and strategies. They are derisive of groups that they view as copycats. They are opinionated about the capabilities of countries to innovate or allow innovation. And they are opinionated about the ability of other people to produce innovative ideas. They are extreme believers in the direction of their chosen technology and view any other person in that technology area as just a hack or copycat.

Many of the stories and concepts included here are stories that are based in the computer-technology arena. Computer technology is just one of the beaches where big waves crash on the shore. The stories translate to other areas of technology, but because my personal experience is in the computer area, I have chosen to illustrate examples from my own personal experience. Discussions with people in other areas have shown me that similar, and sometimes identical, issues apply.

Bright Dawn to the 1960s

In the early 1960s while in high school, I was employed as a janitor at an engineering firm. In addition to cleaning the office space, I observed the various occupations practiced in the firm. The job that I found most interesting was drafting. The firm's draftsmen had incredible tools, large, well-lit tables, and the responsibility of taking the plans and dreams of the engineers and making them into reality. This job had great appeal to me.

In high school, I was at best average. However, I did really well in mechanical drawing (drafting) and felt that I could do well in math. While most of the other students were preparing to go to college, I was considering a career in drafting. Normally, I was very optimistic and easygoing, although at times I could be intense. Many of the other students were high-energy high achievers who were extremely aggressive. Even though I could be very intense, I liked to think that I saved that for times when I needed that little extra bit of intensity. To be hanging around with a bunch of people who tried to operate at such a high level at all times was disconcerting. It seemed a bit disingenuous to think that in early high school years you had a perfect career vision. So there I was, stuck in classes with high achievers. In the end, a large number of these high achievers blossomed into successful career people. It seemed that even a slacker like me might succeed if some of their intellect rubbed off. I was constantly amazed at the success of my former classmates. They were a really smart bunch.

At the end of my senior year, my buddies were going to go to college at Montana State, and with nothing better to do, I signed up. The decision was easy. Montana State had a great engineering department and a lot of courses in math and mechanical drawing.

During this first summer out of high school, I was employed by the Montana State Highway Department. I worked on a survey crew. The highway people tended to be civil engineers who loved building roads. When September came, I enrolled at Montana State University in the electrical engineering (EE) department. EE had a lot of advantages. It required more mathematics and the same amount of mechanical drawing as civil engineering and had the promise of staying out of the elements. Civil engineers had to work outside in all types of conditions, and I felt that being outside all of the time would get old.

Even though I was going to be an EE, I spent the rest of my summers working for the highway department. Though I was pretty average in most subjects, the first summer of working on the highway taught me to become a great reader. The highwaymen read the newspaper at every possible moment. They read it, re-read it, analyzed it, studied the nuance of every sentence, and, in general, tried to make sure they were very up-to-date on what was happening. After a summer of this level of English analysis, I had learned more than I had in high school and was well prepared for college.

I loved college! I had freedom, learning, good friends, and minimal worries.

When I marched off to college, I went with the attitude of success and with an incredible understanding of time management and English. Further, because I had left home to work on the highway, I was already gone from home in the sense that I could go where I wanted and do what I wanted without worrying my parents. The highwaymen had also given me a new outlook on life. Concepts that I viewed as simple were complex to the highwaymen. However, the veracity with which they pursued their occupation was an important lesson for me.

Big Changes

Sometime between the end of my senior year in high school and my sophomore year in college, something changed. It was not just an academic issue or a success issue, but it was something more. Something that began a series of adventures and changes that found me looking for challenges and asking a lot of questions. Something changed that was difficult to measure or describe. Later encounters with people with similar attitudes only reinforced the change and magnified the change until it became a lifestyle.

In 2000, I had the opportunity to have dinner with some of my oldest and dearest friends. Some of these people I had known for so long that I could not remember when we had first met. In particular, one of my friends, a psychiatric professional, and I were discussing the issue of why my attitude was so different from other people we knew. What had changed and why it had occurred were the questions we discussed. He could not explain my attitude, and I found it difficult to explain, but I thought that the issue was pretty simple—passion and optimism with a willingness to take risks. I had a passion for the game. I loved technology. Further, I had an extraordinarily positive attitude to the point where people believed that issues of critical importance were constantly trivialized when dealing with me because of an overwhelmingly positive attitude.

My passion is that I want to play. My passion is that I like to play with winners. I like to win big. My passion is not injured if my team loses. There will always be another game tomorrow, and I will be on the winning team in that game! When playing the game that I know and like, I believe that I am at least as good as any other player. This is not conceit, but overwhelming confidence. If I do my best, my team has as good of a chance as any other team and we'll be in position to win at the end of the game.

The game that I understand is concept development and technology development. I feel confident communicating about technology concepts and benefits, product development, and marketing in the computer field. The closer I get to operating systems and distributed hardware systems, the better I feel. I am in the high-risk product and system development business. I find this an exciting and rewarding area. From my perspective, looking at new technologies and trying to develop a product or system are both risky and rewarding. It is like trying to get up on the big wave to go surfing. Excitement is trying to figure out how to build something that other people need and want. Generally, this involves looking at technology and then trying to conceive what new things can be done. But, more importantly, do other people want to buy the product and how many can we sell? This is like trying to figure out when and where the big waves are going to be breaking and how we can move onto a wave when we are floating in a sea of gurgling, bubbling, rising, and falling water. When do we jump on a technology and try to build a product? Is it a big wave? These are the answers I seek.

I do know that I am going to lose sometimes. Unlike a lot of people, if I am on a losing team I am irritated by the loss, but I am able to instantly put the loss behind me and move to the next challenge. It is not that I do not care that I have lost; it is just that I realize that I will only be on the winning team a certain percentage of the time. Once a proposal has been submitted, I hope to win. I hope that we have given the job our best shot, but I do not get overly concerned whether we win or lose. It is a percentage game from my perspective. My goal is to achieve a large percentage.

I have met and spoken to a number of other people who have had similar viewpoints. This attitude has many incarnations. At a seminar where he was the keynote speaker, I asked Isaac Asimov how he produced such a large volume of written product and how much editing/rework was involved in the process. He told me that when he sat in front of a typewriter and put a piece of paper in the carriage, he knew instantly what was going onto the paper, that it was good, that it needed minimal editing, and that he was done with that chapter/article. He did note that some chapters/stories were better than others, but regardless, he would move on to the next work.

I had a chance encounter with the late Kirby Puckett of the Minnesota Twins at a filling station in the town where we both lived. We chatted about the home-run race between Mark McGuire and Sammy Sosa, and that discussion led into how Kirby felt when he was batting. He said that every time the ball left the pitcher's hand he thought he could hit it. A batting average of .300 is considered a great overall average for major league ball players, which means that they succeed only about 30 percent of the time. Kirby Puckett, with a failure rate approaching 70 percent, was confident and passionate every time the pitcher released the ball. He didn't like to miss, but he didn't spend time worrying because the next pitch was coming his way and he knew that he could hit it.

These are not unusual attitudes. Passion and confidence are key even with a high percentage of failures. This attitude is very prevalent in sports. You see it in the hockey player who is willing to "stick his nose in there" and dig out the puck or the basketball player who wants to take the last shot at the buzzer with the game on the line. In industry, it's the proposal manager who wants to take on the biggest and riskiest product proposal that the firm is developing. The surfer looking for the next big wave takes on one of the riskiest unregulated adventures in modern society. This desire to take risk and to succeed is the key to the game.

This passion and attitude is all over the place. The Marine Corps gunny leading his troops into battle believes he will get them all home safely. A big-time heart surgeon knows he will succeed every time he performs an open-heart surgery. A jet fighter pilot knows success is ensured every time the plane takes off.

At the extreme, this can be a movie-level passion. In the science-fiction classic *Rollerball*, the great Jonathan E could not quit the game because of his passion, and he became bigger than the game. To get rid of Jonathan E, the championship game was played without rules. Clearly, every player but one would be carried off critically injured or dead. Yet, as the anthems are being played, the camera focuses in on the fist of Jonathan E as it begins to beat in time to the music in eager anticipation of the forthcoming game. All of the players and spectators are in awe except Jonathan E, because his passion for the game transcends the risk and consequences. At the end as the only man standing, Jonathan E, in an act of passion and defiance, picks up the ball and scores. That is an attitude that defines passion.

A passion to do what I want and to do it well is what changed my psyche early in college. I love the game. Even though I have lost my fair share, I get up each and every morning ready to play the game. I can afford to lose because I try to capitalize big when I win.

As we will discover later in this book, technology follows a very similar pattern as that of a wave breaking onto the shore. If the stakes are high enough, the people analogy translates into big wave surfers. Big wave surfers have passion and confidence.

Undergraduate School

After the first quarter of college when grades came out, I discovered that I really loved college. Eventually, I became a teacher's assistant in physics. In my junior year, I took twenty-five credits one quarter, but I only got a 3.90 out of 4.0 so I felt bummed out.

Two important things happened to me in the mid-1960s. I went to graduate school, and I met Dr. Robert C. Minnick. I was and am primarily a researcher by nature. I do have the requisite level of book learning, but this is not my forte and at best I find it boring. My goal is to build products out of new technologies.

Dr. Minnick began to direct my future research career. There were a number of nationally recognized faculty members at Montana State University in EE and eventually in computer science. None, however, had the stature of Dr. Minnick, who had studied at Harvard with Howard Aiken, the driving force behind the Harvard Mark series of computers and one of the great pioneers of the computing business. Aiken is credited with development of the all-electronic Mark IV as well as the earlier Mark I, II, and III.

Dr. Minnick also worked at Burroughs with Robert Barton, the chief architect of the Burroughs B5000 series of products and a great influence on a number of products and developers. He conceptualized and developed the first stack architecture computers, a very revolutionary design that used information pushed into a stack structure as opposed to information saved in registers (a flat architecture). Minnick also worked in computer research at Stanford Research Institute. His downfall was mountains. He loved the mountains, and thus, he was at Montana State teaching EE and helping start the computer science/engineering department. Dr. Minnick taught me to surf technology big waves and provided the insight and skills that I eventually used to become a technology big wave surfer.

Dr. Minnick was the prototype of a big wave surfer—a highly professional, well-schooled, experienced scientist who understood the implications of computer technology on products. He was not a manager by training, nor did he have marketing or business development training. Yet he embodied all of those qualities. He also understood that big wave surfers must have a wide variety of experience so that they understand the issues, but the fundamental issue is that technology must leave the lab and move to products so that benefits can flow to its constituency.

Fantastic Experiences and Expectations

A person once said to me that a teacher who has thirty years of experience really may have one year of experience thirty times. Unless teachers seek to modify their courses, they will stagnate. This is true of all professions. So do not let yourself stagnate. Seek challenges. I just took the advice to the extreme. There are a lot of surfers; some seek the big waves. Each wave may look the same, but the waves are different and, in their own way, dangerous. I want to ride the big wave.

A wide variety of experience and the right attitude is a good foundation as you begin to learn the technology art and trade. As I left college in 1969, I had several degrees, but the one that counted was PhDEE. I also had experience as a teaching assistant and a research assistant. I went to Honeywell's research department. In 1973, I went to Univac to work in product development. In 1974, I started as an adjunct faculty member of the computer science department of the University of Minnesota. As 1981 approached, I had completed my initial surf training. I had university and industry research experience, industry product development experience, and university teaching experience.

In 1981, I started my first company and got my introduction to investing, marketing, management, and high-technology engineering. The company specialized in product research, product development, product sales, commercial consulting, and government consulting. Over the years, it also had several engagements in the protection of intellectual property and competitive analysis as well as engagements with venture capitalists and brokerage houses. Currently, my company's focus is on the issue of technology development in the areas of advanced network technology.

When I left Montana State, I had no expectations. There was no grand plan. There was no quest for big riches. The only concepts that I left with were to try to do my best and to learn as much as possible. Along the way, things became different, and it became obvious that the world and the people around me had changed. I began to learn lessons and understand the world through a unique technology perspective. I combined passion, confidence, hard work, and learning as the principles and characteristics that I strived for. I played for the love of the game. Anything that followed was good, but not the primary goal.

In 1969, Minneapolis was the heart of the non-IBM mainframe

business. I remember friends asking me if I thought that it was a good idea to go into the computer business or if it was just a passing fad. Today many of those people use devices such as the iPod to play music. That iPod contains more memory and computing than mainframes did in 1969. Just maybe computers are not a fad.

Today I am still active as a big wave surfer. Eventually, it is risk that stops the big wave surfer from trying to catch the next wave. The surfer may still go to the beach, but the trip is to observe the other surfers, sit on the sand, and listen to the waves. Many of my friends are observers. I am still actively seeking big waves.

Since I started working in the area of computer and system architecture, I have written or led nearly 500 technical proposals (winning more than 200) leading to over $2.5 billion in research, development, and product-derived work. I have consulted on the purchase (by end users) or product introduction (by manufacturers) of more than $10 billion worth of equipment. I was the system architect for the specification of the local area network and distributed processor concepts that resulted in the deployment of a real-time system worth over $7 billion. As time progressed, I saw technology big wave surfing as a metaphor for ways to capitalize on the disruption that technology brings to the product marketplace. Additionally, this thinking led to the creation of extreme ways to develop, manage, market, or invest in the technology product marketplace.

Evolutionary Technology

Technology evolves. It is a wave-rich environment for the surfer because it has waves that are always changing and new concepts that are being developed. As it evolves and changes, opportunities abound. Thus, it is a great place to play the game and surf. The stakes are high. I once asked a broker friend why a certain company was his investment favorite. He explained his technology hypothesis of the company, but the clincher was when he said, "How can you not like this company—it essentially promises to turn shit to gold." That is the ultimate promise of technology, turning a mess into something useful while making a great profit. The closer the product comes to turning shit to gold, the more value added and the higher the financial stakes. The bigger the financial stakes, the bigger the game, the bigger the game, the better the players ... you can see where this is going. The big wave is forming, and the best technology big wave surfers are coming to town. Surf's up, and we need to get started on our adventure!

Chapter Summary

Whether it is an individual, an institution, or a country, we all start with abilities that need to be focused. Over time, we will learn how to perform certain tasks and accept certain risks. Some groups will be more successful than other groups, but you need to learn and understand your own capabilities and tolerance for risk and reward. I favor high-risk activities and focus on the arena of high technology. This book will begin providing a basis for you to understand an extreme perspective on technology big waves and their properties, risks, and rewards.

Chapter 2

Big Wave Surfing Concept

Technology is where the growth is! Technology is a growth industry. As an investor, you need to buy technology because that is where the growth is.

Those statements are not necessarily correct. They may be correct but only in a window of time, also known as a window of opportunity. You do not want to bet your hard-earned money on technology being a growth industry. A given technology has cycles! Do not get caught in the wrong part of the cycle.

In the technology field, you either catch a product cycle or you wait until the next cycle starts. In big wave surfing, you must catch a wave or wait until the next one comes along. In the case of both technology and big wave surfing, it is not every day that a series of cycles or big waves start to hit the shore. In some cases, the waves and technology product cycles may be pretty small and you may not want to try to surf. You will only have a few opportunities for surfing a massive disruption in technology or a set of big waves. When those opportunities happen, you must be alert and nimble to succeed. The issue in big wave surfing is being ready at the beach when the big waves start to hit. The secret in technology big wave surfing is to detect the technology switch from swells to big waves.

A very accurate model of technology is that it evolves and changes. In fact, its development cycle is very similar to a cross-section of waves as they wash up on a beach.

Technology provides growth opportunities but only within the wave structure. Technology is really only a growth industry in the sense of a set of superimposed cyclical developments.

Far out in the ocean there are swells. These swells are similar to concepts that begin to form in a research and product development lab. As the swells reach the shore and the products begin to develop, demand builds and the swells form waves of different sizes. The weather that pushes the swells into shore as well as the beach geography determine the resultant wave size. Weather corresponds to demand creation.

The wave moves into shore as the pressure of consumer demand moves the wave to full height. The wave breaks when other manufacturers enter the market, and the prices disintegrate as the wave crashes onto the shore. Lots of waves crash into the shore with no riders. Similarly lots of technologies that might ignite massive change never reach fruition. Reasons for failure of a technology to launch vary. The reason could be as simple as no one catches the particular wave and the wave becomes obsolete just as another incoming technology takes off. Yet, even as we start down the face of a wave, and catch that new technology, it doesn't mean that it will become a solid product technology. The technology may crash and burn, or it may be lost to another new and innovative technology before it becomes a serious market force.

Technology follows cycles like waves and swells. Different technologies mature at different rates. Like a big wave surfer, you must learn how to surf and develop technologies. You do not start out conceiving new products, just like you do not start your surfing career on sixty-foot waves. You are committed once you launch onto the big wave product cycle and try to turn that technology into a rapidly growing product and company. You cannot turn back; you must ride the wave out, or you will wipe out. With practice, you will learn how to surf big waves.

There is always an opportunity, and you can surf on a lot of beaches. However, there are few legendary surfers in technology and ocean big wave surfing. Two of the best known are Laird Hamilton (big wave surfer) and Bill Gates (technology big wave surfer). Both are legendary figures in their respective disciplines. Yet, there are hundreds of successes in both fields—people who are successful but not superstars. You may have never heard of these other successful people, but there are a lot of them. You do not have to be the superstar to be a great big wave surfer!

Big Wave Structure

The concept of a wave is really simple. **Figure 2-1** (following page) illustrates a big wave and its structure. A wave consists of a large wall of water that is headed to the shore. A number of factors determine the size of the wave, including the underlying beach structure, the prevailing winds, and the size of any storms out in the ocean. However, size is not the only issue associated with a wave structure. A further issue is the size and duration of the churn that forms as the wave breaks into white water and washes onto the shore. Undertow that pulls swimmers back into the ocean is another factor. The structure of the shore or ground underlying the structure of the water is also important. Whether there is sand or coral beneath the wave can have a large effect on the type and duration of the surf as well as the surfer's ability to survive.

Because of such factors, the danger in riding a wave is not

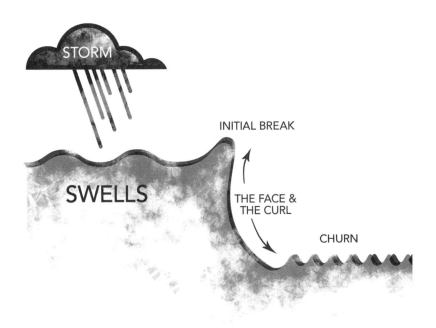

Fig. 2-1: Big Wave Structure

always determined by the height of the wave. Many other factors may come into play, and the tallest wave may not be the most dangerous. The same is true in technology because the tallest wave may be in a benign market. Meanwhile, other large waves may be in a market that's loaded with sharks and coral, and they might be the most dangerous waves to ride. **Figure 2-2** illustrates a technology big wave.

Surging Swells

The fundamental building block of new technology is the work coming out of research and development labs. It is within the lab that ideas are generated and brought to different levels of maturity.

Think of these labs as providing a set of concepts that can be launched at the shore to try to form a wave. The farther out you are, the more you are simply riding up and down the swells with

Fig. 2-2: Technology Big Wave

little direction toward the shore. These swells are, in a research and development sense, ideas that can become the basis of a new product. The farther out the idea, the more work that must be done to launch the swell toward shore. However, a stiff wind from a storm can get a swell moving toward the shore and forming a wave. Consumer demand can have the same effect on a research project as the wind can have on swells. The trick is to establish buzz among early adopters so that the wave begins to push into the shore. As this happens, competition will develop and, if it's meant to, the wave will form. With enough pressure, we form a big wave.

If you are a big wave surfer, you have a serious identity issue to solve. At the very start of the product concept, you may be all by yourself or part of a small team. This is when you are working on figuring out whether a specific swell will turn into a big wave and whether you can generate a big wave, high-growth company from your product concept. At this point, you must have a wide perspective: developer, manager, marketer, and investor. Once you have correctly identified the big wave product and have received some traction on the face of the wave, you can then start to specialize the talents of the team into separate disciplines. When you are trying to spot a big wave, you must do everything. When you ride a big wave, you must get help from a variety of sources. If you have actually spotted a big wave, its rapid growth would overwhelm your singular capacity to ride the wave into a successful product and company.

Emerging Storms

Fundamentally there are swells forming in the ocean at all times. The formation of a storm (technology disruption) causes pressure to push the swells in a specific direction and causes big waves to appear at beaches that have specific structure. In the same way, if a research and development lab can create a disruption and the lab can cause early adopters to use a product and create a buzz, then the new technology gets launched to the shore.

In the ocean, a storm applying pressure to the swells and pushing them in a certain direction causes the big wave. In technology, the disruption creates the buzz of early adopters, which creates the pressure for a technology product big wave.

Big Waves

Swells convert to waves as the shore rises up to the beach and exerts pressure on the swell. A combination of factors can influence the height of the wave. Similarly, trade-offs create product positioning that propels product sales. The comparable technology concept is rapid user adoption, which causes price drops. The faster the price drops, the more users will adopt the product.

When you get a product that quickly moves from early adopters to consumers, you will see a rapid and sustained investment to capture market share and eliminate competition before they can gain a serious foothold in the market. For example, the pocket calculator, cell phone, personal computer, and television markets all developed with a very fast market evolution, and the resultant waves took on steep characteristics as things moved rapidly to a price shootout and rapid product churn.

When the users push (storm) and the rising beach creates a wave is when investors can recognize that a trend may be forming. If a trend looks like it's forming, the investors will tend to jump into the fray.

Initial Break

As the pressure builds and the land rises up out of the earth, the wave will start to crest. This is the wave's initial break. This is when the wave is at or near its peak and investors may flock into the technology, as it may be perceived to be the best investment possible. This is the point that we recognize we can go technology big wave surfing. When investors flock into the technology and the sales growth seems to be going to the moon, the big wave has formed. Investors are looking for this fast-moving technology stock. In fact, many people refer to this investment phenomenon as looking for a hockey stick stock—a stock that has been flat (the blade of the stick) and is now turning up (the handle of the stick). This is the ideal stock pattern, and from an investment perspective, the sharper the rise the better.

When the wave starts dropping quickly and has a very steep slope, the wave is very dangerous because the big wave surfer will not know how fast it will collapse and turn over on the surfer. Danger is here for the investor because the more successful the stock, the more money will flow into the stock and into the business plans and stocks of competitors. Eventually this flow of money and investment will make the product a commodity.

Steep Wave Faces and Curls

The face forms after the initial break when the wave rises up and the surfer can move down the face. As the wave ages and moves to shore, the wave begins to become dangerous and the curl starts to form.

The shakeout begins as the curl forms. In the ocean, the top of the wave will begin to fall over the lower, slower-moving portion of the wave, forming a curl. In the business world, this is the beginning of the end. Eventually, the curl will collapse and the technology will start to be a commodity. Big money begets a large and consolidating industry. As the curl starts to override itself, it is easy to get crushed. This is where you must decide whether to ride into the beach and try not to get crushed or to go back over the top of the wave and into the swells to try to ride another wave. There are different types of surfers who ride big technology waves. The four main examples examined in this book are developers, managers, marketers, and investors.

White Water Churn

White water finally forms as the wave breaks up and moves into shore. This is when the technology starts to be a commodity and only the strong companies with large production runs can survive. This is not an area that I find interesting so I suggest that you find a good textbook on business management practices if you want to know how to run a commodity product company.

Fortunately, back at the beach other waves are forming and probably other beaches are also seeing big waves. Thus, the big wave surfer can always try another beach and another big wave.

The product space has turned into a commodity business on the big wave that has just broken on the last beach.

Big Wave Surf's Up

We have developed a simple model of big wave surfing and technology. The model is important to understand because over the years it's been a successful way to look at technology. I have used and practiced this approach successfully for a number of years and have the battle scars and success to validate the concept. This concept will serve you well in a high-technology street fight and can move you forward quickly, allowing you to skip some classes at the University of Hard Knocks. Big wave surfers are the people who ride big waves. They come in a variety of forms, but generally, the key characteristic is an ability to embrace risk and prosper under extreme circumstances.

Each wave will be unique so you need to understand the basic principles. Because of the potential payoffs, you need to understand the general form of technology innovation. Few people will become true masters of the surf, but a lot of people will ride at least one big wave during their lifetimes.

You are looking for disruption, churn, swells, and storms in the technology arena. If you spot these conditions, you must prepare to sustain your surfing adventure. The big problem will be to spot the wave and, if you spot one, to figure out when it begins to turn to churn.

If you are in the technology industry, you may be in any number of career paths, and we will discuss how to operate in a big wave–oriented environment in the second part of the book.

The chapters that follow discuss disruption, trade-offs, and big wave surfing in general terms. It is the swells of technology storms that emerge from the research and development labs that will cause our big waves.

In the second part of this book, the chapters discuss techniques that you need in your bag of tricks to ride the face of the big wave. These chapters invoke extreme techniques in the performance of these tasks as we are trying to deal with rapidly growing product and company concepts.

As you ride the big wave, either in the ocean or in technology land, the wave will push inexorably to the shore, and eventually, the wave will start to break (technology competition will develop). When the churn of product starts to form, you must find another technology. You can get crushed unless large amounts of money are unleashed as the wave breaks. I do not like the day-to-day grind of running a product company in the high-volume competitive churn. So I try to get back out to surf again. Some of the issues associated with the churn are briefly described in chapter 7.

Embracing change caused by disruption is key to technology big wave surfing!

I cordially invite you to the beach and into the surf. The time has come to catch the big wave. Enjoy the ride and see what thrills are in store as we try to find the biggest waves to ride.

Chapter Summary

This chapter develops and discusses a simple model of a big wave structure. It explains how the analogy of a technology big wave relates to the basic wave structure and sets the concepts that we will explore in the remaining chapters of this book.

Chapter 3

Important Principles for Spotting Big Waves

The wave structure describes a multifaceted, complex, seamless, and continuous process that looks to the observer like a wonderful artistic endeavor. In fact, it is messy. Below, the wave line process is broken apart into principles that can be applied to capabilities required in the technology development business. To spot a big wave, we examine basic principles in three areas: disruption, trade-offs, and the big wave surfing initial break. The details are examined in chapters 4, 5, and 6 respectively.

Swells and storms generate the technology wave input and the product strategies. The basic research in the high-technology industry generates a set of new ideas and principles that allows the technology big wave surfer to survive. The main components of product conception are discussed briefly below.

Principle: Technology Disruption Provides Constant Opportunity

A large economic incentive will spur innovation and cause individuals to try to improve or invent technology. This process is ongoing and leads to disruption of markets and products. The strong and nimble will survive and prosper.

Principle: Technology Trade-Offs Allow Apples to Be Compared to Oranges

No two products or services will be exactly alike. Thus, we must be able to compare and contrast items and technologies that have properties that range in difference from insignificant to important. An apple and an orange can be compared in a number of ways. They are similar because they are both fruits. They differ in a number of ways including texture, growing location, and color.

Principle: Technology Change Creates Multiple Varied Opportunities

The development of a new product or technology will create variations of the product and spin-offs of the technology. If a new category of technology is created, then multiple opportunities can exist over an extended time period. But as time goes by, the competition will heat up as the opportunity is recognized. The development of a big wave initial break will get the product game started. We then figure out how to capitalize on the opportunity.

As an example, we may get our ideas for forthcoming waves by observing attempts to develop extraordinarily complex or unique systems such as those used by the U.S. Space Program. Medical imaging technology and smoke detectors are two results of the space program. The Internet and its spin-offs such as social networks are a direct result of research conducted by the Advanced Research Projects Agency (ARPA) for distributed communication systems.

In these cases, disruption in conventional system design or system performance capabilities led to the development of new technologies. People modified the technologies to fit commercial markets. Completely new sets of products began to be developed based upon these technologies, and society was changed in a variety of ways.

Chapter 4

Technology Disruption

Consider three simple, but very complex, groups: babies, companies, and big waves.

Babies are very similar. They weigh about the same; they don't speak, but they do cry a lot. They have an incessant need for care and feeding. As they grow, environment and education change their capabilities, yet they remain very similar at the DNA level.

Companies trying to catch a technology wave are the same! Rapid company growth is like riding down the face of a big wave—scary and exhilarating. The baby company is much worse than a real baby because its probability of succeeding is very low. The bigger potential for growth, the higher the risk of company failure. At the end of every big wave is a thundering crush of water. Be careful not to get crushed.

Individuals are truly unique in their capabilities and understanding. From their intellectual capacity to their DNA to their fingerprints, people are subtly different, yet very similar. Competing companies are quite similar, but one will end up stronger than the others, and in the corporate arena it is completely legal to kill another (probably weaker) company. In fact, it is encouraged! As similar companies appear on the face of the wave, the face becomes crowded. If the wave is really tall, many surfers head full steam to the same point and all will not survive. Technology big wave surfing is a dangerous extreme sport played by highly similar participants trying to get the best ride without consideration for the remaining surfers. Unless you violate antitrust laws, you can take any market position you want. If you miss the wave, you are out of the game. A single misstep on the wave and you are crushed. When you set out to ride the big wave, you are taking on the forces of nature and cannot step back once you commit.

Disruption creates a lot of opportunity. Many people try to ride the big wave of technology disruption. Most people end up falling into the trap of surfing small waves. You must really try to understand how a technology can disrupt society to find the really big waves. You probably have read or heard about flashy high-tech marketing people. They can be big wave surfers if they are working at the right point in a disruption. The big wave surfer spots a trend and tries to capitalize on its disruption. Surfers just play out the process as it relates to product development and enhancement. Big wave surfers are looking for thrills, challenges, and the big growth that is generated when they find a major disruption in the technology environment. In the technology big wave surfing business, there is serious money at stake based upon individual success.

Every day people evolve. Sometimes they make large leaps. For example, they may learn to program a VCR or TiVo or operate a computer. If they were born working with computers, they are extremely good with them. Otherwise, they may struggle. As a technology emerges, victors start to appear, but the slightest misstep and they can be dispatched. The high-financial stakes cause companies to develop new and innovative technologies. This drive defines products. Research departments try to evolve and grow or develop new leap-frog technologies that start a big wave. Marketing and product positioning create the companies' positions on the wave. Big wave surfers are the key participants in this elusive and most difficult sport.

Few people end up becoming big wave surfers. Surfers come from a wide variety of experience and backgrounds. Some are managers. Some are engineers. Some are financial analysts. But all share a sense of risk excitement and a willingness to take risk. The big wave surfers have brought forth the major inventions of the twentieth and twenty-first centuries. They may not understand what they are involved in, but their success depends upon their ability to evolve as the situation changes. This set of qualities and experiences will be discussed in part II.

Principle: Technology Disruption Provides Constant Opportunity

A large economic incentive will spur innovation and cause individuals to try to improve or invent technology. This process is ongoing and leads to disruption of markets and products. The strong and nimble will survive and prosper.

Big Wave Surfing

There is technology in big wave surfing and in any form of surfing. You have to deal with a lot of issues besides the shape and composition of your board. While trying to catch even bigger waves, people figured out that they could not catch waves unless they had a head start. To solve that problem, Laird Hamilton coinvented tow-in surfing where a watercraft sling shots surfers onto the wave and picks them up at the end of the ride. Big wave surfing purists do not like the idea of tow-in surfing, yet it is practiced almost everywhere big wave surfers gather. Technology surrounds us, and we need to apply its lesson to all of our endeavors.

The area of disruption is highlighted in **Figure 4-1** to illustrate the part that disruption plays in forming a technology big wave. **Figure 4-1** shows that disruption is the first step in the formation of a technology big wave. Forms of disruption vary widely, but the big wave cannot form unless there is a disruption. The bigger the disruption, the better chance that a big wave will form.

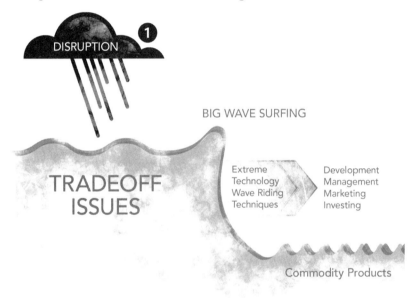

Fig. 4-1: Technology Big Wave Structure—Disruption

In California, there are surfers. On the Hawaiian Islands, there are surfers. And then, there are big wave surfers. On the north shore of Oahu there are a number of beaches that have big waves. My favorite is the Banzai Pipe (the locals call it Pipeline). When I visited the Hawaiian Islands with my family, we would go to the North Shore. I was always amazed at the surfers. Being all alone out in the ocean sitting on a small board, riding the swells, trying to gauge the waves, and then trying to catch a ten- to thirty-foot wave seemed like a very difficult task. Yet when the surfers were on the face of the wave and riding the wave, they seemed to be free from all cares. I'd watch as they placed one hand on the surface of the wave to judge distance. Then, as they worked into the curl, they'd drop down to the bottom of the wave, rocketing out into the froth. If they missed, they would skim along the wave, picking up enough speed to jump back over it and paddle out to start again. To a land lubber from Montana, it seemed like an exciting life.

Mavericks is a big wave surfing beach in Northern California. Mavericks does not have the largest waves in the world, but it is a tricky beach to surf with a lot of danger. On some beaches, waves have been observed as large as seventy feet. Mavericks tends to have smaller, but very dangerous, waves. To understand the dangers of big wave surfing, you need to understand how renowned big wave surfer Mark Foo met a tragic and untimely death on December 23, 1994. He came over from Hawaii to surf the big waves at Mavericks. When he got a late start on an eighteen-foot wave, he wiped out and died.

A big wave does not have to be a giant to be deadly. Any miscalculation, any slight variation of procedures, or any number of factors can cause tragic consequences. The notorious reputation of Mavericks is due primarily to the death of this one renowned big wave surfer. What makes Mavericks so dangerous is a long-sloping ramp on the ocean floor that generates a V-shaped wave that pushes the full energy of the wave across the surface where it collapses the wave into a small, centralized area. Thus, almost any wave becomes a powerful and deadly force to both the experienced and inexperienced riders.

On Maui, I decided to take up surfing. Not having the best balance, I decided to try body surfing, so I purchased a boogie board. On the beach, the surf was up and the boogie board was working pretty well. My confidence was increasing, and I started to like bigger and bigger waves.

As the day went on, I met a couple of Hawaiians who seemed to be more laid back than I was at catching a wave. While we were talking, it became apparent that even as body surfers they were looking to conserve their energy for big waves. These waves could have been six feet tall that day, and their goal was to catch such waves. Thanks to their instruction and assistance, I eventually could catch some of the larger waves.

Every once in a while, I would catch a large wave, but as the day wore on, we seemed to be lying on the boards and waiting for even larger waves. At one point, someone yelled, "This is it," and looking back I saw the biggest wave of the day. Paddling as fast as I could, I caught the wave. That was a huge mistake! I had latched onto a large wave and was being propelled forward at a rapid rate, and then the wave began to break, and I was pushed under. Which way was up? Could I hold my breath long enough? Was I pinned down? Was I going to live? When I pulled myself out of the water, I was missing my sunglasses, my self-confidence, and at least eight of my nine lives.

Think about what it's like to ride a ten-foot wave on a surf board. What is it like to ride a sixty- or seventy-foot wave? A new appreciation of the skill of big wave surfers had been gained. But is that skill and level of risk substantially different from that of an investor in a high-tech start-up? Or is it just a different type of risk? This small adventure pales in comparison to the thrills and danger of riding the big waves. Big wave surfing is an extreme sport practiced by a few unique individuals. It is quite similar to the high-tech industry in that a few individuals take high-risk chances played out on steep growth curves.

Over the years, big wave surfers have taken on bigger and bigger waves. North Shore, Australia, Tahiti, and many other locations have big waves, and when the weather is right and the swells start to form, the surfers gather to see who can get the highest and fastest ride. Today, big wave surfers go after sixty- and seventy-foot waves. A person about six feet tall riding a tiny piece of board down the face of a huge wave is a magnificent achievement. It is the thrill of a lifetime, but a thrill experienced by a select few. Through movies, videos, pictures, and books, the art and science of big wave surfing has been told to mass audiences. In this book, the parallels to technology development are explored. A new world of thought and strategy are explored to provide an insight into the various parts of the technology development spectrum.

One thing that makes surfing difficult is that every wave that breaks on the shore is slightly different. This difference is caused by the fact that the speed of the wave coming in from the swell is modified by the subtleness of the underlying contour of the earth. The friction of the water against the contour of the earth creates an unpredictable wave that rises up and breaks in what looks like a predictable fashion but is really a unique pattern.

In the ocean, there are swells with a rhythm and cycle dictated by the weather, gravity, and topography. As you approach shore, the swells begin to form into waves and the waves are shaped by the ocean floor. Eventually the wave breaks and the water churns into the shore. Technology products follow the same pattern. The researchers are watching the swells of technology and creating the pattern that can become waves of new companies. As the companies and technology mature, the sales cycle evolves into a churning mass of product that loses all differentiation. Because of the economics of mass production and the rapid and widespread adaptation of new technologies, many parts of the technology industry have created big waves. With the big waves, the attendant big wave surfers see excitement and thrive in this risky and dangerous environment. Technology big waves get names such as Desktop Software, Internet Backbone, Heart Pacemakers, Database Software, and Long Distance Services. The results of riding these big waves are similar: massive creation of wealth and power grown right out of the big ocean of technology and ridden to the shores of consumer acceptance.

There are dead surfers associated with a whole series of failed Internet and other technology ventures. For them, despite their best efforts, they failed and wiped out tons of investor money. The best hope they have is to wait for the start of a new wave and to remember that it is better to have surfed and failed than not to have tried. When the next wave starts, they may get another chance under the concept that failed management is better than inexperienced management.

Technology Disruption

Technology disrupts and brings chaos to events that are proceeding along in an orderly fashion. The advent of the personal computer (PC) brought chaos to industry and government. Prior to the PC, the computing resource was controlled by the information technology (IT) departments of industry with their armies of starch-shirted system analysts. Enter the PC, and all of the basic rules are broken. How do you back up the data on the PC? Who is in charge of monitoring the data on the PC? What a great invention to introduce into corporate environments! Further, a whole new set of occupations are created when the PC becomes ubiquitous.

There are many technologies that disrupt the status quo. Early examples include the bow and arrow, cannon, cotton gin, automobile, and factory. More recent examples include the web browser, minicomputer, microcomputer, and PC. Inventions such as the Internet then further disrupt industries as people find different uses such as peer-to-peer file-sharing networks and social networks. The recording and movie industry has struggled for years trying to deal with the genie unleashed in that series of waves. Disruption can spawn waves of technology innovation as people latch onto technology variations.

Disruption has both good and bad properties. It will tend to put one group out of business, but it creates a whole new set of opportunities for other groups. Disruption will come in all shapes and sizes. When it creates a big wave, opportunity will exist in spades and a lot of money will flow into the system, amplifying the opportunity and pain of big wave surfing. In the PC industry, the pain and suffering was widespread.

In the early 1980s, IBM positioned itself to dominate the industry, but small suppliers took over by dominating the low-cost end of the market. The big trade-off was one of speed and cost (from small suppliers) versus reliability (from IBM). The user opted for speed and cost, and the industry evolved quickly. With little to differentiate the products, the wave rapidly burst ashore and deteriorated away from technology and into distribution and low-cost production. Eventually Dell emerged off the wave and out of the churn with the dominating industry position. At the same time, chip technology capability increased to the point that in the battle to get down the wave, the PC market almost wiped out Sun Microsystems (eventually Sun did crash, never adjusting as it was finally and "officially" merged with Oracle in January 2010) along with major portions of the minicomputer, mainframe, and supercomputer markets. For reasons of return on investment, IBM exited the PC business, selling out to a Chinese company.

There is a half-life to a technology, and this is the time when the technology can disrupt the marketplace before it gets destroyed itself. Generally, this time is six to eighteen months. Then the end users will move on to the next wave or generation. It does seem as if the rate of change is increasing as time goes by as new develop-ments continue at a rapid pace.

The minicomputer took its bite out of the mainframe business just like the PC took its bite out of both the minicomputer and the mainframe business. However, there is still a minicomputer and mainframe business, although they are not really growth busi-nesses. The big question is whether the mainframe business will eventually go the way of the buggy whip.

Disruption has a number of consequences that are not obvi-ous to initial observers. Consider the medical advances of the twentieth century. Substantial increases were made in the lifespan of individuals by a variety of advances ranging from pacemakers to radiation therapy for cancer patients. But the technology was only viewed by the general public and corporate management as extending life. Did anyone think about the consequences of this extension of the lifespan when promising retirees lifelong medical care and extensive retirement benefits? In particular, did anyone think about the issues around global competitiveness and the pressure on the bottom line while technology was increasing lifespan and medical and pension costs? One of the biggest problems with the development of a new technology is the side effects that become consequences of the emerging technology. Many technologies are not used for their originally intended purposes.

Many people do not understand or conceptualize disruption without an example. Disruption exists around us at all times. Two easily understood examples of disruption are occurring right now: the long-term necessity to begin the replacement of hydrocarbon fuels and the emergence of high-definition (HD) television. The fuel issue is easily understood. We've run through about half of the known reserves of hydrocarbon fuels and must figure out how to replace the supply. Right now there is not a crisis, but a solution could take fifty years to develop. However, the concept of hybrid vehicles and fuel cells bears watching.

A nearer term example of a disruptive technology is HD television. In 2009, the Federal Communications Commission's decision to change the allocation of the spectrum used for television in the United States became a reality, and we now operate with a well-defined, new spectrum allocation for HD television. Originally, the standard was to take effect quickly, and when it did, the existing analog spectrum would be turned over to the government, which it would use for emergency users such as fire and police radio systems. This seemed like a reasonable plan, but it took nearly twenty years for the cut over to occur.

TECHNOLOGY DISRUPTION

At the same time, the television manufacturers began the development of new generations of technology to exploit the new capabilities possible with digital television. You now need to be a genius to operate and install a new television (alternatively, ask your son or daughter to help you). First, there is the issue of the basic technology. For years, people were still buying analog television sets because they were cheap and getting cheaper. So many people were doing this that the cutover date to only digital transmission was pushed back. Hybrid sets then began to be sold. Even if you bought a digital set there were different standards—standard definition, enhanced definition, and HD. Then the cutover became effective, but you could still use analog sets on cable systems. Once you bought your new HD television, what signal would be transmitted to the television? The newest sets could receive a variety of formats. Are you watching in analog, 16×9, or 4×3? What type of signal does your VCR, DVD, or DVR put out? What connections should you make—composite video, component video, or S-video? How do you connect the surround sound system? What type of television should you purchase—LCD, LED/LCD, plasma, DLP, projection, or tube? Or, should you buy one of the new 3-D television sets?

If you go to the television store, there is a countless set of choices! Which one do you pick?

This whole problem is a classic example of a disruptive technology. It sounds so simple, but with new screen technologies, existing devices, and software (movies on DVD, direct digital download, or videotape), not to mention air, cable, and satellite transmissions as well as equipment manufacturers, the entire technology transformation creates both big waves and churns.

Movies on demand and satellite-based systems are examples of potential big waves. Use of cable modems continues the trend for new phone services. New equipment concepts begin to emerge, such as TiVo devices for recording digital content.

If you look at the back of the television set, you will see the problem. The television looks like a patch panel. If the wires are attached to the patch panel, it looks like an explosion in a spaghetti factory—wires are everywhere! The television needs connections that provide for compatibility for existing devices and connections for devices that put out the new formats.

Over time, the situation should sort itself out, but in the meantime, the user is saddled with the questions of what do I need and what should I buy?

Multiple Waves of Disruption

Disruption of what people think of as the norm can happen at any time. Disruption can take many forms. It may be a new function, or it may be simply a new way of looking at a problem. However, no matter how it occurs, it can have long-term serious changes in what people can buy, use, or even think of as the norm.

A simple case of such a disruption was a power outage in Minnesota during which the lack of a backup power supply caused a patient on a heart pacemaker to die. The attending physician, in an effort to prevent future occurrences, asked Earl Bakken if he could develop a system in which the pacemaker could have a battery backup. This technology innovation eventually led to the devices that became the founding products that caused the formation of Medtronic. Medtronic built the first wearable external cardiac pacemaker in 1957 and began manufacturing the first reliable long-term implantable heart pacemakers in 1960. Today, Medtronic is a major contributor to the health care system that provides a wide variety of medical technology systems to improve the lives of people. However, it began due to a power disruption and its consequences.

A single disruption can cause many further disruptions. A good example is that of packet switching systems. Prior to packet switching, the main mode of communication was circuit switching. Circuit-switching systems developed a circuit between two end points, thus creating a dedicated connection between two end points. This was how telephone networks essentially worked. You dialed up the other end and then had a circuit between the two callers as long as no one terminated the connection.

Originally designed as a specialized communication system that used packets instead of circuits, the Internet has evolved into a necessity of everyday life. It provides everything from simple maps and weather forecasts to email to the world's largest garage sale to social networking sites. The basis of the Internet was ARPANET (Advanced Research Projects Agency Network, U.S. Defense Department), which was the first packet-switching network.

In a packet-switching system, each communication was broken up into packets, which could be sent individually between two points. At the destination, the packets were reassembled in the order they were transmitted in and the communication is then completed. The advantages of the packet-switching system were that the links in the system could be easily shared by more than one user and the packets being sent between two end points did not have to take the same route.

ARPANET's goal was to develop a way that a user could connect from one terminal to several computer systems rather than having to connect from a terminal to a specific computer system. From this humble conceptual start, the project eventually provided email and the birth of the Internet. The simple disruption of allowing one terminal to connect to multiple computers evolved into email, then into the web, then into information utilities, e-commerce, and currently social networking—all connected together. As time goes by, and new uses are found, more disruption will occur. The Internet is one of the best examples of multiple disruption occurrences and of big wave surfing. Each major disruption has provided many opportunities to catch a big technology wealth-creation wave.

Big Waves' Uniqueness

Waves are not only of different size, but also of different duration and frequency. In the case of the Internet, the original design goal was to develop a survivable network that was based upon packet switching. With this goal met, people began to develop applications on top of the basic infrastructure. Simple email evolved as PCs evolved. Then came web services, and eventually came social networks. Along the way, things changed in ways that no one could have envisioned.

In technology, there are always many fronts (beaches) open, such as medical areas, computer areas, network areas, and consumer electronic areas. In each area, there are big waves crashing into the shore. Thus, opportunity abounds.

Opportunity abounds in areas that range from semiconductors to basic materials to process development. Society's needs can be met by a variety of user scenarios. Even pollution has its developments—the need to reduce garbage and hazardous waste dumps. Energy is a big issue, as are medical treatments for an aging population. No matter the time or the state of the economy, there is always opportunity and there will be people trying to catch the next big wave. In fact, from a development point of view, the economy may actually be countercyclical. When companies are doing well and making a lot of money, they tend not to want to spend money on new developments. Thus, new product cycles seem to start after the current product set has been milked to the point that there is not much value left in the product set, and then a massive effort must be made to retool the product set.

We can also have a long period of disruption with disruption embedded within disruption. The current legislative pushes by different factions on the issue of net neutrality could change the entire way the Internet evolves in the future. At this point, no one can tell what may happen!

Technology Abstraction Levels

Technology big wave surfers see the world differently. They seem to have a unique perspective on things. What they see will let them move to the front of the pack. They can figure out where the next big wave is about to occur. They will understand how products must change. This is an ability to understand very abstract thinking as time and technology change.

One of the most important concepts that can be learned from the technology business is the idea of levels of abstraction. When you take math in school, you take the courses in a predetermined order. This is done for one key reason—levels of abstraction. Math is an abstract subject, essentially developing a variety of abstract concepts that allow for the modeling and development of systems. When you are taking your first course in algebra, you search for the solution of the most elemental form of an equation and step through a proof.

The order of the courses is set so that one level of abstraction builds upon the previous levels that you have mastered. However, the problem that becomes apparent as you advance through this structure is that not every individual can advance from one level to the next. You might lose interest, develop other interests, or run out of gas.

Only a very few people will get to the level of understanding that will allow them to take data from the time domain, transform it into the frequency domain, and use that mathematical model to build an accurate three-dimensional model of a physical entity. Who cares, you ask. Well, we just discussed the abstract basis of three-dimensional imaging, which is quite useful in determining land profiles for environment studies, identifying a terrorist from space, guiding a cruise missile through a window, and even allowing a doctor to create and examine a three-dimensional model of your body for medical purposes. But the question is how the first person figured this out. What kind of a person had the vision to try to apply these abstract concepts? How did such an idea move to the front of someone's brain?

Remember the person who sat next to you in algebra who could never solve a simple equation? That person simply ran out of gas. Those types of kids were fortunate if their parents could understand and challenge them in another fashion.

This scene repeats itself many times a day at all levels of abstraction. Over the years, I have seen this happen as my daughter went through school and from students I interacted with at the university both as a teacher and as a fellow student. You need to see things differently to be unique—hopefully, what you see is useful.

Many times, a student is misplaced and on the wrong career path. The advantage of the American school system is that it tries to be fair to students attempting to develop careers. Many times, students are misplaced in technical subjects because they have a desire to be scientists. But no matter how much they want to be physicists, chemists, or engineers, they will never get there. Instead they may end up as great marketing managers, professors, lawyers, plumbers, electricians, or salespeople.

This problem can be brutal. You could be great at one level of abstraction and fail at the next level. That is the nature of society. Some people can walk in the ocean, some can body surf, some can surf small waves, and a very few have what it takes to mount big waves. The difference between walking into the ocean and big wave surfing is levels of abstraction. The current final level of abstraction for big wave surfers is tow-in surfing, where a watercraft is used to get surfers up to speed so they can catch waves that are so big that they are moving too fast to catch by paddling. The difference is the size of the wave. But riding a forty-foot wave appears to be a lot different than towing into a fifty- to sixty-foot wave. The use of a mechanism to help cope with changes in the level of abstraction is not unusual.

Software is a classic example. In early programming courses, programs are simple. In bigger development environments, programs are so complex that they are divided into layers that relate to each other and can be developed separately and in parallel. The ability to design the layers is a skill that requires more capabilities than writing a simple program. But the problem gets worse. Because of the need for reusable code, libraries of modules are introduced and then you need standard interfaces to the library modules. Thus, levels of abstraction become part of the process and stratify the software workforce.

Relative Orders of Effects

One of the big problems in trying to surf a big wave is minutia. The big issue is where and how to catch the big wave. Whether it's sunny or rainy is not really a big deal. Clearly, you would like to surf on a sunny rather than a cloudy or rainy day, but if the big waves are only there on a cloudy, rainy day, you must surf on that day. This leads to the concept of orders of effects.

You can make a list of items that are important, but some of these items are more important than others. For example, if you are going surfing and want to go big wave surfing, you need to find a beach that has big waves. It's simple: no big waves, no big wave surfing!

How many times have you asked someone to explain the basic issue on a specific topic expecting to get a simple answer, and instead you get a dissertation?

Think of the number of times that you have seen a variation on the contest "In twenty-five words or less . . ." It is really difficult to get people to explain something succinctly.

I once had to give a customer a corporate overview of a couple of major projects and had a very limited time. I dutifully began to gather the information necessary for the presentation. I put together what I thought was a pretty good presentation. For one slide, I went to see the designer. I told him that I needed one slide that summarized the concept of the project. He thought for awhile and said that there was no way he could tell me in one slide what the project was about, but he could explain the concept if he had seventy slides.

He assured me that every one of the seventy slides was equally important. I noted that I had only fifteen minutes to talk about five projects, and his was one of the five. There was no way that I could present seven slides in that time, and therefore, no way could I present seventy slides on his project. Eventually I made a slide for his project and gave a presentation with six slides—an introductory slide and five project slides. Each project slide told about the concept, value, and status of the project.

The idea that a concept cannot be summarized is ridiculous. Yet, people do not understand the importance of the big picture. In some circles, this is called an elevator speech. In other circles, it is called a summary. If you cannot explain your concept quickly and simply, you probably do not understand it yourself.

If you are looking to ride a big wave, you must first and foremost have a big wave. All other issues are secondary. We can then discuss the size of the wave, but if the waves are sixty feet high, then most people will agree that it is a big wave. After you have ridden the wave, everyone will view you as a big wave surfer.

Whether you rode the wave in California, Hawaii, or Australia is pretty much immaterial, as is the level of cloud cover on that day.

This really helps to delineate the idea of order of effects. In discussing a topic, items about the topic are more or less meaningful. In looking at the subject, you need to stay on track with the important issues, and not every issue carries the same level of importance. This is a well-known concept from modeling and simulation. In this discipline, you are trying to construct a model of a system and you cannot model every part of the system. Thus, you need to pick out the few factors that are most important in making an accurate model. These are the first order effects. Only if you have the time and computing power will you deal with lower-level effects.

In a simple case, the use of MP3 files with small storage devices and a simple user interface makes the iPod useful. The first order effects involve the physical characteristics coupled with the ability to compress, load, and play back songs. An easy-to-use interface completes the system, and Apple then has the ability to make another major entry into the consumer market.

Technology Change

If you can build or develop a technology, product, or process, it is by definition obsolete. The fact that you can exploit the technology really means you need to be figuring out how to make the next product. The state-of-the-art product you just bought had better be in the process of being obsolete by its manufacturer, or someone else will destroy the market by bringing out a more sophisticated successor.

The fact that you can sell a product brings attention to a specific area of expertise. If you allow yourself the luxury of thinking that you are smarter, faster, or more advanced than your competitors or potential competitors, you are going to lose the big wave.

Once you develop a high-profile product that is new and revolutionary and has mass appeal, there will be a lot of smart and aggressive people who will want a piece of the action. They may have similar technologies or capabilities. If the product's sales take off, there will be a lot of attention and money brought to the product area. The only way you will survive is if you can evolve and extend your product.

The only constant in big wave surfing is change. You must make your own product obsolete. Make it faster and smaller, add more functions, build a lower cost model, or combine the functions of two of your related products. And do it fast. Once you have the least bit of success, your competition will come calling.

The landscape is littered with manufacturers who had a lead and a big developing market and lost that lead. In fact, entire industries have disappeared into the churn as the beach approached. Bowmar built some of the first small calculators. Wang made programmable calculators. Digital Equipment Corporation (DEC) made minicomputers. The beach is littered with tons of companies that made it and then crashed.

Companies crash because they do not evolve fast enough. The management must learn to adapt fast, and that may mean destroying your own products. You cannot believe the amount of money that is available for fast-growing areas of the economy. The stakes are high, and there are companies that believe they can enter markets late and drive over the pioneers by sheer monetary mass and production capacity. The entire Japanese economy is based upon this premise.

The Japanese electronics companies are not known as great innovators. They are, however, great product developers and ruthless competitors. Once they sense a big wave forming, they are able to see the lay of the landscape and then they enter a market with a vengeance. They drive the costs down and the production rates up. How many U.S. manufacturers are there of television sets? At one time, the United States dominated that industry, until the Japanese manufacturers entered the field. Big production companies have a different mindset. They go in for the long haul and drive the competition out of the market. Big wave surfers are in it for the short duration of the high surf and then move onto another beach and another set of waves.

The big wave surfer cannot compete against the big production houses. They're really there to create a concept, create a market, seed the market, start to evolve the market, and jump off the wave looking for the next wave. The big wave surfers cannot compete with the likes of Japanese production. They need to sell or merge the created big wave company as fast as possible because the real high-value monies are made quickly and simply by creating the market and jumping off to a new wave. Maximum monies are made by creating something that someone else will really want and pay a big price for. You must create something that can be sold for its future potential when it is hot. Take Yahoo!, for example. It probably missed the wave when Microsoft offered the company $44 billion in 2008.

The market is changing, and you will not know its state or the efforts of your competitors, so a big wave surfer tries to build a rapidly growing company in a unique space and sell it to someone who can compete with the big guys before the wave breaks.

Ride down the wave at its steepest slope, and get out.

The next wave is coming, and you will get another shot. Get out before you get crushed.

The type of person who thrives in this environment is a person who will take high risks and is very financially oriented. These people are trying to create real value in a big and fast way. I have heard these people described as serial entrepreneurs. People who recognize that change will always occur and they must adapt.

In some cases, these entrepreneurs will evolve themselves and grow to run large companies, but they will probably always wish to get back up on the wave.

Stilted Creatures of Habit

One of the big problems with the big wave surf rider is when you get into a position and notice that the people who should be around you are stuck somewhere else. As you get the company ready to ride the big wave and get that first product launched, you must involve other people, and they may not have the drive or vision of the big wave surfer. They will all have ideas of how things should be done.

They may be right, but without taking risk you will not be able to achieve the kind of growth rates to reach the critical mass that is necessary to dominate a market in the short term.

A simple example is product testing. How much testing is enough before you ship a product? Once you have a successful product and you are about to bring out its successor product, how much testing do you need to do to the new product? Do you just test the new functions, or do you completely retest all functions including the new functions? The answer is really simple. It has to do with your ability to take risk. If your test department grew up in a large, conservative big company, it will want a complete retest. The big wave surfer will only want a new function verification.

If you get yourself bogged down and let some tester control the destiny of the product, you are sunk. You must get a top-of-the-line development staff and get the product out the door. Sometimes you may have to cross your fingers and hope that you did not screw up too badly.

Many times, I've had the problem of having a product that is so far advanced that potential customers never saw anything like it and were willing to buy it on the spot—only to have one of my engineers tell me that the product was not good enough. What someone thinks should be in the product is really irrelevant if someone will buy the product.

You cannot let someone's idea of the perfect product sway your movement forward. You cannot allow the habits, concerns, lack of willingness to take risk, and other foibles of others weigh down your efforts. You must be in position, and you must drive your products and company forward. At some point, someone has to step up and say this is the way it is and I will accept responsibility for the consequences of that decision.

You must break out of the habit of procrastination and believe in your decisions and your product. Procrastination will not get the product to market. Unless you have designed the only product invented that will never need revision or modification, you simply need to break all of your habits that slow down your product introduction. And you need to continue that evolution to new product introductions that will ultimately make your old products obsolete.

Early Adopters/Early Stage Developers

We want to get our new product off the ground fast. As we jump on the wave, we hope to have a very steep slope on the face of the wave because that is how we will create value in our new enterprise. That is, the faster the growth rate we can achieve, the better the valuation of our new company or product. Further, if we have a new concept and want to get it off the ground fast, we will need to find a category of people who are receptive to advanced technologies. These people are known as early adopters. They are the type of people who must have the latest gadget and are willing to take risks. One of the best types of users is to have early adopters who control large systems and need to stay competitive through the constant upgrading and introduction of new technology. We will discuss these people in chapter 11.

Early stage developers are the people who are visionaries, and they come up with unique product concepts. They are people who try to think up new highly useful system concepts and the solution to new problems. In many cases, they conceive of new ways of looking at problems and solutions. We will talk about them in chapter 9, but we need to know and think about their existence.

To get a big wave solution, we will need at least two confluences of events. We will need a radically new solution to a key problem that will provide early adopters a competitive advantage. In the commercial space, we need a jazzed-up potential user base and a new type of product. An example of such consumer products are the Wii, iPhone, iPod, and Windows 95.

The bigger the base of early adopters, the larger the payoff and the faster we can make the product grow so we can get up on that big wave. We want a radical new way of doing business to excite the early adopter user base—we want to jazz the user base. When we try to get the sales channel up and running, we will call it energizing the sales channel because we are trying to excite the sales force about the potential of the product. Really, we are trying to get the sales force excited about the commission potential of the new product. We want to get the salespeople out hunting the early adopters. In particular, it is key to get on board early adopters who will take risks and developers who can manage risks as well as salespeople who can quantify the risks into a value proposition.

Bizarre Characters

When you get into a big wave surfing environment, you will run into a number of characters. Because people are motivated by different things, the number and resultant behavior patterns of big wave surfers is all over the map. Some people are highly financially motivated. Some people are highly image motivated. Others are in it just for the game. But the thing that is truly unique among big wave surfers is that they are driven by technology and willing to take risk. In many ways, they are like little kids. They want to be the best, brightest, and newest user of the toy or the producer of the newest and best toy in the case of the developer and salesperson. Your level of excitement is, in many cases, tied to the perceived value of the new technology and how you think the technology will be used.

This is just like hopping onto the big wave. There is a huge rush as you conquer the big wave. If the wave is steep and you work it, like a serial entrepreneur developing a series of products, there continues to be a large degree of satisfaction. But there are variations on the theme. In some cases, it is the initial drop on the wave or take-off of the product that generates the rush. In other cases, it is the working of the wave and the sales growth and sustainment. In other cases, it is the head-to-head competition as another surfer arrives and you beat back the competition. In all cases, you will need a wide variety of people with highly developed skills to be successful and you will meet some real characters along the way.

Winning Products: Vince Lombardi's Approach

When the technology takes off, there may be several companies at the starting line. As the wave becomes well defined, there may be a series of waves that break with different variations of technology and new companies trying to get started and jump on the wave.

But as the waves break, we get the churn effect, and the waves end up breaking onto the beach as the product becomes a commodity.

The result is that there is only one Cisco, one Microsoft, and one Apple. If we are lucky, there will be a second-place player (who may be a start-up attracted to the wave because of the market dominance and the dropout of all other players). But the real drive of the winners was defined by Vince Lombardi: "Winning isn't everything, it is the only thing."

Win and you are golden, lose and you had better find the next wave! However, once you have become a big wave surfer, almost everyone expects you to lose. There is very little chance that you will not wipe out riding some wave. It is human nature that you will begin to take bigger and bigger chances. Eventually, you will push to the level of failure. Everyone is optimistic, and you believe in yourself and your team. If you are lucky, you will dismount the wave in plenty of time, but sometimes you will get crushed.

Fortunately, getting crushed is as instructive as winning because you cannot know how to win if you don't encounter a few bumps along the road to success. Just remember, your chances of being hired as a big league head coach are greatly increased if you have formerly been a coach even if you were previously fired.

The stakes of big wave surfing are such that a successful entrepreneur may only have to surf once to be set for life, but many take two or three swings at the waves. In some cases, it takes a couple of tries to be successful. Some of the most successful big wave surfers had several tries at the game: megasurfer Bill Gates is known for his persistence in evolving his products and Harry Saal (founder of Network General) made it big on his second try. Nestar was his first try, and unless you are very knowledgeable in local area network history, you have never heard of this try. You may have heard of his second, Network General. Then there are the multiple career surfers such as Bob Metcalfe, the inventor of Ethernet (along with Boggs). He founded 3Com and, after retiring from 3Com, went on to a distinguished career in publishing and venture capital.

Just remember the goal is to win—and if possible, to win BIG!

Locker Rooms

In a serious start-up company, it is necessary to have one big wave surfer spotting the disruption if you are going for the brass ring. You also need a support team! To get started on the wave, you need a marketer, a lead developer, and a charismatic manager. Unless you fill out all three legs of the stool, you will not have a stable entity. At the start, all three positions may be filled by one person, but as the stakes increase, you must fill all positions. One person cannot make all the sales calls, design decisions, and management infrastructure decisions necessary to be successful.

Selecting good teammates is critical to the success of the enterprise.

You need a good board maker. You need good developers to help you navigate the swells. If the wave is really big, you need help to catch the wave. And you need courage to navigate the surface of the giant wave as it drops out from under your board. It is the job of the lead surfer to help the developers identify which of the developing technologies can become a revolutionary technology. Getting the product launched onto the wave is everyone's responsibility. But it is up to marketing to get the board soaring down the wave and up to speed, crushing any competitors before they catch you. Finally, it is the responsibility of the big wave surfer to decide when to move the product set to a commodity status and quit surfing as we try to move to shore. Teamwork cannot be overemphasized; this is a difficult, stressful, and rapidly changing environment.

You must build a quality team with complementary skills.

Quality People

Sometimes it is difficult not to think that the people we are dealing with are nothing but clichés. Some of the most irritating people are the people with the least skin in the game. It is easy for an outsider to say what you should do. It is even easier for the people to explain how you screwed up. The type of person who drove me wild was the guy who, with a flip of his hand, would say something like "just make it happen." A corollary to this statement is, "Well, it's only software." Yes, it is only software. And what kills software is only bugs. In any software, there will be a lot of problems. You have to try to fix all of the potential problems before the product ships—or you'll be fixing them in the next version. You must make it happen.

Over time, it became clear that "make it happen" was not a cliché. It was the attitude that separated success from failure. At some point, you must ship a product to get the rapid sales ramp. Someone must be able to decide when good is good enough and to make it happen. Get that product out. Get to work on the next product. Define the product road map.

No matter what anyone thinks, there is no perfect product. You need to be able to determine what is good enough to sell and what you need to do to overcome sales arguments and make it happen. In a sense, it is a lot like being a trial lawyer. You need to get really prepared, including figuring out what your product is, and get it done and out into the market. Lawyers will tell you that preparation is the key to success. The same is true when you are trying to grow a company fast.

You must make it happen, and not tomorrow. Do not get bogged down by trying to make your products perfect. The only version of your product that will be perfect is the next version—at least it will be more perfect than the current version. The person who can stand up to the developers and customers, as well as marketers, and make the tough choices is going to be the lead surfer, and this person will make it happen for you as you set out on your adventure. If you do not have such a person, you are doomed.

Trustworthy People

As the team is assembled, you need to carefully select all of the people you are going to work with inside the company. Many times, I have done business with people who are abrasive or uncouth, but the only issue that really concerned me was their trustworthiness. Were they honest? Could I trust their judgment?

If they are trustworthy, you can overlook their other faults. If they are dishonest, they will eventually cause you, your company, and your associates to make the front page of the *New York Times*. The only problem is you won't have a business. The only guys who can deal with crooks are the other guys who look good in orange jumpsuits.

Simply said, do not hire dishonest people and do not pay bribes. You want employees to be very aggressive and to push as hard as they can on all fronts, but they must be straight-up, high-quality citizens.

Enough said.

Success Scenarios

Humbleness is a critical attribute. No matter how successful you are, it is important to be humble and thankful for your successes in life. I have had many discussions with my daughter where she was irritated that I was right. The discussion always amazed me. The point that I tried to make to her was that I am very successful on a statistical basis. But I do strike out. Everybody does! However, when I win I try to make the most of my efforts at that time. I try to minimize the cost of my failures. If you are on a big wave and wipe out, you must have techniques and contingency plans to survive. Big wave surfers can die when they wipe out. Technology big wave surfers can destroy the livelihood of a lot of people when they wipe out a company.

Part of the potential solution is the concept of a scenario. Scenarios are critical to the process of big wave surfing. The surfer has to constantly adjust to the perturbations that the underlying structure of the earth causes to the wave. In the curl, surfers will have their hands on the back of the curl so they can feel and sense changes in the wave. The other reason to feel is that it is difficult to see in the curl and you need to know where the surface of the water is. The idea of a scenario is similar. You need to have a scenario that gives you a feel for what will happen when your product is introduced. In fact, you need to develop a set of issues that will occur at the introduction of your product. You need to answer questions like, What will the competition do when we have the next version out? Who is the most likely customer?

Most people do not think these issues through. You need to think them through thoroughly!

Then, you need to understand that you are wrong! No one has seen your scenarios yet, and you are wrong. The environment is so complex and there are so many variables that once you have committed to a product action, your scenario is immediately wrong.

Someone will do something that will cause your assumptions to be incorrect. Once I was involved with a new product introduction. A big question in the introduction strategy was, Will the other competitor sue us because it perceives that we may have a patent violation (which we did not have)? Everyone in management and marketing agreed that was the least likely scenario, because of the cost. Everyone felt the other company would lower its price and try to drive us out of the market before we could ramp up production. Within four hours of our product introduction, we were sued for patent infringement, violation of several trade secret agreements (we had resold its product previously), and a number of other issues. The price strategy never occurred. You just can never tell.

When I enter into a new venture, I make a set of scenarios and possible outcomes. I do not recommend making only one scenario. I recognize that the scenarios will have to change as time goes on. The set of possible scenarios will constantly change. And we may have missed the most important possible scenarios. We may not even have figured out the real possible scenarios; we can never tell what may happen. Once you start down a path and the real deal starts to unfold, you must adapt and revise your scenarios.

The trick then is to be adaptive as the scenarios change. You must adapt as the competition or possible competition changes. Unless you change, the wave will overtake you and you will end up being crushed by the wave of water.

Unknown and Unpredictable Side Effects

Walking by a serene pond and throwing in a rock will cause ripples to move out toward the edge. Hidden artifacts within the pond will disturb the movement of the wave. On a beach, the surface of the beach, hidden coral, and other physical effects will affect the size and movement of the wave.

In a similar way, once you introduce, start to sell, develop, announce, or do anything with your product, you have modified the product environment. You have no idea what's about to happen. Even if you have thought through a set of scenarios, you still don't know what will really happen. Though you cannot predict the future, you can try to bound its effects and understand the range of options that you will face. Like when you throw the rock into a pond, the very act of starting your company and putting out your first product will cause ripples in the environment. And you have no way of knowing what the possible effects will be.

Perpetual Incremental Change

Once you have launched your initial product, you have embarked on a course where you must support and evolve the product. Many times, there are people who believe that all you have to do is launch your product and sit back and reap the rewards. You, however, have just entered into a course of action that will require at the least some changes to support the product.

In most cases, the product that a company starts out with is just an initial development effort. For example, the car industry is always coming out with new products. Therefore, you should expect the same from a technology company. Otherwise the company will fail. The problem is that no one wants to be the last person to buy a new product, and thus, product plans must be closely guarded and kept out of the hands of both customers and competitors.

One of the best system designers who led a large design team used to say that you need to embark on a course of broadening the product line. You need to (before a product is introduced) have complete plans for your next product. You need to adopt a plan of incremental change at the very minimum. You should have plans for a lower cost product, a higher function product, and a product that integrates completely new concepts so that you can keep the competition off balance. In his words, you need to take a look at your product and find as many ways that you can build slightly different product versions and get them to be priced at a variety of price points for maximum coverage of the customer space. Look at the number of versions of the iPod that Apple has introduced.

As in the ocean, each wave is slightly different, and as you start down the wave, you must make slight incremental adjustments to stay up on the wave. After you bring out your product, you are into a game of constant obsolescence and evolution of your product.

If you do not adopt this course, your competitors will overrun your position.

Chapter Summary

Because of the pervasive effect of technology on the day-to-day lives of people, the economic effect of changes in the relative position of technology products can be huge. We are trying to find disruptions in technology that will allow us to get a jump on our competitors in launching down a steep wave surface. Disruptions can come in many forms and be caused by a variety of factors. In a number of cases, the disruptions have come as a result of legislative or judicial rulings. We need to be on constant alert for any major change in the technology environment regardless of its source. The size of the possible economic effects on individuals' wealth status is so large that a lot of smart people are constantly on the lookout for disruption regardless of its source. In many cases, sources of disruption are relatively clear. What's not clear is which company will be able to effectively and profitably capitalize on a specific disruption.

Chapter 5

Trade-Off Issues Associated with Big Waves

There is no perfect product or service. And if there were such a perfect product, it would only last for a short time in the state of perfection because someone would come up with a better idea. Thus, it is critical to understand that everything is really a trade-off of relative capabilities, features, and desires. In fact, when conceiving a product, you can really divide the space of trade-offs into two parts: musts and wants. Musts are your real requirements. Wants are features that are nice but do not really affect the basic operation of the system.

It is important to understand what the application must really do. In fact, it is critical to coordinate the must against the capabilities of your product. If your product does not solve all of customers' musts, it's dead in the water. In this chapter, we'll look at

Principle: Technology Trade-Offs Allow Apples to Be Compared to Oranges

No two products or services will be exactly alike. Thus, we must be able to compare technologies that have properties that range from insignificant to important. An apple and an orange can be compared in a number of ways. They are similar because they are both fruits. They differ in a number of ways including texture, growing location, taste, and color.

how to build comparisons and we'll discuss some initial design issues before we take a detailed look at how to develop and market our product. And, we'll also talk about trade-offs.

Trade-Off Answer— "It Depends"

Leonard Kleinrock, the early scholar/developer of the Arpanet's packet-switching concept (the predecessor to the Internet), is on the phone. Kleinrock runs one of the first and most successful seminar businesses in the technology area. He wants to add a section to his most successful seminar on the issue of local area network (LAN) technology, and he is calling to see if I will do that section of the seminar.

This encounter will lead to one of the most insightful discussions that influenced this book. The discussion centers around the concept of a trade-off.

There is no problem with signing up to do a seminar or part of a seminar for Kleinrock. His organization is first class, the instructors are first class, and the students are well satisfied. Thus, there is no reason to be anxious about this call. Well, there is this one little issue: the students.

Kleinrock is running a really tough seminar to teach. The seminar purports to cover the entire field of network technology from traffic engineering to architecture to protocols, and he has assembled a world-class staff. The seminar takes four days. Each day is taught by a different instructor, and Kleinrock has coordinated the lecture notes of the instructors. What gives one pause is that the seminar is advertised as Experts on Networks and claims to have the best instructor in each of the four major topic areas in the network world. Could you imagine walking into a company such as IBM, Digital Equipment Corporation (DEC), or Intel as one of the instructors of the seminar titled Experts on Networks? That is risk taking.

The problem is with the students. What if a student is smarter than the advertised expert instructor, stumps the instructor, or asks one or more questions that the instructor cannot answer? Thinking about the possibilities would just drive one nuts. Yet, for a couple of years Kleinrock has been successfully running this seminar. How does he do it? Consider the big problem: Technology is always changing so at the time you start a seminar, you are not sure that something will not be changing. Not only that, some of the students are from manufacturers so they must know more about trends and current or future products than the instructor. The real issue is how to present the information in a way that is fair and provides added value.

In fact, the issue is how to answer a question in this highly volatile world that is rapidly changing. Eventually a deal was cut to participate as an instructor in these seminars and away we went. The key to the deal was a simple statement by Kleinrock: It depends!

"It depends" was Kleinrock's stock answer to almost every question. The answer is be careful when you answer a question and take a position in proverbial quicksand, especially when you may not have the entire context. A better approach is to provide a spectrum of answers. This is the trade-off. Answers are dependent upon the context.

An old engineering question is, How do you compare apples and oranges?

In reality the answer is simple. It depends on what you want to compare: roundness, firmness, color, or some other attribute.

In fact, you can actually compare apples and steak. Clearly, a steak loses if the questioner is a vegetarian.

The issue is setting parameters for the comparison and understanding that the correct answer will depend on the parameters that are important to you.

Given two items, we may not be able to get an answer to even a simple question of which item is better. Consider this simple question: Which is better for you to eat, an apple or an orange? This is an example of a problem and a solution. At one level, you cannot compare an apple and an orange. They are different. We can list some of their differences. They can grow in different climates. They have different skin types. Their skins are of different thicknesses. We can see that they are different in color both inside the skin and the skin itself. They taste differently. However, we can compare a number of parameters and, based on them, we can pick the one that we like the best according to our criteria!

Similarly, for technology implementation, the best choice depends on your context and needs.

Fig. 5-1: Technology Big Wave Structure—Tradeoff Issues

Figure 5-1 illustrates how we are moving along the technology big wave structure. At this point, we have spotted a disruption and are about to consider the first aspects of the product/company that we are trying to establish. We are looking at ways to get into position to surf the big wave. We are trying to decide what the disruption will provide and the necessary trade-offs to build a new product.

Trade-Off Question—"What Were They Thinking?"

A thing of great beauty is the 1959 caddy convertible. A favorite of almost everyone who sees it is the convertible with a continental kit. This car must be as long as a freight train. It has some vertical tail fins that each sport twin bullet taillights that are large enough to stick a small animal through its side. The trunk is so large that it must hold four or five people being dropped off with cement overshoes at a mafia funeral. The 1959 Caddy is without a doubt one of the greatest feats of engineering in the era of Detroit iron.

Seeing such a beast begs the question: What were they thinking?

What set of trade-offs could have possibly caused an automaker to build such a machine? Is it fuel efficiency? Is it style? Is it passenger/trunk capacity? Is it a sense of beauty? Or is it future engineering?

Just what could cause such a design? Think of the concept of the 1959 Cadillac. What set of parameters or measures could be invoked to let someone buy such a car? Well, if you wanted a big car, this was the one. If fuel efficiency was not an issue, this car could pass that trade-off. But probably the issue that created the design was the idea of a high-tech future and space travel. The 1959 Caddy exudes fast travel and a jet-like elegance.

It in no way considers any trade-offs associated with the concept of fuel economy, but fuel economy was not an issue in 1959.

Today, few people would buy such a car unless it was a hybrid. Can you imagine a 1959 Cadillac convertible with a continental kit running a four cylinder hybrid engine? Importantly, trade-offs are not just relative comparisons in a context at a point in time, they evolve over time. The trade-off that makes sense at one point in time can look pretty foolish at a different time.

Real-World Hard Facts

There are a number of positions that are hard for people to really understand. One truism that I have found is that people, especially engineers, have difficulty understanding the concept of installed base. A hardware base that is dominated by one concept limits your product development choices and your ability to develop product trade-offs. This is because the designers' choices become limited.

As a predominantly software- and systems-oriented guy, my attitude has always been to deal with the installed base as defined by the major manufacturers. There are people who modify and evolve the installed base. They also introduce new concepts and generally improve the installed base. They are to be admired, because performing such tasks requires extensive capital and huge risk taking in what is essentially a commodity market. For example, the semiconductor business is both a high-risk and a gutsy environment in which to do business with low payoffs. Intel controls the majority of the installed processor base. Consider the number of companies that have come and gone in the processor space over time. Even a venerable great company such as DEC eventually succumbed to the vagaries of this market. IBM also had to change its business model. Semiconductors became so powerful that the majority of processor design is now done by Intel, and other companies just use their chips.

In the short term, any significant change in the installed hardware base is not possible. Over time, there may be small and incremental changes, but the architecture can only evolve slowly once an architecture catches on. The advent of the personal computer (PC) made some subtle changes to this argument. In fact, the most significant design aspect of the PC was the inclusion of the bus with card slots that allowed users to tailor their PCs by adding little cards with specific capabilities to their systems. If you needed more memory, you added a memory card. If you needed more inputs/outputs (I/O), you added an I/O card. In fact, one of the first products of Microsoft was a simple add-on card for the Apple II computer, the Microsoft Z-80 Softcard introduced on April 2, 1980. The most significant design legacy of the Apple company may have been the inclusion of an open bus structure for the Apple II. Then they closed up their system with the Mac.

There's no clearer example of the power of the installed base than Intel's continual evolution of the x86 computer chip architecture. Success against this basic architecture is almost nonexistent because Intel has increased chip densities and speeds in a constant evolution since 1972 with the introduction of the Intel 8008.

Over time, the slots in the PC became useful for higher speed communications and the LAN industry developed. The desire to connect LANs together led to the development of bridges and routers. That, coupled with the development of the ARPANET, eventually led to the Internet. But during this period, the basic architecture of the hardware essentially only underwent incremental changes.

No matter what the hardware designers wished, there were few significant changes in the installed hardware base due to the dominance of Intel!

Great Pyramid of Personnel—
Synthesis, Analysis, Encyclopedia

Over time, it becomes clear that all people do not have similar capabilities. The differences in people make for an interesting world. It would be a very dull world if everyone looked the same or had the same intelligence. The differences in people are greatly magnified in the high-technology industry. This is an industry that is focused upon performance and driven by money. However, more than anything it is an industry that can incredibly reward people who develop and implement new science. This is accomplished by personal satisfaction, income, stock, and other motivations like power. Yet the high-tech industry is an incredibly conservative industry. No one wants to risk large sums of money on ideas that have no demand. Yet, the ideas that will really pay may have no previous history. Look at some recent successes in generating wealth such as MySpace, Facebook, YouTube, and search companies like Google.

YouTube, Facebook, and MySpace are simple implementations of applications layered on top of the Internet. Search engines like Google and Yahoo! make their money selling ads. They are simply electronic advertisement technologies that try to predict what items you will be interested in based upon your search.

However, none of these applications would be possible without the enabling technology of the Internet.

But how did we get the Internet?

We get it by people inventing new technology. This section discusses the most basic and simple distinctions between the kinds of people who are trying to create basic technologies.

The technology world seems to be divided into three classes of people: the synthesizers, analysts, and encyclopedists. Even though the workers in the industry tend to be similarly educated, they still fall into these three simple classes of capabilities and attitudes.

It is necessary that big wave surfers be synthesizers. However, they must also be quite practical. Analysts, however, can be just surfers as they are helpful, but not qualified to actually ride a big wave. They do not move up to the required level of risk taking. Encyclopedists are like the grandmothers of big wave surfers. They fret all the time. They worry about the surfers' safety, they worry about whether the surfers are well trained, and unwittingly, they try to keep the surfers out of the ocean.

There appears to be very few synthesizers and an incredible number of encyclopedists. I would estimate that encyclopedists make up 85 percent of the workers in the technology industry, analysts make up 14.99 percent, and synthesizers make up about 0.01 percent of the high-tech workforce. Have these numbers been confirmed? My observations of hundreds, if not thousands, of engineers over a large number of years led to this conclusion.

In fact, it is the distribution of such personnel that creates the opportunity.

First, let us describe the overall characteristics of the classes.

Synthesizers are people who can think about ideas and develop new concepts or variations of concepts. They develop new ways to apply, develop, modify, or build new technologies and applications on top of existing technologies. These technologies allow for new functions to be constructed and developed. The ideas can be simple, like taking advances in semiconductor technology to make calculators the size of cigarette packs. Alternatively, they might develop a new paradigm of communications like packet switching, which enables the Internet.

Analysts, however, do not seem to be able to come up with new ideas. They do seem to have the ability to explain how the new idea relates to other products, ideas, and patents. Analysts are very important people in the structure of technology development. They deal in reality and can say, "If we did this, this is how our solution would compare to other solutions and we would have the following advantages and disadvantages." As an idea develops, the analysts will be the ones carrying the ball onto the competitive playing field. They will have to do the grunt work to implement and describe the ideas developed by the synthesizer. If you are a synthesizer, then the analysts are your friends. They will be able to counter the competitive thrusts from the competition.

Encyclopedists are the bane of the technology business. The encyclopedist has a reason why every idea is not unique, no technology is worthy of developing, and everything is just a variation on someone else's idea. Encyclopedists look at the past. They lay out the literature, other products, the state of the art, and other code words that prove your concept is not unique. They tell you why the idea will not work. They think they are synthesizers or analyzers, but if they get the attention of management, they will kill every idea that comes from the technical staff. To them, no technology idea is unique or good enough. The problem in technology companies is that many times the encyclopedist looks like the reasoned scientist and the synthesizer looks like the flakey dreamer.

Many times, the company gatekeeper is an encyclopedist. This is the kiss of death for the company, because the encyclopedist will just beat down the rest of the technology staff. The counter to this problem is a synthesizer with a past track record and a strong personality. The synthesizer also needs to be politically astute to fend off the encyclopedists, while engaging the analysts who can help the synthesizer make the product move forward.

A successful company will have a strong synthesizer in the role of key technologist.

The larger the company, the higher the probability that an encyclopedist will get into a key gatekeeper role due to their studied scientific bent. They fit well into large companies. Synthesizers fit best in small companies where their innovation, flexibility, and ideas are appreciated.

Dad's Directions—Cut the Crap

One of the trade-off issues in building and designing a system is the give and take among designers. It's the old story that no two people see or value a feature the same way. So it's important to have a strong leader with vision who can lead and shepherd the process. Sometimes, this can be like herding cats. It's usually difficult to figure out what features the product should have. Yet, it's critical to get enough functions into the product to successfully launch the product into the market. In many cases, the product definition will be done by one person. At some point, you will have to get other people involved. They may have differing opinions about the features, but at an early stage, you must develop a consensus. This is often a time-consuming and frustrating process. It is, however, key to getting a good design.

Once you have the design, it is important to move on to development and marketing. Sometimes you'll encounter people who want to change the design. Once you commit, you can't go back. Unless you discover a fatal error, you must move ahead as fast as possible.

If such issues come up, it is important to have a lead designer. Eventually the lead must make the decision on how to proceed. This can be very difficult. If you are the lead, you need a signal so everyone understands that the discussions are over and we need to get back to work. In many cases, I've seen the lead say, "Cut the crap; let's get back to work."

You may have heard that phrase before from your dad when he said, "Cut the crap," and then gave you the look. I had not realized how universal this was until one day when my daughter came home from her friend's house and said, "You wouldn't believe what my friend's dad said. He said, 'Cut the crap.'" I laughed when she asked if there was a school where this was taught to dads. When I asked if her friend had also gotten "the look," she said yes. I thought there must be a secret dad school where dads and designers were taught this very useful technique. After this, I started listening to dads and was quite surprised how often I heard this phrase in public places.

When a lead designer utters the phrase, the discussion is over. The trade-offs have been made, and the design is moving to its final stage.

If you do not think this decision making and toughness is necessary, you are wrong. In so many cases, engineers and software designers cannot give up the product. They just cannot let the product go because there is always another feature to be added. This problem is prevalent in the engineering environment.

In the military industrial complex, there is a name for this problem: requirements creep. The problem with the design of a large-scale system is that everyone wants it to be perfect. Well, that is just not going to happen. If it were going to happen, the tooth fairy would deliver the system. You have to learn how to develop systems and functions in an incremental fashion. That's why software has multiple releases, and we're lucky that the releases are numbered in ascending order. Consider the problem if Microsoft had started with release two and numbered in descending order each time a new release had come out. Would we be at version -100? To further confuse things, designers invented subreleases and service packs to let people do their own upgrades to fix software bugs. Releases prove that the world is not perfect, and no product can afford to start out with every possible feature.

In some cases, a sharply worded comment and the look of death is not the only result of a final or interim design meeting. An explanation of how smart someone is, but how difficult they are to deal with, can be a prelude to firing. The craziest case that I am aware of is a situation where a month before product introduction, one of the designers decided that the design was incorrect. In his opinion, the entire design should be scrapped and the product rebuilt. In fact, the designer staked his career on that decision. After the meeting, the person was never invited back to the project and quickly left the project and company.

Once the direction has been set, all of the designers and implementers need to get on board or leave because there is not much room for second guessing. It is time to start designing and implementing.

Wounded Rabbits

After you have the design in the bag, you normally make a presentation to a group of your associates, your bosses, or your potential customers. This is a very difficult process. Everyone wants to put their two cents in, and the more that the reviewers know, the more they want to make a point in the review process. Or, a customer may want to show their associates how smart they are and how quickly they understand your product or design.

The biggest hazard in this circumstance is the Wounded Rabbit Syndrome. I don't know if psychologists have a name for such a syndrome, but in the late 1960s, a teacher who was a specialist in technical presentations taught in his class that the key to an effective technical presentation was the first question that you would face. His said you must nail the first question. If you did not nail the question, you would be just like a wounded rabbit.

Let us consider the wounded rabbit. Alongside the road, a crowd has gathered and everyone is looking at a sweet little rabbit that has been injured. It may or may not be critically injured, but it is injured to the point where it is clearly incapacitated.

What happens next is really dependent on one person. If one person comforts the rabbit, everyone will have sympathy for the rabbit. But if one person kicks the rabbit, everyone will pile on and stomp the life out of the rabbit. Human nature is such that this does seem true. Anyone who has read William Golding's book

Lord of the Flies will recognize this dark aspect of human nature.

What happens next depends on your response to the first question. If you have a well-thought-out immediate response delivered in a confident and knowledgeable manner, you'll be successful. If you fail and look vulnerable, anyone in the audience opposed to your position will try to stomp you. At that point, you will have an uphill battle to reestablish yourself.

In fact, I have never seen people who got off to a bad start recover. They just get stomped.

In many cases, a smart lead designer will plant a softball question in the audience so they can hit a home run with the first question. At that point, there is no stampeding that day.

One of the best trial lawyers I know claims this is just a variation of the well-prepared lawyer. In a complex product with many variables, you need to make sure you are prepared and do not become the wounded rabbit.

You must understand the trade-offs that went into your product and be able to articulate and defend these trade-offs.

Lion Hunters and Assistant Trainers

In many cases, I have had little prior training to perform the types of jobs that were required of me and have sought the help of highly skilled professionals. Many times, these professionals were friends of mine so that I could gauge the quality of their professional opinions. In the early 1980s, I encountered alternative personalities: the wounded rabbit killer, the assistant trainer, and the lion hunter. I had encountered these personalities earlier in my career and, like the wounded rabbit killer, could not put a name to the phenomena.

When I was working for computer manufacturers, there would be meetings that just baffled me. In the case of a complete system design review, we would get bogged down and some people would just get beat beyond recognition over simple issues. Initially I was concerned about these design reviews, but after a couple of them, they became a giant source of amusement.

When I started my own company, I was doing a lot of presentations and seminars. A friend who was a motivational speaker offered to improve my skills. I was about to be trained by Steve "Big Tuna" Lundin, the author of the immensely popular book *Fish*. As we prepared the seminar, he asked how I prepared for a speaker's worst nightmare, the lion hunter and the assistant trainer. I didn't know about lion hunters and assistant trainers. Once he explained, things became clearer. Lion hunters are people who want to prove that they are smarter than the speaker. If lion hunters can they will try to take out the speaker during the presentation.

The other problem children are the assistant trainers. They are the audience members who try to help the presenter deliver the presentation. They may elaborate on a point that the speaker was making.

The problem with these characters is that while the lion hunter is trying to take you out, the assistant trainer, while being helpful, chews up the clock and wastes time. It is important if you give a presentation or lead a group that you control these characters so that you are not the wounded rabbit. The key is preparation! Whether you are discussing a product in front of a customer or leading a design team, you must know your stuff and be able to defend your positions.

The Big Tuna was instructive. The Big Tuna added a number of questions to my evaluation form. After the seminar, the Big Tuna gave his immediate conclusion: one of the worst seminars he had ever attended. The viewgraphs were crummy, the presentation lacked pizzazz, the jokes and stories were stupid, and he could not believe that the audience had stayed for the entire seminar. While I took care of some administrative issues, the Big Tuna compiled the evaluation forms and prepared to give me a detailed critique to help me get better. When I joined him in the bar, he said he thought all of his previous comments were correct. The only thing he could say was that the evaluation scores were the best he had ever seen and there was nothing he could do to help me.

The Big Tuna concluded that when presenting boring subjects like design trade-offs, be organized and develop your arguments so they're understandable and defendable. Then you will have no problems with lion hunters, assistant trainers, or wounded rabbit killers. As the years have gone by, I have encountered the Big Tuna on many airplanes. He always asks to see my materials if he thinks I have been giving a presentation. His conclusion to this day is that my slides are still crummy, my delivery is still probably boring, and my stories are clearly still dull. But he has never argued with the evaluation forms.

It's all about preparation when you have to explain complex subjects like trade-offs.

Government Research to University/Industry Research to Business Product to Consumer

Massive amounts of money are required to do fundamental research that eventually turn into finished products. Generally, commercial enterprises do not have the vision to do a lot of fundamental research. It seems that many major developments are spinoffs of military research. Or they may be the spin-off of a special program that does not seem solvable. Consider military and space programs. They have given us major advances in the commercial industry because commercial firms have been adept at turning the fundamental developments from the programs into consumer products. For example, without the laser you do not have DVD players. Without special military and space program research, you do not have the laser. There are a lot of examples of spin-off products from fundamental research.

In many cases, a consumer product starts as a government requirement. Normally, a university or industrial research lab picks up the requirement and provides that initial solution to a business that commercializes the product to the consumer.

One of the greatest examples is the Internet. The Internet started as a government research project to establish a new way of communicating information between disparate computers. One of the first applications for this new way of communicating was email. Then this communications medium morphed into the World Wide Web, and as they say, the rest is history.

This transition never gets to take place without the vision of a government champion and the cooperation of a number of university and industry partners. This type of development cannot be legislated or orchestrated. In many ways, it simply depends upon some evolution of a fundamental development that drives the technology into the consumer space.

Some of our greatest inventions were initially developed off of a government vision! The group in the government that has the greatest need for advanced technologies is the military. The military has the incentive to take risks and the need to develop technology that will give it an advantage on the battlefield. Consider the development of global positioning systems. They were not developed to allow you to wander around the countryside; they were originally developed by the U.S. military to develop guided weapons systems or to locate its own troops. There are tons of such examples ranging from lasers to communications satellites.

Technology Cycles

There are cycles of technology. Just because one product is in the lead today does not mean it will be the leading product tomorrow. In many cases, trends go in cycles. What is a trailblazing high-growth company today is tomorrow's laggard. You can be on top one minute, and a simple change of abstraction or a revolutionary product will put you at the bottom of the pile. The designers of the new product have your success as a guide and will really want to get to the top of that pile. You'll want your picture on the surfing magazine cover riding down that really big wave. You probably do not care about the cover of *Reader's Digest* or any popular magazine, but you do care whose picture is on the front page of that special issue of the big wave surfing magazine.

The same can be said of a company. At one time, IBM was the leading computer company in the world. In the mid-1980s, it was the envy of every other computer company. It had a string of high-growth years. It was poised to extend its dominance of the industry and vanquish its competitors. Instead, it got vanquished by a simple extension of computing power to the desktop. The power shifted out of the big glass-enclosed computer rooms with raised floors onto the desktop.

Today Cisco, Google, and Microsoft sit in the position of IBM, and it is inevitable that something in the product cycle will turn. They will probably fall on hard times as they miss new capabilities brought on by different products with different looks. What will change in the cycle we do not know for sure. These companies are very large and successful. Thus, there are a lot of people looking for storms that are new technologies hoping to vanquish the current successful companies. This battle can be fought by products that differ by cost or function, or with new abstractions. But there is always another technology wave with big wave surfers hoping to ride to glory by taking out one of the major growth companies. Microsoft failed to capitalize on early Internet capabilities such as the search function that Google capitalized. Google failed to predict social networks.

How these cycles will occur we cannot really say until after the fact, but the cycle will occur and in a manner that no one can really predict.

Eventually IBM grew so big that to grow it needed to create the equivalent of a Digital Equipment Corporation (DEC) each year. At that time, in the 1980s, DEC was over $1 billion a year in sales and the world's leading minicomputer manufacturer. But IBM missed the start of the PC industry, and while trying to play catch-up to Apple, IBM just stopped growing. The company had grown too fat to make effective and viable decisions. Even though IBM is still a good company, it has not returned to its glory years and probably never will.

Product Cycles—Wheel of Reincarnation

In the classic 1982 book on computer architecture *Computer Structures: Principles and Examples*, editors Daniel P. Siewiorek, C. Gordon Bell, and Allen Newell address the issue of cycles in product development. They look at the problems of the constantly changing relationship between parts of a computing system. Their resulting concept is the wheel of reincarnation. This is a wheel that is constantly rotating through the changing trade-offs between memory, processing power, and I/O capabilities. This concept is one of the best statements of the design cycle in existence. The idea that new concepts are always driving the design environment is key.

Every time there is an advance in the technology, something will change that will allow you to enter with a new or revised product. The change in technology can affect the system abstraction in a variety of ways. The introduction of high-speed I/O in LANs along with evolving trends in wide area network technology caused workgroup systems to evolve into full-blown Internet ecommerce systems.

There is a constant change in technology, and it is incumbent on designers to think about the ramifications and how to exploit these changes.

What new type of products can we come up with? What problems does a new product cause, and how can we solve these problems? How can we incorporate old concepts in a more efficient manner? What previous functions could we reimplement that would make for a major cost, performance, or functionality change? And would these changes allow us to get a jump on our competition?

This thinking process will allow us to implement or reimplement new ideas and new technology to strengthen our new product against a competitive product.

Massive Disruption—Carterfone Decision

Tom Carter—have you ever heard of him? Ma Bell—have you ever heard of her?

Ma Bell was a nickname for AT&T, the phone company. Ma Bell ruled the world like a crazed nun in a Catholic grade school ruled the classroom with a metal-edged ruler. Nobody would go up against the vaunted Ma Bell for fear of punishment. She made sure that no one connected to her telephone lines, and we had a high-quality, albeit very expensive, phone system. If you messed with Ma Bell, your knuckles would get rapped with that great big ruler and you would be found with broken hands and bleeding knuckles. Ma Bell ruled her domain.

Tom Carter is one example of an extremely important pioneer who essentially created an industry, yet few people have ever heard of Tom. Tom designed a simple system that eventually caused an industry revolution. Tom worked in the oil industry and was a creative and practical person. Yet his contribution to technology is essential to telecommunications. Without Tom, the business of telecommunications, the Internet, and the computer industry would look very different. In the old days, Ma Bell controlled communications. She had a death grip, a total stranglehold, on communications in the United States. Outside the United States, national phone systems had a similar grip, but like Ma Bell, they too were eventually dispatched, although they fought very hard and it took longer to dispatch these tyrants.

Tom had the problem of communicating between oil rigs in the Gulf of Mexico and corporate workers on land. The conventional way this occurred was someone would call on a radio to another person on shore. That person would call the office and then relay messages between the home office and the oil rig. Pretty clumsy! Tom Carter invented the Carterfone to solve this very problem. The Carterfone would allow a radio to dial through to a phone in the office without a person being in the loop. You would call to shore; they would dial the number and then place both the phone handset and the radio receiver into a coupling device, the Carterfone.

Before the invention of the Carterfone, all communications were controlled by Ma Bell. She controlled the technology, the lines, the infrastructure, and with the help of the government she also controlled the tariffs. Ma Bell was a regulated utility, and her job was to provide a highly reliable, high-quality, universal (and expensive) service. In fact, Ma Bell was one of the greatest and most profitable corporations in America.

The rules said that Ma Bell owned the lines of communications. The Carterfone attached acoustically to Ma's lines and went about its business until that fateful day when Ma discovered that she had a wayward child that was misbehaving. Ma immediately tried to put a stop to the bad behavior, and Tom fought back. (Previously, Ma Bell had successfully killed a device that attached to the phone's mouthpiece similar to cupping your hand around the mouthpiece. Eventually this decision was set aside by the courts, but the Hush-A-Phone decision emboldened Ma Bell to continue to defend her turf with a vengeance.) Eventually, the Federal Communications Commission and its faceless government employees toiling in the bureaucracy came out with the Carterfone decision. The Carterfone decision allowed any organization to connect to the lines of Ma Bell as long as they met the specifications of Ma Bell. Ma was required to publish these specifications.

The rest is history—MCI, Sprint, PBXs (Private Branch Exchanges), computer communications, etc.

The Carterfone Decision, Federal Communications Commission ruling 13 F.C.C.2d 420, in 1968 allowed for the selling of devices that could connect to the Ma Bell–controlled phone system using a protective coupler. That opened the market to a phone system containing customer-owned equipment. In effect, any lawful device (a device that met Ma Bell's specifications) was allowed.

Thus, we saw the proliferation of devices such as Anderson-Jacobson acoustic couplers, a wide variety of modems, fax machines, and eventually PBX and other devices that would enable a wide variety of communications.

Without the Carterfone decision, the entire telecommunications industry from equipment manufacturers to long-distance resellers to cell phones to the Internet may not have existed.

Sometimes the start of a big wave is a simple administrative decision that allows for the proliferation of technology. This FCC administrative decision allowed for the creation of these new products and technologies. Without Tom Carter, there are trillions of dollars and thousands of companies that may not have existed. If you think this is just a small, old historical reference to an arcane fact, think again. Skype is trying to get the decision applied to the wireless network, and others are using it to try to break the vendor lock in the voice and data network businesses. The Carterfone decision will continue to allow entrepreneurs to innovate in the telecommunications space for decades to come.

Amazing Visionaries and Vannevar Bush

There are numerous examples of visionaries. Some get it right, and some completely miss the boat. Other visionaries are adaptable, and many are very forward looking.

As the computer industry evolved, there were a number of classic visionaries in major segments of the industry.

In the emerging mainframe market, the head of IBM had one of the best quotations (possibly an urban myth of a quote because it seems quite difficult to find an actual citation for the comment Watson is alleged to have made) indicating the level of understanding that people had of this early new industry. The quote attributed to Thomas Watson Sr. in 1943 is, "I think there is a world market for maybe five computers." IBM and its management, as well as its competitors, clearly did not have a firm grip on the future of the computer industry. But perseverance paid off for IBM.

When the minicomputer industry came along, DEC came into prominence, and in the midst of its success, it underestimated the PC industry. In 1977, Ken Olson, the founder and president of DEC, weighed in on the PC industry at a meeting of the World Future Society with the following quote: "There is no need for any individual to have a computer in his home." This quote was made famous when it was published in *Time* magazine after the World Future Society meeting. Later, DEC would fall on hard times and eventually be taken out of the computer industry as it got absorbed by Compaq, which was eventually swallowed by Hewlett-Packard.

Even Bill Gates gets an occasional surprise. His quote (as reported in CNET News July 2, 1998) about the Internet is very telling: "Sometimes we do get taken by surprise. For example, when the Internet came along, we had it as a fifth or sixth priority."

Clearly, all of the above people and their companies were successful and were successful for an extended period of time. One of the keys to their success was the ability to evolve over a period of time and keep reinventing their companies. No one has really been as successful as Bill Gates in terms of reinventing and repositioning his corporate abilities and assets for an extended period of time.

There are other visionaries that look so far forward that their visions cannot be acted on and don't come true in exact form. However, their concepts are significant because they predict trends or sense a swell in the technology ocean.

One important concept was the idea of a statistical machine. Emanuel Goldberg's Statistical Machine, a photographic-based document search engine that searched metadata stored on microfilm, was described in U.S. patent 1,838,389 on December 29, 1931. This patent contained some of the earliest known concepts that could be used to form a basis for current Internet-based workstations.

Other ideas for workstations were proposed in the 1930s. A microfilm-based workstation was proposed by Leonard Townsend during 1938.

Both the Goldberg machine and the Townsend machine may be considered predecessors of the proposed memex machine. Memex was a late 1930s concept proposed by Vannevar Bush. Bush was an early engineering pioneer and the first head of the National Defense Research Council, which was the formal forerunner to the American concept of a defense-related research and development industry. His proposed memex device has been criticized by some as a knock-off of the Goldberg and Townsend machines, but it contains a lot of advanced concepts. Memex was a workstation-like device that was based upon the idea of associative addressing. It contains similar abstract concepts of addressing what would-be forerunners of the HTML ideas used in the World Wide Web.

In "As we may think," published in the *Atlantic Monthly* magazine in July of 1945, Bush predicted that "Wholly new forms of encyclopedias will appear; ready made with a mesh of associative trails running through them, ready to be dropped into the memex and there amplified." Bush is an example of an early visionary. But the concepts he developed were way before his time. The ability to look ahead and consider other ways to envision a system or concept is at the heart of performing trade-off analysis for future product development.

There are a wide variety of visionaries. Some of the visionaries take theory to practice, such as the founders of Apple, Microsoft, Oracle, and other major companies. Yet even these people misjudge technology. Visionaries tend to underestimate the future, the rate of change, and how the future will work out. But if you can get even one big wave and ride it for a little time, you will find great success can occur rather quickly.

Design Trade-Offs—Dynamic Tension— I/O, Memory, CPU, Software

There are constant changes within the capability of the hardware that are available to designers. As components get ahead of other parts necessary to build a product, the kinds of products that can be built change rapidly.

But even further development has changed the entire product scene. The key development is that hardware is essentially free. "Free," you say, "that can't be. Look at what I paid to buy product X."

Well it is true, hardware is essentially free. Consider, the power contained in an iPod or the power of the microprocessors that run your car engine or the amount of processing power in a digital radio. You are carrying supercomputers around in your pocket or driving them around in your car. The design strategy (employed by CDC or Cray Computer) for a supercomputer always used to be that the first model would cost $10,000,000 and no software was included. Your iPod has more memory and your PC has more processing power than the old-time supercomputer.

The simple fact that computing power is free has let companies make user interfaces that are intuitive (at least to a teenager) and let the computer move into all aspects of society. Think of the simple and ubiquitous iPod. Its memory is measured in gigabytes, and depending on the model, its screen displays colorful motion video and stores entire movies. In the heyday of the supercomputer, it was a great trick to be able to store and replay simple songs with a synthetic sound system that sounded like a fuzzy kazoo.

This rapid progress of technology has added a new dimension to the main design elements of a system, and that is to rapidly and cheaply implement software. This has led to the concept of reusable objects and open source software. The cost of software has also been driven down to basically free.

Part of this cost reduction is due to volume considerations. If you can design a product that has true mass appeal, the cost will drop like a stone and the market will quickly expand. What at one time was huge volume is now commonplace due to computer games and other technology applications.

Yet, there is this constant tension between I/O, processing power, memory, and software. The easier you want to make the interface, for example, the more you must narrow the functions available or the more processing power and memory must be devoted to the interface. Eventually, designers have had to come up with truly unique interfaces such as on the iPhone and iPod. In these interfaces, many functions are provided by dragging items in a list rather than searching through the list, and thus, it takes a bit of getting used to the interface to really use the product. In a large majority of cases, designers are able to build into the product functions that will never be used by the average user due to the large amount of free capabilities provided in the basic hardware device.

As we progress on our journey, remember that there are now very difficult design choices due to very complex interactions between the various hardware parts and the software.

I do not want to claim that all software and hardware are

free. There are some very expensive systems that are developed, but these tend to be low-volume, extremely reliable systems for military applications or the operation of nuclear power plants. What makes these systems so expensive is the desire to achieve reliabilities that allow the systems to run for years without a failure and the fact that each system may be customized for a particular requirement. In such cases, hardware is expensive and software is incredibly expensive!

Trade-Offs—Simply a Matter of Programming

The goal of modern programming is to hide from the user the details and complexities of the underlying applications. This is achieved by building abstractions that can be reused generally, called *objects* or collections of objects called *object class libraries*. In developing applications, you will attempt to build the underlying fundamental structure of the program to use previously developed objects and then try to reuse as many objects as possible. It is through this structural way of doing business that the cost of software has come down to reasonable levels. The capability of the general programming population has dropped so the average programmer is not faced with a start-from-scratch program that has high economic incentives based on the success of the program or its future derivatives.

Thus, the type of programmer or system designer that you will need to get into the product development business will be a different breed. They must not only be able to program, but also conceive of the class libraries and how to implement them to set up the systems. Yet, many managers will not differentiate these skill levels necessary to set the product in motion. In many cases, they will only look at the time in man months that it takes to develop a program. As I have been told numerous times, it is simply a matter of programming. Well, it isn't. It is a matter of sizing the job, figuring out who on your staff can accomplish what amount of work in a fixed amount of time, and getting the personal commitments of the staff to complete this job in a timely fashion. This is an art. But it is critical to the development of the product and will make or break the new company. Trade-offs will have to occur because everyone will want to be the lead programmer, but few are truly capable of doing that function. Plus, the jobs will have to be configured based upon individual characteristics.

In the recent past, programming was done by highly skilled practitioners who spent years developing their art and capabilities, but now there are a large number of programmers who have been schooled in the higher levels of abstractions who have no basic idea of how the programs work. This is not a problem if you are going to develop a program that is really a tailoring of an application to an Oracle database or an SAP application. These can be, and in most cases are, time-consuming, expensive undertakings, but in comparison to developing a communications driver for a specific interface card containing a new chip set, they are really simple tasks. In the case of the database, you need to set up the fields and relationships and build the retrieval algorithms and then build the applications. Eventually, you need to tune the application and deploy it.

There can be massive amounts of work to accomplish this task. In fact, the job may cost anywhere from five to twenty times the cost of the basic Oracle product for the development, operation, training, and deployment of the product. But the underlying work is not really that difficult as long as the lead programmers have built a detailed specification of the systems functions and partitioned the work properly. There are many tools to help you. The job really boils down to driving out the functions and verifying their implementation. This type of work goes on all of the time, and there are large numbers of capable programmers available to do this type of work.

On the other hand, building that new communications driver is another problem. It requires not only the programming skills that would make you a good programmer in any high-level environment, but also a detailed understanding of how the software will fit onto the hardware. In fact, the lower the level of the programming that is required, the more critical the trade-offs and run-time efficiency of the application. Consider an application that is implemented in a set of structures that can be essentially layered. If the top layer is not efficient, say it runs 10 percent slower than desired, that may not be a huge problem. But if at each layer of a multilayered application there is a 10 percent drop, then the speed of the program slows down dramatically. So it is critical to make the programs efficient at each level, but it is critical to make the lowest levels of the application very efficient, and we need a different breed of programmer for the lowest level of programming.

Once we were involved with a lawsuit where programming skills were critical. The object of the investigation was to find how certain machine features were used. The other investigators involved in the case were looking at things from a conventional manner. They had all of the right information. When we brought in our information, they were in a state of shock because we had uncovered the information they'd been searching for. They had done all of the right things. But what they had not understood was that the information they needed was detailed programming at the system level. These programmers would not develop features in a conventional manner. They would be programmers who concentrated on high-performance critical infrastructure development and that information would not be contained in a conventional book.

Changes in the programming environment will cause economic dislocation. Any time a new abstraction occurs, there will be developers who understand the technology, and these programmers will get to charge a lot of money. A classic case was when LANs were first popular. Novell developed a program to certify Novell engineers. They could not certify these engineers fast enough, so an economic dislocation occurred and a certified engineer could command twice the billing rate of a noncertified engineer. In fact, many engineers quit their jobs when they became certified and later were unemployed when Novell got its certification process up to speed and started to crank out certified engineers at a rapid pace. In the short term, the people who quit were able to command a very high price. The Novell people were quite clever because they created a high demand for their training and then got to reap the economic benefits of providing the training. In reality, the training was really very simple and did not provide the certified engineers much real understanding of how the product worked or could be tuned to work better. I often remarked to some of my associates that the engineers were trained like I was originally trained by my dad to set the valves of my car.

Before cars were controlled by computers and worked as well as they do today, you had to do a lot of expensive maintenance. One of the least desirable jobs was setting your valve clearances. At the time, I was driving a 1956 Corvette that had a 265 V8 bored out to 283 cubic inches. Because I set the valves myself, I had learned from my dad to warm up the motor, remove the valve covers, and then back off each valve until you heard it tap. You then turned it down until the noise disappeared. You then turned down the valve ¼ of a turn three times, waiting for the lifter to pump up between each turn. If you were going racing and wanted to get higher RPMs, you could go down four turns. There was also a set sequence of turning down the valves.

This is how Novell trained its engineers. They were given a set of concepts and a formula without a lot of understanding of how the system fundamentals could work and perform at an acceptable level. If your trade-off was real performance, I would call a friend simply known as the Griff, who was a motorhead of the first order.

He would come over with the Chevrolet spec book and a set of tools. With that book, we would find the settings of the valves in microns and we would set each valve with a micrometer to get the precision that we would need for the performance level that we wanted. We could use the mic to set to Chevy's spec, or we could tweak the spec a little but tweak on thousandths of inches. It's a trade-off on how deep you really want to go into the innards of the system environment. Not everyone will need to know how many thousandths of an inch we need to set the valves, but somewhere there is someone who does have to know.

When phones were first introduced, Bell Labs did studies to determine how long a phone number should be. They concluded that phone numbers needed to be a maximum of seven numbers and characters because people had trouble remembering longer strings. Yet there are a wide variety of capabilities, and in particular, there are a real wide variety of programmers. So it is important to understand their capabilities and to set the workload accordingly. People learn to remember and do things differently and at different rates. One of the most critical trade-offs that must be made in a development environment is apportioning the work so that everything gets done at the appropriate time. You cannot leave an unproven programmer in your critical path.

Copying is flattery. Some of the best programmers are some of the best copiers that I have ever seen. It is important in the development of a major program or system to not reinvent the wheel and to learn from your previous mistakes. Your lead programmer must be able to point the junior people to where they need to concentrate their efforts to get the problem solved. Experience and battle scars along with overall capabilities will get your project done on time.

It is only within the above framework that anyone can view the trade-offs necessary to set your development schedule as simply a matter of programming.

Two-Tape Turing Machines vs. Go-Fast Hardware

A problem as you develop your product is how fast it should perform. One of the problems that I have had with programmers and system developers is that they all want to deal with the functions of the application. They do not want to get involved with making the system go fast enough to deliver the performance required by the user. Part of this problem is that people do not understand how to modify algorithms to make them execute fast on a particular computer. In fact, every programmer that I have met has the tendency to want to build their algorithm to run fast by optimizing the algorithm for a specific machine. To develop good software, you need to develop it so that it will run fast across a wide variety of hardware configurations.

Turing machines were first described by Alan Turing in 1937. Turing was an English mathematician and described a fundamental mechanism of computation that involved symbols on a tape and controlling the tape to produce the essence of an algorithm. Even though you could conceivably compute any algorithm using a Turing Machine, it would be extremely cumbersome and time consuming.

As time passed, people developed concepts for other forms and models of automated systems. One advanced form of a Turing Machine was that of a two-tape Turing machine. This machine used multiple (two) tapes because the use of two tapes made programming easier and execution faster.

Thus, we had the idea that we could modify the performance of the algorithm by changing parameters of the basic system upon which it ran.

Enter the concept that I will call go-fast hardware. This is really a variation on high-speed power boats. There are a number of high-performance, primarily ocean-going speed boats. An example of boats is the Fountain Power Boats built by Reggie

Fountain. These boats are designed to run at very high speeds on the oceans and are generically referred to as go-fast boats. If you want to go some distance in the ocean, you can use a variety of boats, which have similar overall characteristics. For example, they float, have engines, hold people, and have a certain bow size. If you want to go between two places in a hurry, you could just simply upgrade your boat to a go-fast boat by applying a lot of money to your boat purchase. But the trade-off is that you will use a lot of fuel to go fast.

Similarly, if you have a program that you want to go faster, the simplest solution is to buy a faster system that contains a faster processor and lots of high-speed memory. At a later time, you can begin working on modifying the algorithm.

Remember, you can do lots of computations with theoretical systems like Turing machines, but in reality you can never beat a go-fast processor. You do not get computations for free. You must pay the price for go-fast hardware, but in most cases, your performance in running a program is based upon how fast the basic hardware runs. Generally, one of the best ways to speed up an application is to buy a lot of high-speed memory.

Mathematical Proofs—If A Then B

When describing a product or presenting a concept to a customer, I do not like to leave the forum without having developed a position so that marketing and sales can close the sale. The job of the senior technology leader is to get the marketing staff into position to close the sale. It is the job of the technical staff to launch marketing onto the wave.

The secret is to approach the entire problem well prepared, but fundamentally from the point of view of a mathematician. Explain your view of the correct trade-off (that forms the basis of your product) as a mathematical proof. The hypothesis is that if your problem is A then the solution to your problem is B, and guess what, we are selling B. Further, there is no other product that solves A. Thus, you need to immediately buy our product B. The trick here is to understand the customer's problem and to learn how to approach this problem in a manner that illustrates that your product is the only solution to the customer's problem!

The idea of a proof-based strategy is not unique to the technology industry. I have seen it in many other industries and with a variety of products. While picking up some parts for a Corvette at the local Chevrolet dealer, I ended up talking to one of the sales guys and we got into a discussion of how a Chevrolet dealer could sell a high-end car like the Corvette against other cars with more cache. The salesperson shared with me a copy of his sales manual. In the manual, there were a set of scenarios that illustrated the capabilities of the Corvette against a lot of other vehicles. Function, cost, performance, and total cost of ownership comparisons were included in the manual. The manual had all of the requisite sales points laid out in an easy-to-use format that provided the salesperson with the ability to counter almost any argument that could prevent the customer from selecting the Corvette. It made the salesperson's job quite easy if you had an interested customer.

In selling a big wave product, the strategy from engineering the product to selling the product is quite similar to constructing the Corvette sales manual. You need to construct a product that is unique. The product must have the requisite performance and functional characteristics, and then you must demonstrate the proper value-added and cost benefits.

In thinking about the product, you need to think about how to position the product like a proof. The design and benefits must work in the sales environment. So you can tell your customer, if you need a product that does A, then our product is your only choice because we are the only company that does A.

You want to demonstrate that the product has a set of functions that are useful to a particular customer and then show the customer the advantages of implementing these functions.

From the design to the sale, you need to approach the problem as a proof. Postulate the customer's needs, and verify the needs of a class of customers. While you design the product, you can aim the product for a set of problems that have an economic benefit. When looking at the design, make sure that every part of the design meets some part of the customer's need. When the product is complete, you can then prove that the product solves a real and pressing problem in a cost-effective manner.

Thus at every part of the process, you want to ask whether feature Z contributes to the solution B. Is feature Z unique? Finally, when approaching the customer you can carefully lay out the argument that if you have this problem, then you need features that give you solutions to the problems associated with A. Our product has been designed and implemented to solve problem A and its derivative problems. Thus, you should buy B because it solves your problem. And, we are prepared to deliver B to you.

Trade-Off Scenarios

Scenarios are one of the most useful tools in the area of trade-offs.

Consider the simple concept of dropping a stone into the middle of a silent pond. If the pond is a perfect circle and we drop the stone into the center, a set of ripples will emerge that go toward the pond edge at a consistent pace arriving at the same time. This is our perfect pond scenario.

In the real world, however, the pond is not perfect. In fact, to get a perfect pond we need to make a lot more assumptions than we did in the previous paragraph. We need assumptions about depth, as well as assumptions about the angle the stone drops into the water. Eventually, we may need to make a lot more assumptions, but we don't need to go any further with our assumptions to illustrate this point.

In the analogy above, we developed and described our perfect pond scenario. But how would the ripples proceed to the edges if the pond had a nonuniform depth? What if the stone entered the pond at an angle and the pond had a nonuniform depth? Further, if we had included those details in the scenario, other issues could affect the result, like whether a stick was penetrating the water at some point. The scenarios can go on ad infinitum. What would happen, for example, if suddenly another person had dropped a boulder into the water?

A scenario is only as good as the quality of the assumptions behind the scenario. If you mess up the assumptions, you will be surprised at the results. The ability of people to misunderstand the value and predictive capacity of scenarios is legendary. This has led to people talking about concepts such as the Law of Unintended Consequences or the saying that "The best-laid plans of mice and men sometimes go awry."

The reason that scenarios are important is that you do not want to blindly embark on a course of action without thinking about the consequences. What will the competition do? Is there another variation or a similar product that could be introduced? Do we have the right pricing strategy? These are the types of questions we need to ask as we develop our product development and introduction strategies.

But scenarios have even broader application. In general, technical scenarios are relatively simple and usually easy to figure out. For example, what is the effect of a new set of instructions in a computer? Or what is the effect of a new memory technology? In chapter 9, we will discuss the length of time that it took for semiconductor memories to displace core memories and some of the innovations that people developed for core memories. Core memory developers were an inventive and feisty lot, and it took years for semiconductor memories to displace them. However, the point is that once you conduct a scenario and begin to implement it, you should expect that the other side will react in any number of ways to counter your advantages. No stakeholder from the other side will let you win without a struggle.

Even if the scenario mechanism is far from perfect, it is an important drill for you to go through. As you develop and implement products, you must try to understand the consequences of your actions. Once you take an action and the other side reacts, you need to revisit your scenarios to adjust and counter the actions of the competition. In a sense, Newton was wrong. In the product business, for every action there is a variety of reactions of consequence. Newton had a more straightforward problem and thus encountered a reaction that was equal and opposite.

Now if simple scenarios require periodic updating and adjusting, then more complex scenarios will require more adjustment. You should never underestimate what some group will do in response to your actions. (Politicians should take note; they are the worst at figuring out people's reactions.)

Classic examples of bad scenario planning or failure to adjust to people's reactions abound. The biggest example is regulation or lack thereof in the investment banking community by government agencies in various nations. This list is endless: wars; bonus payments to AIG managers; auto makers flying to Washington, D.C., in their private jets looking for government money; and bubbles created in housing, stocks, and raw materials. The list could go on and on. You need to look at scenarios as a tool to quantify your responses and counter the competition.

It is important to have a plan and at least one set of scenarios for failure. Everyone who I know always sticks with the rosy scenarios. But what would you do if things worked out badly? You need to develop a broad set of scenarios that encompass many possible results.

For example, you can file for a provisional patent. That shields your information from public view for close to a year, and it establishes your date for rights to the technology. Of course, after a year you have to file a regular patent application to protect the technology. So if you are introducing a new technology, you will probably do a search for filed and granted patents. You do need to think about what happens the day after you introduce your new product and you discover that there was a provisional patent to the same technology and it predates your invention. I am not suggesting that you should be overly concerned, but it would be useful if you thought about these issues ahead of time.

For example, we once introduced a product to a small market on a specific date and created a trademark. About a month later, at a trade show, I was walking past the booth of a large computer manufacturer who was introducing a similar product and using a term that we had just trademarked. The net result was we were both kind of embarrassed. We had not thought that we would have to devote resources to trying to force the other company to make changes, and the other company had not thought that anyone else would come up with some of the same images. We had a long and not very fruitful phone conversation. At the end of the conversation, our competitor understood that we really owned the trademark and it offered us a very large sum of money to assign it to them. This made me quite happy. At that point, we had only shipped about ten copies of the product and I thought that it would be easy for us to assign the trademark and move on. However, when the other stakeholders looked at the offer they felt it was inadequate because when they calculated the costs to make their changes, the large company was offering us an amount that was way below its costs. The company was surprised when we refused the offer (because it was a significant amount of money), and we then countered with an offer about four times what the company had proposed. We thought that our offer was fair. The company thought we should roll over because it was the big company. Needless to say, it had to change and was unhappy. I ended up unhappy because its resultant marketing blitz rendered our product irrelevant. We won on principal and lost on execution. Our trade-off was that our image and brand name was more important than the other company's money.

First-Order Effects

In most businesses, everything can seem black and white. Did we get the sale? Did Jane get the project done on time? How are we going to meet our quarterly earnings goal?

Many questions, issues, and directions may be black and white, but are they important? Some trade-offs are more important than others.

Did we get the sale? This is obviously an important question, but what if we had two sales pending? One sale is for $100 and the other sale is for $10,000. It's an important question if our average sale is $100. But if our average sale is $10,000 and the sale being discussed is $100, then no one cares. Unless the $100 sale is a buy-in for our first national account that will enable the entire launch of a new product line, then the sale is important.

Likewise, if Jane's project is simply watering a plant in the entry of the office space, it is probably not important. If you talk to an investment banker, there will never be a goal as important as meeting a quarterly earnings goal!

The question is, why are some decisions, issues, and challenges more important than others?

There are some sayings that you have heard that are very important. Don't sweat the small stuff. Who cares? Is it really important? What are the three most important issues?

These types of statements are just one way of saying that in a business all issues and decisions are not equally important. The key trade-off is whether your product does what the user needs and whether you can convince the user to buy your product.

For example, in introducing a new product on a specific date, it is vitally important that the product be complete and work properly. Whether the graphic artist misprinted the background as aqua instead of light blue and we did not have time to change the material is an important issue that needs to be addressed and fixed at the first available opportunity, but it is not the most critical issue.

In any project, some items are more important than others. These are the first-order effects.

In selecting something to eat, there are first-order effects such as do we want fruit, are we hungry, and are we allergic to something. Issues like do we want our meat cooked rare, medium, or well done are secondary issues.

Well, not all of the time! At certain restaurants, we might be concerned about the issues of E. coli. However, if we go to restaurants that have historically good records of health inspections and have reputable managements, then the worry about E. coli is way down on the list of concerns.

One of the most difficult problems is figuring out what the most important issues are. What issues will really affect the outcome of your project? Does the project need a technical breakthrough? Is it dependent upon a certain supplier? Figuring out these issues is critically important and one reason that projects fail.

Any given project can have a list of concerns and issues associated with it. It then becomes a management responsibility to build a cohesive list based upon priority, time constraints, and other criteria. The fact that Joe may have to take his child to a baseball game on Tuesday is an important issue to Joe and little Joey, but it's not an important issue for the project schedule. The need for marketing to meet with the customer and agree on the final price of the product on Tuesday is a critical issue and needs to be factored into the manufacturing schedule if it changes the production run. It's not necessarily a critical issue to the engineering development plan because production issues may not affect them.

What tends to happen in an organization is that the people involved in the project submit their concerns. These concerns are summarized into groups, and major issues from these summaries go through a resolution process. Where the project gets derailed is when the list gets too big or issues of low importance get placed into the mix. Generally, there are only a few real project drivers. In a simple case, the first order is whether we can develop and make the product work. After we get a working prototype, the issues become whether we produce it in a cost-effective manner, how we get early adoptor buzz, and whether we have patent protection.

Risk Management

Every time you enter into a trade-off in your product development cycle, you are looking at risks. If you take out a feature or function, you run the risk that the competition will include that capability in their product. On the other hand, if you include the function and the customer doesn't want the function but you paid some price (either in cost or performance of the product), then you will probably lose.

Risk is at the crux of any set of trade-offs. Technical people want to look at a set of trade-offs just from the technical point of view. This is an interesting point of view in product trade-offs, but it's not necessarily the most important issue. You need to view trade-offs in the total context of the product. Can we actually make it work? Will we have enough features or some type of technical advantage? Will the customers find it useful? How fast will the competition react? Did we select the right price?

Each of these questions illustrates risk. If we make the trade-off and we are wrong, we risk making the product unattractive to customers. When we make a trade-off, we make a judgment about the desirability of the product. The risk is that an undesirable product will not sell. Actually, there are many cases of undesirable products selling and selling well. Sometimes they turn out to be unique and the customer has no choice but to buy the product. In other cases, a bad product can be a winner if the product has a lot of potential customers and very low expectations. For example, a product controlled by a monopoly can be very successful but not be a very good product.

Nothing illustrates the issue of risk in trade-offs more than Windows versus Linux systems. Many technical people view Linux as a far superior product to Windows (whichever version is available at a specific time). However, there is a vast difference in end-user knowledge of both systems. Windows is far simpler for most people to use because they are familiar with the system. Thus, as a trade-off, ease of use trumps technical product. In fact, the vast marketing machine that pumps up Windows convinces the end users that they don't have to be concerned about technical issues such as security, low-cost upgrade paths, quality of the software, etc.

Windows has managed to create a dichotomy in the user community. System implementers generally favor Linux-based servers and the end user favors Windows for its ease of use and graphical user interface. Many other vendors try to give away office applications needed by end users, but the concept of seamless integration and compatibility of Windows products skews the results toward using the Windows products.

The issue is simple. If I pick a product that is not a Windows-certified product, will it work?

Just writing a proposal can involve risk management. There are a wide variety of proposals that are necessary to sell a product. For example, there is an exclusionary proposal and there is also an inclusionary proposal. The exclusionary proposal is written when the customer is trying to buy a single product that meets a set of criteria. In this case, the result is winner takes all. When writing this proposal, you must make sure that you build a finely crafted proposal that displays all of the advantages and none of the disadvantages of your product. When your product is selected by the customers, the other vendors are no longer in the picture.

The inclusionary proposal is designed to get your product on a preferred-vendor list along with a group of other similar products. In this case, your proposal may be a simple specification sheet, a check-off list illustrating that your product meets the requirements and a cost sheet. As long as your product meets the requirements, it gets on the preferred-vendor list and is available for any buyers wanting that product type.

Writing these two types of proposals exposes you to very different risk scenarios. In one case, the game is over for the competition. In the other case, the game is just starting because buyers must pick your product off the list. The amount of effort that you need for either position is different.

The way that you approach the proposal and the amount of resources required also reflect a different level of risk.

Another simple example of risk management is porting software. Consider the case of moving—or porting—software. What happens when your software is running on an obsolete piece of hardware because the manufacturer stops making it? You now have two problems, particularly if you have to port your software to new and faster hardware. First, will the old software run on the new hardware? And second, can we make changes to the old software so when it's ported to the new hardware it will run faster and better?

If the old software does not run on the new hardware, you are in a highly risky situation and you must immediately fix the software. If the software runs on the new hardware, you have less risk and more time to update the software to take advantage of the new features.

Risk is a key ingredient in making your trade-off and development decisions truly decisions. You need to understand and quantify your choices and the risk they bring.

Product Development—Not Rocket Science

Development of a product can seem to be rocket science. Many products, however, are simple evolutions of an old concept. You look at the available building blocks and select the appropriate elements based upon your manufacturing capabilities. There are not really a lot of new things that happen in product development. The easiest development strategy is the path of least resistance. Many product ideas are simple variations on a theme. It is a lot easier to design a product that is a variation on a previous product. Take a competing product, and add something to it to make your product unique.

The underlying enabling technologies of most products are in constant flux. Once you start, you will find that the product contains technologies that can be modified or changed. Thus, you can generate a whole series of new products with slight variations on their basic theme. This is important because if you don't make your product obsolete, your competitors will.

I once met a rocket scientist who designed propulsion systems for rockets. He was an expert in propulsion systems both liquid fueled and solid propellant. I was curious about his background and what made him decide to go into his field. We joked about what a good cocktail party gimmick he had because he was an actual rocket scientist. After getting quite a chuckle over the fun you could have with that title, we talked about how little new technology there really was in the world. He explained that there was not a lot of technology in rocket science. He said the trade-off between an explosion and a rocket launch was how you controlled the explosion of the material that you were about to set off. If you made the material burn really fast, you had an explosion. If you made it burn too slowly, you had a messy fire. But if you could figure out how to make it burn at the correct rate, you could have a tube that blew fire out of one end creating a vast amount of thrust. This tube could then take off to the skies, bringing with it a spectacular show. My rocket scientist said the design of the propulsion system was really a set of trade-offs that had been around since the time that fireworks were invented. Thinking about it, I had to agree—rocket science is overrated. The fact that it is difficult and requires attention to detail is separate from the fact that rocket science is really just a set of trade-offs made in a specific fashion once you get all of the details correct.

The obvious problem is that if you miss some design details, the rocket can become a giant stick of dynamite (so to speak). But the trade-offs can be detailed, and given a reasonably skilled design team, even you can build a rocket. In the early days of the rocket program, the science of trade-offs was not really well understood and it took a few tries before people got it right. That's why a number of rockets failed to get off the ground and blew up on the launch pad.

Once designers made a functional rocket and successfully launched it into space, it became an easy process to duplicate. But the problem changed when the trade-offs changed. It is not good enough to just build a successful rocket that launches into space with a payload. What you want to build is a rocket that for a given propulsion system carries a maximum load. This cuts down on your margin of safety and makes launching the rocket a real adventure. The best case is to launch the rocket with only one pound of fuel to spare. But if you miscalculate, you have a real problem.

Over time, space launches began to look easy because the engineers really understood their technology. Rocket science is not difficult. However, as you begin to put other constraints on the product, such as a certain payload size, the resulting design becomes much more difficult. With the right constraints, development of any product can become an exercise in real rocket science as you try to juggle all of the parameters necessary to get the product to perform specific functions.

Clear Trade-Offs

When I was growing up, certain manufacturers would have contests and have participants explain why their product was good, why the person bought the product, or the product's benefits in twenty-five words or less. This was a very easy contest to develop and organize. You have a simple set of rules, and at a certain time, you receive some entries that you must read. For lack of better terminology, let's call these entries *innovations* and *trade-offs*.

Generally, most of the innovations and trade-offs are going to be garbage. Either the writers did not understand the contest or they came up with nothing that was very innovative.

Additionally, many of the statements are really similar. For example, they may say that the product tastes good, is lightweight, or serves a unique need. But given a large enough set of entries, you will find someone who does truly have a unique view and an innovative statement so that we can announce a contest winner. The winning entry does not have to be truly unique; it just must encapsulate the critical uniqueness of the product.

This simple contest deals directly with the most difficult problems associated with trade-off issues. That is, what is the uniqueness of the product that we are trying to sell?

Let me give you some examples of the trade-off problem.

Once I had to meet with a customer and the customer was in the proccss of selecting a product set to move forward in his system. We had five or six products that spanned a range of useful solutions for this particular customer, and we already had products in the system. Because the customer had already selected us, he just wanted to validate and go over our product positioning. Further, he was really busy and needed to have a brief summary of the products and their status. Because I would have only thirty minutes to deliver our message, I decided that the best approach was to have one slide that summarized each product individually. With five or six slides, I then had the time to briefly highlight the importance of each product and still have time for a few questions.

So I got each lead developer to give me a slide about their particular product. This is difficult for designers to do. They want to give you more information than you need for such a presentation. Many times, it is obvious that designers have no clue about the uniqueness of their particular products. They will describe the product in detail but cannot tell anyone what is special or how it relates to other products. The designers could tell you everything about the product's detailed functions but nothing about why you should care about the product. They cannot understand why the customer does not want to spend hours going over the details of their product.

Eventually, I developed a statement about the innovation features of each product. What was needed was a statement that talked about the importance of the product in a system context, not how the product worked in detail. To deal with the trade-offs that end up in the system, the system's owner needs to understand the product concepts, not how they work in detail.

Another time we developed a product that our technical staff felt was revolutionary because it made sure that systems that booted up were correct and the system itself did not contain a virus. All that was necessary was for the single major manufacturer of the extant product technology to completely change how it did business. The technical staff felt that because I knew the president of the product company I should go to the president and present the idea, and the company would then fall in line with our position.

Not being shy about making such a pitch, I explored the idea.

The idea was great technically, but not very practical. I never called on the president of the company because when we examined the idea there was no advantage. The new concept was not cheaper. It took longer to operate than other similar products. It required a complete change to the manufacturer's production technology. Frankly, it was a great technology idea with no real user benefits. The staff was just floored when we went through an extensive list of issues and could not find one clear advantage. There was no real way to sell the idea. There was no set of trade-offs that would have presented an advantage to the manufacturer. There was no way of describing any innovation that made sense for actual product deployment.

Another example of a trade-off situation was a job that we performed for a major manufacturer. In the heat of battle, it had gone ahead and bought another company for its great technology and market position. After six months, sales had slid and this major company could not figure out what to do. We were brought in to develop a set of lists that would emphasize the uniqueness of the company's products. As we went over each and every product, we developed a detailed position on how the products could be deployed in a unique fashion. Getting ready to present the information to the president of the major company, we prepared a slide that had seven points that completely summarized the unique features of the company's products. We then prepared a report and a set of over 100 slides that gave our analysis in detail. In discussing the details of the presentation to the president of the company, the people who hired us could not believe that I expected to use only one slide during the entire presentation. Because that one slide encapsulated the critical positioning of the product set and its relationships to its competitors, I expected that there would be no need to show additional slides. The critical issue was to describe how the products were unique and how they fit into the market.

The ability to explain a product or its market positioning succinctly is extremely important as the fundamental basis of trade-off analysis. It is not an exact science but allows designers and marketers to simply explain the importance of a product or how its capabilities relate to other products.

Chapter Summary

In successfully developing a new product or concept, the designer of a successful product will have to consider a number of trade-offs. But a successful product may be a simple extension of trade-offs applied to existing products. You will never be able to create and ride a big wave if you do not provide a simple concept that has a compelling user value. Trade-offs need to be considered in the context of whether we can build a compelling new product that will form a big wave structure. We need to examine the disruption that we have encountered or spotted and understand that we can build a new product. The product features constitute our trade-offs. We must create a compelling product, thus forming a big wave that we can ride.

Chapter 6

Big Wave Surfing

Every day I look around to see what is happening in the world, and there are a lot of new technology and products being developed. I remember when the first pocket calculators came out. I remember when the first color televisions became available. I remember when the first computer-based engine control modules appeared in cars. Make your own list, and as you do, you will find that from one day to the next there may not appear to be much change in the technology surrounding our everyday lives, yet there is an incredible amount of change in a very short time. Further, as technology changes and a critical mass of users is established, the cost of the technology will come down at an astounding rate. This chapter will try to capture and summarize technology change from a user perspective. The ocean is very big, and in the middle of the ocean, there are always swells churning and opportunities abounding. Opportunity abounds in all kinds of fields ranging from computers to energy. New drilling and recovery methods for natural gas and oil deposits are as important as the changes to the social networking fabric of the Internet. Consider the changes in the personal computer (PC) business or the energy industry. Opportunity abounds; the question to be answered is the size of the opportunities.

Principle: Technology Change Creates Multiple Varied Opportunities

The development of a new product or technology will create variations of the product and spin-offs of the technology. If a new category of technology is created, then multiple opportunities can exist over an extended time period. But as time goes by, the competition will heat up as the opportunity is recognized. The development of a big wave initial break will get the product game started. We then figure out how to capitalize on the opportunity.

Brewing Storms

There is an incredible economic incentive for people to innovate. A large segment of the population seems to be naturally curious. Thus, there seems to be a wide variety of developments occurring at all times. In big companies, the process is institutionalized. In small companies, it is a matter of survival. The small company must innovate, or it will be overrun by much larger and better financed companies. Many individual inventors get into the mix of developers as they try to make devices that will make their lives better and easier or develop inventions they can patent or market. At the smaller end, the process is institutionalized in the form of specialized investment pools, namely venture capital, private money, or assistance from friends and family.

No matter how or where you fit into the mix, there are opportunities. In **Figure 6-1**, we are right at the breaking point where the big wave is forming. Competition will determine the slope of the wave, and we are hoping to catch and ride a steeply sloped wave with a high return on our investment.

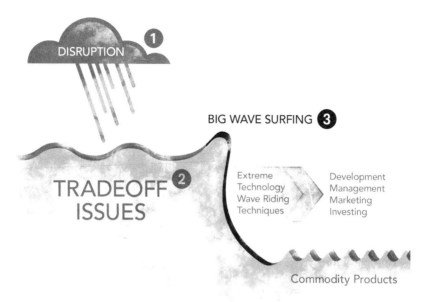

Fig. 6-1: Technology Big Wave Structure—Big Wave Surfing

The number of people trying to develop and exploit technologies is very high. Some of these people are highly professional and have a well-developed plan, and others are simply dreamers. Regardless of which category you are in, there are always opportunities. However, you might be in the wrong location to exploit the opportunities. Just as in the ocean, there are always weather changes such as the sun coming up, heat adding to a particular spot in the ocean, or a change in wind speed that causes changes in the type of waves breaking onto beaches worldwide. Even though waves are always breaking onto beaches, there are not always big waves.

Periodically, there are large storms in the Pacific, and when wind and sun conditions turn just right, big swells form and big waves are pushed onto the beaches. Due to the geological structure of the coastline, there are certain beaches that when the weather conditions are just so they end up with big waves breaking onto the shore.

When this happens, big wave surfers come from all over the globe to ride the giant waves. But there are certain areas of the world that tend to get the big waves when the weather is just right: Oahu's north shore, Mavericks in California, and parts of Australia's Gold Coast. Similarly, there are areas of technology that are fertile: medical devices, pharmaceuticals, computer technology, software, energy storage, and alternative energy production, to name a few. There are also other applications of technology that provide assistance in developing and furthering other technologies. Typical of this is the use of advance recovery technologies in the recovery of oil.

Because of the potential economic effects on a person's life, just like certain beaches tend to have the big waves when the storms come up, certain technologies tend to gather crowds of people trying to cause the next big success story. People tend to specialize, and they learn to spot when the storm of a new technology is kicking up or has the potential to kick up a new set of products and thus financial developments.

Backing these surfers are sets of support staff, venture capitalists, and angel investors. Further, there are a wide range of development tools. Just like an ocean big wave surfer must have the right conditions and equipment along with the right training and attitude, the technology big wave surfer must have the right attitude and the right resources, including the right team of associates at the right time to catch and ride the wave.

The real issue is to find the start of a storm. Because, when a storm starts, the beach will become crowded quickly. There are many areas of activity and tons of people looking to find the next storm. Because of the way storms form, not all beaches get the big waves at the same time. Similarly in technology, the storms brewing in medical devices will not necessarily be occurring at the same time as the storms in computer software. Based upon intellectual property and other barriers to entry, waves will be of varying size. The length of time that big waves will roll onto the beach can be of different durations.

The key issue to understand is that there always does seem to be a storm brewing, and detecting the occurrence of a storm can be difficult, so we need to be vigilant across a number of technology areas.

Big Swells

If we are to be successful in riding big waves, we must first discover how to find big waves. There is a lot of noise in the environment. Out in the ocean, there is a constant movement of water. These movements form swells. It is only when the swells get a major push toward the shore that a wave forms. The more force behind the swells as they move toward the shore, the better our chance of getting a big wave to form.

In the technology world, demands and adaption of technology by users cause the big wave to form. If you can generate a huge user demand, you can create a massive product structure and rapid growth. It is important to differentiate between two often confused concepts. There is a difference between a swell that will create a big wave and the churn that is going into the shore.

A swell usually involves a new or seriously modified technology that will bring on a new or highly modified industry. An example of this is the development of the PC, specifically the Apple II computer, which fueled the emerging growth of the personal computing company Apple. The Apple II was a major breakthrough and essentially moved the PC from the realm of the hobbyist into the mainstream of small business. IBM eventually grabbed onto the concept, and the entire PC industry was born.

An example of churn is the iPhone. In this case, although Apple brought out one of the coolest products in the phone industry, the product was not a game changer for the revenue stream of the phone industry. The phone industry had already become a low-growth industry in which you gain major market share primarily by stealing other companies' customers. Even though the iPhone was a big hit, its effect was on Apple's earnings and not on creating an entirely new industry.

Our probabilities of finding a big wave are higher when a new product forms a new industry.

There are ways to find the trends that are swells. It is a simple issue of looking for trends in the technology areas. Go to conferences and trade expositions that provide overviews of technology trends. Go to trade shows in the technology area for which you have interest. There are a lot of ways to sense trends. The big issue is whether we can ascertain when a trend will actually form a big wave.

In addition to having and determining a sense of technology directions, we need to be able to pick out technologies that have a chance of being game changers. There are ways to spot the technologies that have potential to be game changers. One of the key issues is whether we can actually spot both a technology solution and a customer need. One way to find the need is to look for problems that need to be solved. How are we going to find such a list of problems? For example, in the security industry in the area of information assurance, the Information Security Research Council produces a list of hard problems that need to be solved and the list is updated periodically.

The solution to spotting the swells is to work it from both ends. What are the big problems that need solutions to move forward, and what are the technologies that enable these solutions? When you can make the connection, you then need to begin an analysis of market size—only then can you decide if there is a possibility of a big wave forming.

Beware of a solution looking for a problem when there is no problem that anyone cares about.

Smart People

One of the problems with big wave surfing is that it attracts a lot of people who train to ride the wave. They get very good at surfing. They learn to develop techniques that allow them to ride big waves and manage the risks and uncertainties associated with the unknown wave's variant behavior. Sometimes big wave surfers get lucky, and they have climbed up onto the biggest wave of the day. This wave poses unknown challenges and payoffs if the surfer can just complete the ride. It is the same in the high-technology business. But what differentiates a great technology big wave surfer from an ordinary technology surfer is vision, persistence, and marketing. Great technology big wave surfers must be the total package to succeed. And they cannot get discouraged by their losses.

In high tech, there are a lot of smart people who have trained for years in a variety of business- and technology-related disciplines. They are looking for the same swells and big waves that you are looking for. They work for a variety of companies and have a lot of motivation to find that next big wave. The competition to find and ride that big wave is as intense as the competition to find and ride that real big wave in the ocean. Yet, there are techniques that will get you into the game. We have talked about how to spot the swells. Clearly, others also know how to spot the swells, but they may choose not to act. There are a variety of reasons that people do not act: They underestimate the potential of a technology, they miss the window of opportunity to push the technology into product, or they just simply do not understand the technology. You cannot assume that someone who specializes in medical technology understands software technology. It is difficult to understand multiple technologies in-depth. There are people who claim that a good manager can manage anything, but if you are at the bleeding edge of a technology, you must understand the technology.

That is not to say that given enough time to work on

understanding a technology that you will not be able to become an expert in a reasonable amount of time. However, you must work at the problem of acquiring the necessary capabilities. In a sense, it is easier to become an expert in a new field because there are less experts in that field. If you get into the field early enough, you can define portions of the field and become the expert on how the field develops.

At one point, one of my best engineers had to go to a procurement briefing. The customer was going to outline its problem and allow potential vendors who had only a part of the solution to meet with the current vendors and form partnerships. This engineer was one of the brightest engineers I had ever dealt with. He had great ideas, thought ahead about alternatives, and could describe many ways to build the basic product concepts he came up with. However, he did have one small shortcoming: He had little customer experience. So it was decided that he would accompany marketing to the meeting. When he went to the meeting, he had felt good about our chances and was really enthused. When he came back, he was frustrated and incensed. During the discussions, he found that a lot of other vendors had stolen his basic idea.

The problem was that the other developers and companies had never been exposed or briefed on his idea, so how could they steal it? At some point in the product development cycle, information flows freely about customer needs and wants. Most developers have access to the same or similar parts and techniques, and there are a lot of smart people, so you should expect that a lot of people will come to the same or similar conclusions. When this was explained to our engineer, it made the trauma of the briefing a little bit better, but there was still a high level of frustration when reality set in.

You should not underestimate the intelligence of your competition, but you should not overestimate the first mover time advantage because once an idea becomes visible, it is easy to imitate.

In addition to smarts, you will need luck to ride the big wave.

You may be the best surfer, but if you are sick, on a different continent, or on vacation with your wife when the world's largest wave breaks onto the shore, you will never be known for riding the biggest wave.

It is not enough to be smart, you must also be lucky and opportunistic to recognize and capitalize on the opportunity.

Change Rates

When you look at the shoreline of a beach, you will generally be in an area where the topographical structure is relatively fixed. The coral reefs, the slope of the sand, the depth of the water, the high-tide and low-tide elevations probably do not vary a lot. What varies is the height of a wave as it breaks onto the shore.

When big waves are driven onto the shore by a storm at sea, the size of the wave is determined by wind, sun, and other forces that are out at sea and are pushing the waves onto the shore. The net result of this is that as the height of the wave increases, the slope of the face of the wave becomes steeper. This idea of slope is critical as the slope defines the dangers of a big wave. It is one thing to find a small wave with a steep face, as you will only be on it for a very short period of time and it generally will not be very dangerous to ride. It is quite another thing to climb onto a big sixty-or seventy-foot wave that has a steep slope and is moving toward the shore at a rapid rate. The danger in big wave surfing comes from a combination of the height, slope, rate of movement toward the shore, and a lot of other variables. Further, each time you climb on the wave everything is just a little different, including your position on the wave.

There is an incredible similarity with technology and big wave surfing. Each company, industry, and rate of change causes a similar effect. The rate of change is analogous to the growth slope of the companies or industry, and what we are looking for is a disruptive technology that will create a new industry and a set of companies (or at least one new company) with a very high growth rate. We want to create and ride that growth rate as far and as long as we can. That is the ideal scenario. In general, the more disruptive the technology, the higher the probability that we can create a rapid growth rate. Sometimes the growth rate will end up being industry-wide, and sometimes it will be limited to a single company. We should not care about whether the growth rate is industry-wide or from a single company.

We want a shift in the marketplace. We want disruption! We want the storm to push the wave onto the shore with a major amount of force so that a big wave will form. We want to see an entire series of these waves from one industry breaking onto the shore.

Swell Types

There are a wide variety of combinations of events that will cause a big wave or a set of big waves. These mechanisms are generally well understood. It can be as simple as making a product faster. In this case, the probability of causing a big wave is not very large. There may be a lot of competing products, and making your product faster will probably not make a large change in the marketplace and its growth rate. Other types of swells that can cause new products are performance improvements, cost improvements, additional functions, new functions, completely new product ideas, out-of-the-box strategies, and legislative decisions.

However, if you are in a developing industry and you can make your product significantly faster than a competitor's product, you may affect not only the other company's prospects but also the prospects of the entire industry.

Sometimes entirely new markets may be created. For example, the whole field of nanomaterials emerged in a product sense in the late 2000s. Who knows what new and great products and companies will emerge from this area? If swells push to the shore in this arena, all types of new opportunities will be available. This becomes a game of risk and reward. If you are innovative enough and take the right risks, you will prosper and achieve the maximum return on your investment.

You can go at the problem in a number of ways. But the waves that have a high probability of success demand unconventional thinking. You can always take a crack at the problem of making a faster-growing company or industry with conventional ways of thinking. Typically, you would add new functions to your product, make it faster, or add functions that are in your competitors' products.

The bigger issue is whether you can think completely out of the box. Is there a completely new product concept that can be developed? Are there entirely new product categories that we have not thought about? What if you took an existing product and tried to determine what that product would look like under a new set of technology assumptions?

You need to begin thinking about new ways of looking at products.

For example, what are the effects of legislation on particular product categories? In many cases, a simple change of the processes or set assumptions under which a company operates will create massive opportunities. In particular, legislative aspects will have a huge effect on the medical device industry. When thinking out of the box, you cannot underestimate the effect of something as simple as a legislative change.

Further, you need to think about what happens with your assumptions as rules change. Just remember that for any given set of rules or assumptions, you can expect that the environment will change constantly as the wave you jump on moves toward the shore.

Big Wave Riding

The scary part is not the preparation; it is actually being on the wave.

Think about what we are trying to do. Have you ever been in a company or involved with a product where we are going to try to change the fundamental structure that we operate under by multiples? I am not talking about changing a company's revenue by 2, 3, or 10 percent in a year. I am talking about changing the total revenue of a company by 200, 300, or 1,000 percent in a year. The goal is to make a significant change—factors of hundreds of percents.

And to go right back at it and do it again the following year until the wave of product technology runs up onto the shore!

It does not really matter how big the company is. In fact, little companies are more of a challenge than larger companies because they have less corporate infrastructure. In a big company, there is inertia and processes that make it difficult to make a radical change. In a large company, it is relatively impossible to do the kind of thing that I want to do.

In a small company, it is possible to make a radical revenue change and it is possible to make a similar change in the next year. In fact, if you have enough capital, it is possible to do it several years in a row. I was once involved with a small company that had several consecutive successful years. At one point in the process, one of the employees came to me and said, "We are not going to try to do this again, are we?"

The answer at that point was no. However, what caused the employee's concern was that we had started with nothing and in less than two years we had jumped to a high run rate, and we were so undercapitalized that our biggest concern was collecting money for the payroll. We had a 100 percent growth year. We followed that up with a 200 percent growth year. We followed that up with a 100 percent growth year. In fact, we went from a nonissue in a particular market segment to the leading provider of the products that we were making, and we had a number of Fortune 500 companies coming to visit us to see our business strategies.

But there was a significant amount of pain and personal stress involved in making a company grow at such a rapid rate. Once you learn what is important, it becomes a repeatable process. If you have a new technology that is unique, you can outrun the other people in your market space and create a massive amount of interest and profit growth. Unfortunately, even if you start out small and get one of these technologies to grow rapidly, you will soon have to either stabilize the growth or let someone else run out the product set.

In some cases, industries and products are really transient and you end up having to manage the failure of the business as well as the rapid growth. If you do not spot the wave turning over on top of you, you can end up getting crushed.

Chapters 8–12 will elaborate on the issues in creating and riding big technology waves. However, the ubiquitous nature of the Internet has allowed the stakes to grow bigger than ever, but the ability of people to figure out how to make a profit out of huge revenue streams still seems to elude them.

Pipe Riding

It is not just enough to get a big year or take a drop on that big wave. Many people can get that one good year. To really make it stick is the key. You must achieve the effect of compound interest. You have to get multiple high-growth years. A series of high-growth years even coming from a low base is the key as they establish you as the real deal. The real deal commands a premium. The real deal gets to go time after time until the real deal wears out or gets bored. The real deal knows that you are only as good as what you are doing today. Fame and fortune are fleeting aspects of life, and you must keep establishing your position.

It is not good enough to ride a single wave because most surfing contests are judged by a series of waves, and you will not know ahead of time if you caught the biggest one that is available to be ridden that day. Physical conditioning is a key part of the sport. Just like in the technology arena, your chances and opportunities are not always there. The Eddie is a big wave surfing contest held (or attempted to be held) annually on the north shore of Oahu. To have a viable contest requires that at a certain time (early December) there must be waves exceeding twenty-five feet. By big wave standards, these are pretty small (sometimes riders go for waves that are above sixty feet), but they are big enough for a great surfer to demonstrate a varied set of skills. Successful riders make multiple runs, and the prize can be $1 million. However, only about 35 percent of the time is there an actual contest because the waves and weather do not always cooperate. But winning the Eddie provides more than money. It provides a lot of prestige because of its history (it is considered the Super Bowl of big wave surfing because it is named after one of the early greats of big wave surfing) and the fact that all of the serious big wave surfers want to win the prize.

When you come over the top of that big wave, you are now on the slope and you want to demonstrate your technique and your form. This is the process that you need to install to ensure that you are putting out a quality product.

You ride the wave down, and then you can ride along the wave at various angles. If you are really adventuresome, you can slow down and ride back into the pipe as the water cascades over you and then you need to shootout of the pipe and accelerate further down the wave. At some point, you will have to pick up enough speed to hop back over the top of the wave or shoot into shore, or you will get crushed. This is like the beginning of the end of your product cycle, and you need to develop a feel for how far you can push your product before you need to bring out the next model.

As you look at the surfers in or near the pipe, you will see that they have their hands out touching the vertical surface of the wave. It is difficult to see where the surface of the water is. All colors begin to blur, and the noise associated with a big wave is deafening. The same thing happens in the product line. Everything is moving fast, and there is a lot of noise in the environment. Just like big wave surfing, intuition and measurements let you make the instantaneous decisions necessary to stay on top of your game and keep the maximum velocity that you are trying to obtain in terms of the growth of your company.

Wave Face

Due to the nature of a wave, you can ride it for quite a while. While the wave may only be sixty feet high, it can be quite wide, and you can move along the wave in a horizontal manner burning up the energy you obtained as you shot down the wave's face. You can also add energy by body movement on your board. Thus, you don't have to shoot straight down the face of the wave. You can use the energy to move back up the wave.

Likewise, when you are building your company or product, you will not have a straight path to success. You will sometimes move sideways. Sometimes you will have to add new energy to your system because you may have to bring out another product or a new variation of your product, or completely change your strategy. These are all issues that you will face because every wave is slightly different.

Just like the big wave surfer, you still have to make rapid correct decisions to avoid getting slammed into the ground. Unlike the surfer who wipes out, you will probably not face death, although you may feel like you faced massive destruction. One of the key issues that you will face is that unlike a surfer, you have competitors who take no prisoners. The product and high-growth technology business is a blood sport due to the economic effects of the possibility of success.

If you are successful, the technology equivalent of the momentum and energy generated by the big wave surfer is financial freedom to make personal choices that you find exhilarating.

White Water Churn

As the wave finally gets close to shore, the water will begin to churn. This is the same effect that you see when your product starts to age. This is decision time. You have ridden the big wave. You have survived the big drop. You have made it toward the shore and ridden through the pipe. Now you need to make a decision. Are you done?

The question is simply, "Are you ready to quit?" If you choose to ride into shore in the churn, you have survived and can eventually get off the board.

You can choose to go back out. If you either have the momentum to drive yourself back out to the swells or the watercraft to tow you back out to the swells, you can probably get in another run at a big wave.

The reality is that, in general, big wave surfers are not good at running companies. They are good at getting them going and getting them growing. They can manage change, and they can conceive of new products, but they have difficulty running companies as they find it boring to actually run a company for a long time at a slow growth rate. There is a lot of excitement in starting and causing a company to have a high growth rate. Running a slow-growth company and dealing with the day-to-day mundane issues that accompany such a job is simply boring!

Big wave surfers know when to quit. If they are tired or a shark appears, then they need to go to shore. Similarly, technology big wave surfers need to know when to quit. If the margins are deteriorating, the competition is nipping at your heels, or you have a new great idea, it is time to move on to another beach and another set of waves. If you are a concept person, do not waste your time trying to run a company. Get back to generating ideas and having fun.

Wave Structures

No matter how many times you have been involved with a company starting up, seen a start-up, or known the founders of a start-up company, you will always see different nuisances to the problem of making a company grow fast.

You can never figure out whether you have grabbed onto the real deal. You can catch a lot of waves, but you will find that in many cases, the probability of a wipeout is very high. The number of times that you are in the right area, have a great product, and still wipe out is very high.

I have been involved with a number of start-ups and have friends who have collectively started over 100 companies, and I am always amazed at how the start-ups play out.

In most cases, it takes longer, costs more, and yields far less than your business plan predicts, even with your worst-case predictions.

You cannot figure out in advance how any part of the process will play out. I have lost money on start-ups that I had considered to be sure things. I have made money on start-ups that I felt were one step above the bottom of the ocean. In fact, one company that I bought stock in was a company started by a friend of mine that I invested in only as a favor because it was not looking for a lot money and I wanted to maintain a relationship with the founders. This company struggled for a year, changed management (I was involved in setting up the incentive plan for the new management), struggled for another two years, and then took off making one of the best percentage gainers in any portfolio I have ever owned.

But as the company launched, I had continually tried to cut

my loses. I never thought it could succeed. It just happened to get the right amount of cache, get the right product, and encounter no setbacks.

In many cases, it is a classic case of the best laid plans going awry.

Flipped Graphic

If you think about the wave structure, what we are attempting to do is very simple: Flip and modify the graphic into a stock chart as shown in **Figure 6-2**. The steeper the wave, the better off we are in the short term. In fact, we want to create a situation in which, from an investment perspective as illustrated in figure 6-2, we monetize the rapid growth of our chosen technology as the wave continues to push into the shore; we get off the wave before the growth slows and the stock appreciation slows.

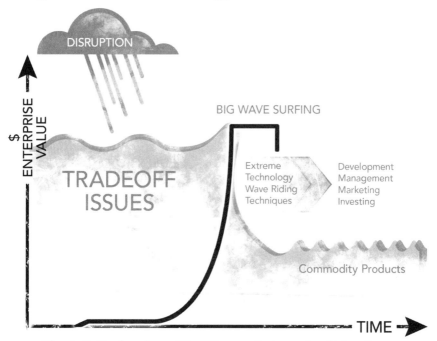

Fig. 6-2: Technology Big Wave—Enterprise Valuation

This book is about generating companies with high growth rates, which means their stocks have a high rate of appreciation. We then want to monetize that stock value. For lack of a better measure, we will talk as if we are using a stock value as a measure of the value of a company. In the case of a private company, we assume that the owners of the private shares will figure out how to monetize the stock. Thus a graphic depicting a stock chart will be the concept that we will be discussing.

We want a stock that has a flat bottom for a period of time and then takes off at a very high rate of change. We want to be out of the stock when the rate growth begins to level off. In **Figure 6-2**, the stock chart is just the flip side of the big wave breaking onto the shore. It is like a hockey stick superimposed upon the wave with the bend in the stick starting as the wave starts to break. Our best scenario is if the blade is short (we are quick to the market) and the shaft of the stick is long (our economic return is high) and the bend between the blade and shaft has a rapid turn (our product launches quickly).

Daredevil Surfers

Some days there will be a series of big waves that break on a beach, but some days there will be complete change in the fundamental structure of entire industries. In these cases, the situation is reminiscent of a tsunami.

We have seen at least two of these events in the last thirty years: the Internet (since the early 1990s) and the PC revolution (starting in the late 1970s). Both of these events were positive developments.

As I have noted, there are many areas of technology or its application that can be the beneficiary of big waves. Other examples of tsunami events include the use of computers to be able to generate derivative securities and model them efficiently. In this case, the daredevils who tried to ride the wave almost took down the entire financial system. The effect of these large wave structures is that they are like a tsunami in the sense that they can create death and destruction on a widespread scale.

In the case of the Internet and the PC, a lot of money was made and most companies adjusted to the realities of the marketplace. In the case of the financial meltdown, millions of people were ripped off by the bankers to enrich a small number of people on Wall Street who created the fiasco.

Innovation Statement

When looking at a product, you need to understand not only what the product does, but also why the customer should care—the statement of innovation.

What makes your product different, unique, better, easier to use, etc.? Do not try to be cute. Do not try to obfuscate what is important about your product. Why is your product innovative? What is it that I should be looking for that will make my life better?

Years ago, the mainframe was the computer solution of choice. Then along came the minicomputer. What was the innovation provided by the minicomputer? It let users who were unable to afford a mainframe have a cost-effective entry into the data-processing world. Eventually, even the mainframe manufacturers brought out minicomputers.

Then along came the microcomputer. What was its innovation? It let users who were unable to afford a minicomputer have a cost-effective entry into the data-processing world. The counter to the market problems caused by microcomputers was that the mainframe and minicomputer manufacturers brought out their own microcomputers.

Then along came the PC. What was its innovation? It let users directly control their entry into the data-processing world, but it had a problem. Because the PC had none of the system administration functions that users expected, server farms were born and computers that had the capabilities of mainframes, minicomputers, and microcomputers ended up coming back to life. The other manufacturers reacted. They brought out their own PCs. And then all manufacturers brought out their own server systems.

Eventually it became solely a price shootout, and some venerable manufacturers, Digital Equipment Corporation and Compaq Computer, were eventually bought out in the inevitable consolidations that resulted from this set of technology cycles.

So the innovations of one technology can become the problems of another technology, and the technology cycle will go full circle. Another wave will hit the beach, and some surfers will wipe out.

It is important to be able to specify what you think your innovation is, but you should not assume that your innovation will be long lasting.

Value Addition

We have talked about what will make your product different and successful, but can we actually quantify the importance of a product? What makes a product different? As we have discussed, there are a variety of factors that make a product different or make someone want to buy a product.

However, it comes down to a question of value. Value may be a perception, but to a buyer, it is a real factor. The challenge we need to overcome is to create the concept of value. If we can create the concept, then we can begin to measure the value that our product adds.

It is via the concept of value added that we will enable the sales department to sell our product. Value added will not necessarily be something as simple as an increase in speed or performance.

If we make the claim that the product is faster than another product, we can differentiate the products. Differentiation on the simple basis of speed is really an attempt to discuss the product on the basis of a feature. We want to discuss the benefit of the product to the customer. Our value added would be that we can cut the transaction cost of the system by 30 percent. That will play better than trying to claim that our product is 30 percent faster than a competitor's product. Differences correspond to features. We want to concentrate on the issues of value added, i.e., what is the benefit to the user? We must couch our arguments in terms of benefits, not features.

The issue is that a faster product may not necessarily provide a benefit in terms of processing more work. What if the faster product then needs more overhead or has more complexity that saps the basic speed upgrade?

Consider this: How many times have you upgraded your PC's processor and not gotten the full speed out of your system? You double your processor's speed, and the overall system barely runs faster because of the cool new features provided by Microsoft Windows and the new security features. Your system does not run any faster and may actually run slower even after the upgrade. The feature of a faster processor speed did not end up as a benefit of an overall system speed up.

Isn't it cool how new features can destroy the benefits you believe you achieved by getting that fast new hardware? A value-added approach to the design of the system would be to make sure that the new software packages actually allowed the user to take advantage of the faster processor instead of sopping up the new hardware capabilities by doing overhead tasks.

When trying to quantify the benefits of a new product or system, you need to work on the overall end user benefits not the specific mechanisms that are the feature benefits. Each user benefit may well be supported by a series of features, and a feature enhancement may actually support several benefits.

When discussing your innovation and value added, you must be able to explain why you are building the product, what the product is or does, an example of how the product benefits the user, and how you build or differentiate the product. You should also be able to describe how the product uses technology, how the technology leads to new features, what benefits the features provide, how the benefits create value for the customer, and how new systems capabilities are created that lead to sales.

Technology Hangover

We cannot underestimate the competition. Generally, we have been talking about the potential competitors, but there may be existing competitors. In many cases, one way to create a big wave effect is to find a process that can be improved by technology. Then you put out your new product and the money rolls in.

Well, at least part of the scenario may be correct.

If you are targeting an existing process or product, you must factor in the hangover effect. Just because you bring out your new product, you should not expect the competition to roll over. You are trying to eliminate their livelihood by taking away sales and killing their product line.

In the case of similar new products, the competitors will try to push product differentiation and put your product in a poor light. The competition will do whatever it needs to stop your product from getting traction so that they do not have to face your product in any significant way in the marketplace. A great trick is to develop an abstraction that describes your product but implicitly degrades the other company's product just in the terminology that you use to describe your product. An example is when Novell coined the term *true file server* to describe its system, leading to the impression that all other competitors had an inferior product. Somehow the competitors' servers were not true file servers. Amazingly, this tactic put all the other vendors on the defensive, and eventually, Novell took its place in the spotlight of rapid growth.

The real area in which you may underestimate the competition is when you are trying to replace an existing product. If you assume that just because you are in the ocean and there is a storm that is pushing big waves onto the shore that you will automatically catch the big wave, you are mistaken. Similarly, if you think that the existing solutions that are currently in the marketplace will roll over and just let you into the market, you are mistaken. The existing product vendors are going to fight you. You may have put their back to the wall, but they are not going to give up easily. How are they going to accomplish this? The first strategy is for them to improve their products.

The product improvements may take many forms. They may add new functions. They may bring out easier-to-use products. They could even bring out new products that make their current products obsolete.

Another way they can attack the problem is to change their manufacturing processes. One company I worked for had a great-selling product that was very simple and easy to copy. Its strategy was to keep running on the brand name it owned and to bracket the competition with two maneuvers. First, it would keep bringing out a set of product variations to keep the competition off balance. Second, for all products that were selling in high volume, the company would go through a product improvement cycle each year designed to make the products better and cheaper. Then, if necessary, it could do whatever it needed to keep its market share at the correct level.

You should in no way underestimate how tough the competition will be when they have their backs against the wall.

Elevator Speech/Note Card

As described previously, many times I have found myself needing to give a briefing to one of our customers. The customer simply wanted an overview of a set of technologies that we were working on. Sometimes we were trying to integrate these technologies into an advanced product that we were not sure would even work. We knew that we could make it work functionally, but could we make it perform in a way that would make the technology transition worthwhile for the customer? Many times the customer had a simple request, and that request was to give the group an overview of the key technologies in a thirty-minute presentation. This was really a no brainer. We would have four or five technologies that needed to be briefed along with how we planned to put them together.

It is easy to build a presentation that is long, but it is another trick to build small, self-contained nuggets of information about technology.

In many cases, and in business books, these small nuggets are known as elevator speeches—the type of speech you might give on a short elevator ride when you have an important person captive for a very short period of time.

This concept is really an old concept. For years, there were contests that required the entrant to describe, comment on, and explain the advantages of a product in twenty-five words or less. That is the key to the elevator speech. Can you explain your concept and its advantages in twenty-five words or less?

Try explaining your product in twenty-five words or less, and you will soon find that you can describe the key features of your product simply and succinctly.

Another trick is to see if you can describe your concept on a single 3" × 5" note card or on a cocktail napkin. There are large numbers of new products or product improvements not withstanding entire companies that have been founded on the basis of a diagram put onto a cocktail napkin.

Real World

The real world does not change a lot on any given day. It is the combined effect of many little changes that will cause a special day or time frame in which the big wave occurs. When that day occurs, you must gather to ride the waves. In the real world, the norm is the status quo—disruption modifies the status quo and provides opportunity.

Consider the number of days in which there are really big waves. On most days, there are tons of waves that are breaking onto a lot of beaches in the world. This activity is caused by the lunar movement and general aspects of the tides and weather. Sometimes storms cause big waves to form, but this is a very rare event. Then there is that rare moment where the normal ocean actions line up in perfect harmony and truly big waves hit certain beaches. Because there are monitors in the ocean, particularly the Pacific Ocean, the potential emergence of big waves headed for certain beaches can be predicted, and the surfers gather.

The real world works the same way. Generally, there is some amount of progress in research and development occurring every day. Technologies are being developed and perfected every day. But periodically, someone comes up with a new product or concept that starts to accelerate sales. This is always an ongoing process and, in a majority of cases, yields small incremental progress in terms of product sales. Thus, there are very small sales changes (increases or decreases) occurring all of the time based upon a continually changing product environment. But sometimes change that starts to look incremental accelerates, and for a given technology, the surf's up and big waves start to form for you to ride. It is, however, usually business as usual. Just like really big waves, there are a very few times in which there are big waves forming.

In the technology area, disruptive technologies have the potential to cause the big waves. If you have a disruptive technology and there can be a real user need developed, you stand a chance of breaking out from the crowd and riding a big wave. Just like big waves that form in the ocean, each wave has a time duration, and the number and duration of waves breaking onto the beach is a short-term event that you must exploit when you are given the opportunity.

Not all disruptions may be technology driven. In some cases, the disruption may be driven by a change in something as simple as a law. In some cases, the disruption may be a side effect or unintended consequence of a law. Not all disruptions are positive. Or if they are positive for one group, they may not be positive for another group. A classic example is the repeal of the Glass-Siegel Act, which allowed the big Wall Street firms to amalgamate and form the basis for our mortgage melt down. The change in the law allowed the big banks to grow really big and fast and make huge amounts of money for a small group of people. Coupled with computers and mathematical models, it also led to a variety of bizarre mortgages and eventually the downfall of our economy. Yet a number of people who figured out the problem also made huge amounts of money on the collapse.

In the big wave surfing world, there has always been disruption. People have designed different boards: smaller, skinnier, and thinner. In addition, they have also changed the boards' material and shaped them differently. However, one of the most significant innovations was co-invented by Laird Hamilton—tow-in surfing. Eventually as waves get really high, you cannot paddle fast enough to catch the wave, so Laird came up with the idea of using a watercraft to sling shot the surfer onto the wave. There is a debate over whether tow-in surfing is a legitimate form, but the only way

PART ONE: SPOTTING BIG WAVES

you get onto a sixty-foot wave is with a sling shot. Tow-in surfing brought serious technology innovation to big wave surfing.

Chapter Summary

Disruption is the key. Whenever you have a status quo and get a storm, there will be waves to ride. If they get big, then the disruption will have been either large or significant in terms of changing the environment for some type of product or process. However, the real world wants to remain static. Change is difficult for people, and generally change is difficult to spot.

The key issue you must understand is that you will have trouble spotting a big wave, so you must observe a lot of waves and get a feel for the process that creates big waves. Looking for the value added by a technology to society is the key. The more people want and need to embrace the resultant product offerings derived from a particular technology, the higher the probability of a big wave being formed.

Chapter 7

Big Wave Surfing Future

Where we go from here is unknown.

No End

Somewhere in the world, there are engineers working on a variety of ideas every second of the day. Some are just reengineered ideas of their companys' products, and some are new technologies that engineers hope will be breakthrough technologies in the marketplace. Regardless of the direction or sophistication of the technology, the engineers are trying to position themselves for rapid and dominating market growth. For the majority of these engineers, this will just be another set of products that, if they are lucky, will move into the market. For the lucky few, they are starting to see the formation of a new wave structure because they have found the holy grail of a new technology wave and are about to launch onto a new technology adventure similar to the launch of such companies as Facebook, Apple, and Google. At some point, these engineers will have stories told about them and will become mythical figures living on as legends of the technology industry.

Disruption causes the opportunity. Innovation defines the products. Your ability to evolve, change, and embrace these new technology directions partially determines your success. Some companies fail. My Osborne computer was the pride of my eye when I first bought it. Osborne Computer was a superstar company for about two years, and then it failed to make the leap to the next generation of portable computers (PCs). The time window can be small, yet the stakes are high.

The number of really big wave surfers is small (probably 0.001 percent to 0.0001 percent of the population), but their effect is large when they are successful. There are a lot of good surfers who could ride the wave but just are not at the right place at the right time. If you are the person who rides the biggest wave, you will be remembered by everyone. Even if no one knows of your exploits, you can still be very successful.

Jobs are the issue. Disruption will change the status quo, and jobs will be both lost and gained. This issue came into focus for me one day after I had just completed a seminar on office automation and was talking with the participants. One participant was hanging back and finally was the last person to talk to me. She told me how much she enjoyed the seminar and that she thought I had a particularly clever way of presenting the information. What intrigued her was the way I presented the benefits of what would become the office automation revolution that started with the PC industry. I presented the information in a fashion that emphasized the increase in quality and productivity. This participant had been sent to the seminar by her boss and had started her working life as a secretary. She had worked her way up to being an administrative assistant and had obtained a junior college degree. She was currently working on a four-year degree in business.

As we discussed some of the issues in the seminar, she was concerned that I had (in her opinion) skipped over the fact that the technologies were going to have a very disruptive effect on the lives of many people in her position and that my use of the term *increased productivity* translated into needing fewer people to do a given job. She was concerned whether I understood this fact and was being careful about this issue and if I understood the potential effect on workers in industry.

I assured her that I fully understood the effect, but I chose to present the information in a manner that was nonconfrontational and would not start an argument in the seminar. I felt that it was incumbent on the workers who could possibly be displaced to be alert to technology change in their profession to learn new tools and techniques to remain employed.

Any time there is change, there are winners and losers. This was very disconcerting to her, but she had no basis to prove that you should always stay with the status quo. If you stay with the status quo, you are destined to put yourself into the churn and you will become a loser to the low-cost producer. In a corporate and a personal sense, you must learn to deal with disruption and innovation because no matter what you want to happen, change will occur. Disruption will cause change, and your ability to innovate will determine your place in the pecking order of success. If you are running an operation and you choose to ignore progress, you will most certainly go out of business. If you are an employee of a firm and you fail to embrace change, you risk losing your job.

The first automated spreadsheet program, VisiCalc, had a tremendous effect on the industry and on the office workers of the world. Not only did it allow for people to build great financial models, but it also made them look authoritative. However, the program really could not change the basic premise of garbage in garbage out. If you do not have good data and a good model, you still have garbage. VisiCalc eventually was overrun by Lotus 1-2-3, which was overrun by Excel. You have to run fast, in both technical matters and marketing, to live a long and prosperous life.

Bob Metcalfe, coinventor of the Ethernet, said that because we have the solution now we need to have the problem that we are solving. Over time, that problem appeared and the concept of networking and the Internet took off. With the rise of social networks and numerous other applications, the future of networking seems secure. But all was not easy going. In the early 1980s, the future of networking was anything but certain. 3com, the company that Bob Metcalfe founded, was one of the leading manufacturers of Ethernet equipment and, in fact, was the first company to provide an Ethernet interface on a single board for under $1,000. The question that you might consider now is, At that moment, how many people envisioned single chip Ethernet interfaces built right into the equipment or envisioned gigabit Ethernet interfaces?"

The great search at the dawn of networking was for the Holy Grail of applications. Currently, many people think this is the set of Internet based applications. Finding the Mother of all Applications will bring out the big wave surfers.

Technology continues to make progress, so there is no end in sight. Yet our vision of where we are going is not clear. I think we're still searching for the holy grail.

Massive Excess

No matter what we do or try, we do not necessarily see how things are going to turn out. Even when we have and observe an event that lets us understand the status quo, we need to be wary of unintended consequences. We try to conceive every possible outcome, but we are only able to verbalize things that we have seen in the past.

We advance through the space of new products in fits and

starts. The primary mode of advancement is fiddling with the current state of the art and trying to position a product concept against a "what if" need. That is, based upon what we see in the environment, can we piece together a number of related technologies to get a new product? Or is our product really an extension of an existing concept with updated technology? Over time, the sum of our product improvements and technology insertions provides us with a new product that we hope will take off big in the marketplace.

Sometimes the products take off and then flame out. Sometimes the products take off and the early producers fail as a company. Classic examples of such product categories are fax machines and calculators, which exhibited rapid growth and then quickly became commodities with rapid price drops. Similarly, the industries of disk and random access memory producers were dominated with flam outs as these products turned into commodities.

Once the money guys sense blood in the water, they rapidly converge just like sharks. Money flows, and the companies move forward. But excess is in the air. Once a company is seen as successful, the wave becomes crowded, but investors must be wary because the market will take it up as far as possible. The price of a perceived successful and emerging wave of new products becomes expensive fast, just before it hits the commodity graveyard.

Gluttony Innovation

There's an old joke about how a project or product development will progress. This is known as the six stages of a project. There are a number of variations on this theme, but a common variation goes like this: The six stages of a successful project are enthusiasm, confusion, disillusionment, search for the guilty, punishment of the innocent, and promotion of the nonparticipants. There is so much truth to this that it is sometimes difficult to take it as humor. But when you view a successful project in its abstract form, you see that big wave surfing is not limited to just technology. It may also apply to power grabs, political structures, social networks, and finance. In fact, the Great Recession is due to the mass of innovation created over the last few years by the latest versions of our Wall Street gang and their political brethren. But this is neither the first nor the last financial crisis that will occur. Hopefully, the next crisis will not be so large as to nearly bring down civilization.

If you believe our venerable government officials, the only solution was to flood the financial system with cash. Because the amount of bailout funds was on the same order of magnitude as the bonuses of the big bankers of Wall Street, one wonders what was accomplished.

There I was one morning in 2010 watching the live broadcast of the Financial Crisis Inquiry Commission (FCIC). The commission was investigating the causes of the financial meltdown and what could be done to prevent such goings on in the future. If you believe the conventional wisdom, then the entire economy of the world had nearly been brought down by the invisible evil doers—no one would admit that they were actually part of the fiasco.

In the July 2009 issue of *Vanity Fair*, Joseph Stiglitz (Nobel Laureate in economics) discusses the relationship between Wall Street banks and the four horsemen of the apocalypse. There are a number of variations of the horseman theme that are discussed in modern society including in comic books and rassling and on Wall Street, but the original concept comes from the Bible. In the Bible, the horsemen are death, famine, pestilence, and war. In his article, Stiglitz denotes them as greed, mendacity, stupidity, and arrogance. After watching the testimony of four of our great Wall Street firms, I felt that there may be better groupings: disdain, idiocy, deceit, and avarice; or annihilation, misery, plague, and enmity; or destruction, paucity, scourge, and strife.

It is clear that the Wall Street bankers do not understand their effect. They do believe that they are justified to do what they want. Innovation should not damage the world. It needs to lead to a better world. Somewhere along the line that astute Wall Street firm Burnem, Lynchem, Sackem, & Pillage convinced itself that it did no wrong but that it was a victim of some awful tragedy and should be bailed out. With the assistance of its venerable legal firm Dewey, Screwem, & Howe, it pictured itself as a great innovator who got screwed by the system when everything it did was according to the rules.

It got so bad during the testimony that the Big Buck Bankers of Wall Street even explained how they did not do anything wrong, but in fact were victims. The FCIC will undoubtedly produce a report that will be the basis for new rules. These rules will start another round of financial innovation, and in the future, there will be another crisis. All of it was accomplished legally because when you develop a set of rules, you open the door for innovation. Further, the Democrat Wall Street guys are no different than the Republican Wall Street guys. What you hope is that you can hide below the radar of their greed and not get hurt by their bad behavior. They will continue to innovate, and eventually, they will all use the same algorithm and their model will fail and all hell will break loose.

The FCIC should be renamed to the Financial Crime Institutionalization Committee. It will build a new set of rules to be bent and morphed to the benefit of financial innovation that will be dangerous to your health. The rules may not even be enforced, so be careful investing. We need to consider ourselves lucky that this cast of characters was relegated to just running money. What would have been the result if they were in the biological agent business?

There was not only one way to solve the crisis. There were other more innovative scenarios.

Why not use the National Hockey League (NHL) scenario? When a game gets out of control and the players are yapping at each other, the referee has been known to step back and utter the three dreaded words, "Let them fight." The political class would not like that, but maybe then we would not have guys lying, cheating, and stealing without regard to the consequences. Many people frame the argument as one of Wall Street versus Main Street, but maybe the real innovation is that a financial firm gets to be a big wave surfer and creates innovation because it gets so big that it cannot fail. The company knows it will get bailed out. Big wave surfers wipe out, and companies will fail, but Wall Street doesn't fail. Maybe the NHL scenario would have been better than the bailout scenario. Maybe not, but we will never know.

Just like generals who study history and then fight the current war using the tools, weapons, and tactics of the last war, the governments in countries where the financial crisis occurred used the tactics from previous crises. They just flooded the system with money and stuck the taxpayers with the bill for the bailout of Big Buck Banker and his buddies. I wanted to see the bankers fight it out. I cannot conceive of too big to fail. There is no wave too big to ride! At one point, I thought that maybe we would see Wall Street stormed by the peasants of Main Street. Envision the scene, the peasants running down Wall Street, pitchforks and torches in hand, looking for the monsters. It happened in Thailand when the radicals burned down the building that housed the stock market.

The bankers of Wall Street violated many entrepreneurs' fundamental rules of innovation. The robots in Isaac Asimov's novels have rules about harming humans and society. A robot is not allowed to harm a human. Innovators try to do good. They do not try to bring down society, other humans, or the financial system! They may cause disruption, but the intent is to make their products and the world better!

Going Forward

The effect of a wave structure to technology development is that they are always breaking upon a shore. Whether they are small, medium, or large, big is an issue of perspective, but there will eventually be a time when the waves will be big. At that time, we must be prepared to capitalize on our good fortune and be at the right beach at the right time. Much of our time will be spent in boredom intermixed with seconds of exhilaration. But we must remain vigilant and on guard to get up on that next wave. Because waves breaking onto the beach can change in size depending upon factors far out in the ocean, we must be alert and ready to move at the drop of a hat.

When I worked at the Univac Corporation, the symbol of aggressiveness was a modified cartoon hanging on your office wall. In the original cartoon, there were two buzzards sitting on a branch and the caption read, "Patience Hell; I'm going to kill something." In the product development version it said, "Patience Hell; I'm going to build something." That latter attitude will serve you well if you are a big wave surfer. You need to practice every day, even if the waves are not large. You never know when the surf will be really large.

The nature of innovation cannot be taught. You can go to the biggest and highest quality business schools and learn from the best and brightest professors. You can have classmates who are well above average, and still you will not learn how to be an innovator or entrepreneur. You will never learn how to become a big wave surfer. You may learn to be a surfer, but being a big wave surfer requires that you go beyond the normal capabilities. Being a big wave surfer requires that you have just that little bit extra that cannot be taught but has to be found within you. If you are lucky, you evolve into a big wave surfer and just happen to be on the beach when the biggest wave in history hits.

Consider other fields in which it takes more that just skill to be at the top of your game. A lot of people can play the guitar or sing. Some of them go on television shows such as *America's Got Talent* or *American Idol*. But what do you think would be the outcome if in the early 1960s such shows existed and the Rolling Stones, the Beatles, or Bob Dylan went on these shows? Would they win? Or were they just another act, but in some magic moment they ended up being highly successful? Maybe they were extremely good song writers and arrangers and not the world's best singers.

Expect the unexpected when it comes to big wave surfing, innovation, and entrepreneurship. In 1980, I was involved in teaching a course at the Technische Universitat Munchen. This course was an intense two-week short course given on the subject of distributed processing. In the time leading up to the course, the lecture notes and assignments were divided among eight lecturers. Unfortunately, in the assignment of the lecturers, I was assigned to give the summation of the entire course in the last lecture. This was a challenge because as we had developed the course, it was clear that we agreed upon some things and would never agree on other things. As I sat through the entire course, it became apparent that this was going to be a very complex task. As the course proceeded, I tried to capture the essence of not just the course preparation sessions, the course lecture, and the interaction between the students and the lecturers, but also the real-time interaction between the lecturers and the students.

Eventually I hit upon an idea to summarize the course. It was a simple organizational structure that began with a small set of definitions labeled "What we defined." This was followed up with a set of technical constructs that we had conviction about "What we think we know." Then there was a list of things that we thought we knew about "What we conjecture." And in a burst of intellectual honesty, we talked about "What we think we do not know." Then based upon our opinions (there were a lot of them) we discussed

"What we advise" followed up with "What we should know." Lastly, we spoke about "What we do not agree upon."

In the business of innovation, big wave surfing, and entrepreneurship, you just do not know what is going to happen next. You should never be surprised, but you need to be prepared. You cannot train for the unknown otherwise it would be known. You can train and practice for things that you have seen before, and things that may be incrementally different from what you've seen before. You will encounter versions of what you think could be deltas off of what you had seen before, but you will never know the unexpected until you see it.

If you have any doubt about your ability to predict things, you need only to ask yourself, How many companies failed to capitalize on the Internet? Why did BP end up at the center of the biggest oil spill in history? and What caused the recent flash crash on Wall Street? You can work as hard as you want, but at some point you must have luck and great timing as well as the right technology wave to end up as a big wave surfer.

The United States has had to reinvent itself a number of times. We have been an agricultural society and a manufacturing society. To maintain our standard of living, we must become the leading innovation society because we do not compete well in the other arenas. When the government talks about job creation, the only real thing it can do is be supportive of the innovation environment. In a society where a month seems like a lifetime, you cannot make a thirty- or forty-year career plan unless you can continually reinvent yourself. The environment is in a continual state of disruption.

Chapter Summary

Somewhere in the world, the technology surf's up.

No matter the circumstances, there always have been people working on innovation and taking risks. Jobs are created and destroyed. Companies grow and prosper as well as die slow and painful deaths. It is incumbent upon you to understand the real world and what you can do to change your own circumstances. You need to understand that you control more of your destiny than you think you do. We live in an innovation culture that rewards big wave surfers, and if you apply yourself, you have a shot at a big wave. I encourage you to give it a try and hope that some of the information contained in this book will help you as you learn to surf and seek out a big wave.

Surf's up, and I will see you at the beach.

PART TWO

Riding
Big
Waves

PART TWO: RIDING BIG WAVES

Once we have spotted what we believe is a big wave, we need to ride the wave. Because we are limiting our examination to technology big waves, there are four major types of technology big wave surfers: developers, managers, marketers, and investors.

Big wave surfers who are riding down the face of an ocean wave are well-conditioned athletes with courage and skill. They train and experiment for years before being able to jump onto that big wave for a thrill ride. If you are a technology big wave surfer, you can get up onto bigger waves at a faster pace if you have seen a lot of products developed and problems solved.

This part of the book concentrates on techniques that should be in the bag of tricks used by technology big wave surfers. Some of these techniques may seem unconventional and extreme, but we are trying to ride a big wave and there is extensive risk. These techniques will work! Our sole focus is on techniques and characteristics that will allow us to succeed once we have found a wave to ride.

In this part, we will examine some of the traits and characteristics, as well as techniques and pitfalls, that each group of big surfers needs to be aware of to successfully ride a big wave.

Riding a technology big wave is the process we go through to build, manage, and market new technology products as we try to build a rapidly growing concern.

The process of developing the ability to ride a big wave involves experience, training, and building on the previous experiences of others. Thus, I have interspersed traits and characteristics of technology big wave surfers into the chapters as well as discussing tactics and lessons learned.

Chapter 8

Principles for Riding Big Waves

Once we have identified a wave structure, we must begin to ride the structure. There are different participants who ride the technology big wave. The main categories of players that set out on the big wave are the developers and the development team, the technical management, the marketing staff, and the investors supplying money to the product process.

Each of these groups has a unique outlook that we will discuss. However, there are some lessons that I have learned over the years about how to work in various disciplines in fast-growing companies. The lessons of how to achieve a fast growth rate and the sacrifices that growth may cause are described in the sections that follow. Because we are trying to get results in a short time frame and achieve high growth rates, many of the techniques that I will be suggesting are not normal. They are extreme and should not necessarily be applied to companies that are trying to grow and prosper in conventional circumstances.

The swells and the storms have generated our technology waves and product opportunities. Now we must make the most of these opportunities.

Principle: Development Is Evolutionary, not Revolutionary

Most development of new technology is evolutionary. The developers take a new concept and graft it onto an existing concept or evolve an existing concept in a novel way. Given this strategy, it is possible to create a product that is unique and new without spending huge development costs.

Principle: Big Wave Management Must Be Proactive

You must be proactive. Most every management that I have seen is reactive. Their goal is to milk their current products for high growth until they are able to get better jobs. Thus, they want to evolve their current product at the lowest investment cost possible. They become vulnerable to innovative, agile start-up companies with unique products. Big wave management must be proactive. To survive and prosper, you must seize the moment and get your product to the market in the front of the product cycle. If you are riding a big wave, you must anticipate and be aggressive.

Principle: Marketing Requires Early Adopter Buzz

To really launch a new product, it is incumbent that you create a marketing buzz. This requires identifying and selling to key individuals who are early adopters. You must identify a champion at the customer site who has the purchasing authority or ability to determine what product to purchase. Preferably, the early adopter will not only be able to assess risk and accept risk, but also will champion your new product for deployment in a system.

Principle: They'll Take Your Money

The finance industry has developed procedures that are aimed at managing corporate development and product risk. They also have developed a strategy that is designed to ensure that they move their risks to other people. Whether your technology has matured to the point of cashing out as a publicly traded company or is simply a promising emerging company, the money guys are not fools. Whenever possible, they are trying to take your money.

The key to creating a big wave is to find a unique concept in a research and development lab. Nurture the idea until you get a unique product so that you can create a product with distinct value. With this unique value, you then need to find an early adopter who can see the value in grabbing the capabilities that you have created. Getting a number of early adopters to push the product into their respective organizations will then get the buzz necessary to launch the product into the market in a big way. If the product has a broad market, you will be riding a big wave, but watch out because the competition is not far behind, the wave may start to break soon, and you may drown as the competition floods in.

Examples of the skill sets necessary to ride a big wave abound, but the critical element is a depth of focus. There are so many smart people and so much money chasing high-risk, high-reward investment returns that the big wave surfing environment is highly competitive. The difference between success and failure can be as small as whether you got your product announced first and excited the marketplace.

You will need to run hard and fast to avoid getting crushed by the wave. Fortunately, we are able to understand the skill sets necessary to ride big technology waves by looking at the results and techniques used by others who surfed before us. The following chapters (9 through 12) will convey a number of the most useful techniques to allow you to ride a big wave.

Chapter 9

Extreme Technology Development

In this chapter, we are going to look at the process of developing a product. In this chapter, the big wave surfer is a product developer.

We will be looking at extreme ways to build a product and the lessons that have been learned or observed during years of trying to build products quickly. In general, the big wave surfer is trying to ride a wave, and in this chapter, the big wave surfer is in the development side of the business. For the big wave surfer in the ocean, the satisfaction is conquering risk and having a great ride. For the entrepreneur, the satisfaction is developing the product and, hopefully, making a great living.

The key issue and the most important thing you can do is to get your product to market. "Obvious," you say. "The only way you can sell a product is to get it to market." Well, yes, you are correct. But it is not that easy. There is a tendency for engineers, managers, and marketing professionals to all try for perfection. Perfection is the enemy of success. You will never find the perfect wave. You will never know its height or ferocity when you get started on the wave. You will never know how to ride it until you are on top getting ready to start down the face. You will never know what was until you ride down to the bottom. The number of people that I know who develop and build perfect products is imaginary. The number of people that I know who successfully build and sell products is small. You can make a perfect product, but it will be obsolete by the time that you get it to market. Good enough is the only solution to product development.

If you do not believe this, you need only to look at Microsoft. Here is a very large and successful company that was built around an operating system (Microsoft DOS) where the designers placed the system state information into the high-order bytes of the initial physical memory limitation dictated by the IBM personal computer (PC). From a computer design professional's perspective, you would not produce such a design. For Microsoft to adopt it and for IBM to sell it is astounding. Still Microsoft is very successful. This shows that given an aggressive marketing department, a lot of demand for new technology, and multiple attempts to get the product "right," people can make a successful product and company even though they do not provide the best technical solutions. Sometimes in the product world it is really about being good enough.

If you are on the face of the wave, you must stay focused otherwise you lose your advantage. Getting your product out is the key issue, and speed is of the essence. If you do not get your product out, you will miss the wave.

Even though you are trying to bring out a product that will hit the market running and be a huge success, the best product may be just an incremental improvement on an existing product. For example, Apple made a huge smash into the smart phone market with its iPhone. The technology (with the exception of the touch screen) was not revolutionary. Yet Apple got a hugely popular product launched at the expense of its competitors.

Successful products must be simple and easy to understand, and thus, they may be extensions of existing concepts with a unique twist to tie up the unique product idea.

One of the critical issues in riding a big wave is knowing when to get off the wave. There are no well-defined rules and signs. Just as it is difficult to spot a big wave, it is difficult to figure out when to get off the wave. In the development process, signs that the wave is starting to turn over are concerns over product compatibility to prior product versions, requests for the engineering staff to reengineer the product to reduce production costs, and appearances of similar products on the market (all signs that you may want to find another wave).

Opportunity Windows

Everyone wants to think well of themselves; however, no matter how smart you are and how much you believe in yourself, you are probably not the smartest person in the world. There are a lot of smart people, and given that you've thought of a new and unique idea, you need to rec-

Principle: Development Is Evolutionary, Not Revolutionary

Most development of new technology is evolutionary. The developers take a new concept and graft it onto an existing concept or evolve an existing concept in a novel way. Given this strategy, it is possible to create a product that is unique and new without spending huge development costs.

ognize that a lot of other smart people are thinking of similar ideas. The competition is not far behind. **Figure 9-1** illustrates the position on the wave as the big wave surfer starts to ride the wave. It all starts with a development idea for a product, and generally, the person with the vision to create such an idea is a developer. In later chapters, we will discuss other functional positions: management (chapter 10), marketing (chapter 11), and investing (chapter 12). Getting a great ride on a big wave starts with a developer!

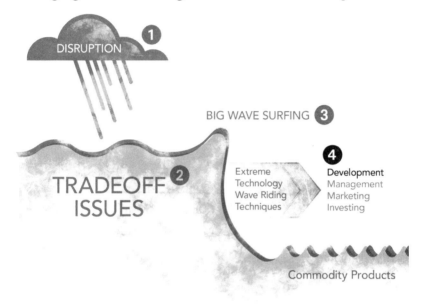

Fig. 9-1: Technology Big Wave Structure—Development

"We can't show our prototype to anyone because they will steal our idea." This is one of the worst sentences I have ever heard. If you can't show people your idea or product, how can you sell it? There are people in the development business who think their developments are so wonderful that no one else will ever come up with the same or a similar idea. This attitude is wrong and will only cause you grief as the competition comes up with similar and possibly better ideas.

There is a lot of herd mentality in the technical development business, just like there are similar patterns in other businesses. But in the technology business, a lot of the ideas and products are really derivative products or products that are driven by people trying to develop products that fit into needs being articulated very loudly in user forums that are quite public and open to large numbers of developers.

The major system houses also make it very clear what their needs are, and thus, you will find that for any problem or requirement, there are a lot of people making noise about what types of problems need to be solved.

In this environment, it is difficult to come up with a truly unique idea. There are definite windows of opportunity that open up, and some developers get a new product into the window, and others do not.

To have the idea that your idea is truly unique and no one will ever come up with it is a nonstarter. You must get your concept out to the public market. You must build an articulate and pervasive case as to why your product is the winning concept. You must also get your product into a couple of key sites so that the buzz starts about your product and not your competitors' products. For example, early on Apple invested heavily in the niche education market because the company realized it could "train" early adopters on its systems.

The window of opportunity is constantly opening and closing. It opens quickly, but because of the tremendous financial stakes and the total amount of information about user needs, it quickly closes. You must get your product defined, prototyped, and into the market fast. Otherwise that window will close.

Just like trying to ride a big wave. Waves are constantly moving toward the beach and breaking up. If you miss getting up on a wave, you must search or wait for the next wave. Luckily, there are a number of technology areas that will allow you to develop and market new and innovative products. However, you must get to the start and get up on that wave. If you do not, you have missed that wave and its window of opportunity.

Developers who want to hide or keep secret their new ideas are doomed to failure. To make a new idea work, you must get the idea prototyped and into the market as fast as possible to avoid being left out when the window closes.

Design Process

At one point during my career, I became very interested in how to make a design decision. During the process of making design decisions, each decision that you make will both affect the design and narrow your allowable choice of other decisions. If you make one decision, what happens to the design? If you make another, does the design have to take a completely different track?

In fact, it seemed to me that there was a structure to design. There seemed to be a sequence in which decisions should logically be completed. You cannot make a decision about what operating system you can choose if you do not know what hardware you will be running. If you pick a particular piece of hardware and it has limited choices of operating systems available, then you must settle for one of the available operating systems. However, if you deem that the operating system is very important, then you should select the operating system before you pick the hardware. This decision about which part to pick first can have very different results in how the end product looks.

Because different companies and groups of developers have different skill sets, the process for designing a product is very different. It is based upon the biases of the designers.

Yet when you go into a company, you will find that most companies have a design process. This process implicitly encapsulates the personalities and biases of the designers. Yet the company will be able to tell you how the process works and how many previous times the process has provided the company a viable product.

I found the idea of design process to be quite important because it also allowed me to control design decisions. At many points in the design, you are going to have to defend the design and compare it to other products. In some cases, these design reviews, customer presentations, marketing meetings, etc. will become quite contentious. I did not like this sequence of events because I found it counterproductive to explain or argue my position. Thus, I began to develop a set of design processes that I felt should be followed. I created a set of systematic approaches that attempted to describe some of the key decisions and the order of these decisions. This included the next logical decision and ways to describe the design as a set of related decisions. By having my framework or set of systematic approaches, I could describe the design in a very structured and organized fashion. Not many of the other designers I encountered took this approach. When they had to describe their designs or products at meetings or design reviews, they consistently fell short of the mark. The design process is intended to make you organized and prepared.

Because different groups have different capabilities and biases, there is no right design process. If you are a hardware company, you will start with the hardware decisions first. That will dictate your software architecture. You then have to pick your input/output (I/O) devices and the software drivers along with how you will interface the applications to the operating system.

If you are a software company, you will try to make decisions that provide flexibility on what hardware platforms you can run the software on.

In any case, you need some sort of process to keep track of the decisions and the order in which they are made. Only then will you be able to see how your design evolves.

A very large company has a very formal, well-developed, and institutionalized design process that includes all types of design reviews. Typically, these types of companies will have preliminary and critical design reviews. In a small company, there will probably be an informal meeting of the design team once a week, and the necessary decisions will be ironed out at that meeting. In any case, it is important to have your design process written down. In the small company, it may simply be a list of key decisions, the order, and date at which these decisions must be made. It doesn't have to be (and should not be) a large, formal process!

If we arc at the start of a wave and are deciding whether we are going to ride down the face of the current wave or wait until the next one, we will not have an extensive amount of time to make a formal process and argue over the niceties of that process and the attendant decisions. We need to have the courage of our convictions and experience. Set up a list of decisions, assign them, and get on with the design. It is critical to minimize the size of the team that will be making these decisions. Too many people with input into the decision process will slow you down. Even with a great idea, you can spend so much time making a decision that you'll miss the wave.

Life Cycle

When you are developing a product, you have a wide variety of issues to consider. Development is not just about building the product and selling it. You have a complete set of other issues that you must address. For example, how do you repair a product that fails or fix a bug in a piece of software once the product has been deployed?

Further, there may be sets of collateral information that need to be developed. What type of training is required? Do you have online or hard-copy manuals? An entire set of questions needs to be associated with the product development before the product can be launched.

This is really a simple part of the product development business. You need to begin with your product concept. Taking the basic concept, you need to generate a concept of operations that describes how the product is used, functions, etc.

Once you have the basic product concept nailed down, you need to make up a complete list of ideas about how you are going to build and support the product. How are you going to install it? How are you going to update it? There is a myriad of such questions.

You can envision the process of what you do with your product from cradle to grave. You need to build scenarios that take the product through its life cycle to figure out the possibilities and how the product could evolve over time.

On many big government systems, you find that there is a concept called *life cycle costs,* where people who do procurement try to figure out the total cost of ownership of the system. This is a really good exercise because it tries to illuminate the total costs that you encounter as you bring on a new piece of equipment or process. In many cases, the cost of ownership is dominated by the attendant costs not the basic product cost. As the designer of a product, you need to be aware of these costs and issues.

When trying to figure out how the product will evolve and its costs over a lifetime of the product cycle, you need to not only envision the basic costs, but also project variations of the basic product. This includes new product models and changes in the customer environment. One of the big issues you will face is maintenance. The really big questions are, "What is the cost of maintenance, and how long will you support a product?" In the case of software, you will probably choose to discontinue support of a version after a new version (or after two new versions) has come out. In the case of hardware, you want to support the hardware for as long as possible.

I have a friend whose company made a hardware product. As the PC industry matured, the hardware product became obsolete. The company successfully converted its customer base to a new PC-based hardware system. However, that still left a large number of customers who failed to convert to PC-based solutions. Thus, the company began to perform extended maintenance on the old hardware. The company also had a number of competitors who had used the old hardware and to varying degrees had switched their customers to newer PC-based solutions.

The company finally became the only firm that provided maintenance on this old hardware base for not only its customers but also its competitors' customers. At one point, trying to get parts became difficult, so the company bought as much obsolete equipment as it could find. Finally, the company developed newer technologies that could replace key parts of the older equipment. The end result was that more than 40 percent of the company's revenue and nearly 80 percent of the company's profits came from maintaining obsolete hardware.

You must really consider all of the details of your product plan. Try to figure out the potential scenarios, because you never know how long a particular product will hang on in the marketplace.

Hierarchical Cores

One of the major design problems that product developers will encounter is the rate of change in technology. In some senses, it moves really fast. If you are introducing a new product, you must move fast. However, if you have an existing product, you still have to move fast, but you may be more in the arena of value engineering and not so much in the area of raw technology development.

In the early 1970s, I learned an invaluable lesson about rate of change. I was in a group that was developing concepts for new computer systems and predicting what technologies would be ready and cost effective for certain points of time in the future. We were a very aggressive group and had a lot of advanced technology ideas that would become deployed in a large number of systems. One of the areas we were studying was the effect of semiconductor technology on memory design. We had a number of systems that were developed and deployed by our divisions that needed a variety of memory technologies. In addition to raw storage capacity, our products needed special features in the area of memory, which made memory technology a very big deal to us.

One of the technologies that we were working on was semiconductor memories and their abilities with regard to volatility. Volatility is the ability of a memory technology to retain its information when the system loses power. This is not a big deal now because many memory technologies have nonvolatile properties. But in the old days, things were different.

There were a lot of competing memory technologies at the time, and they had different properties. There were core memories, which were made from little donut-shaped iron ferrite cores that were strung in a pattern to form the memory. However, core memories had physical limitations on the size of the memory because a core could be only so small. That limitation would be dictated by the size of the hole through which you had to thread the wires that would be used to provide the electronic signal necessary to read and write information. An advantage of the core technology was that the magnetic orientation of the core would stay even if the power was turned off.

Our group was interested in semiconductor memories, which had a lot of advantages. If you had an application that could stand the use of volatile data, semiconductor memories held a lot of promise. (Eventually nonvolatile semiconductor memories came about, but that was about twenty-five years after we were worrying about this problem.) Semiconductor memories provided a great deal of density and allowed for massive data storage. There were various schemes to maintain power and, thus, take advantage of the size advantage of these memories.

Our division had a further need for more exotic memories, so we looked at plated wire memories. These memories seemed to have the best of all worlds. However, they were difficult to manufacture and did not have any chance of going into mass production, which would have lowered their costs. But if one of your major applications was to develop a space-borne computer system, you needed memories that were radiation hardened, nonvolatile, and small. Plated wire was your only choice at the time. However, the division really wanted a denser approach, and that caused the push for our semiconductor investigations.

We were pushing hard on the concept of the new memory technology when a friend invited me to his company to see a demonstration of the way it conceived of new memory technology.

My friend was a big proponent of technology change and evolution but felt that you could never underestimate the ingenuity of a factory that learned how to build and milk a specific technology. It not only had to milk the technology but also had to produce state-of-the-art products at the fastest rate possible.

During the time I had known him, his company was also working on new memory technology concepts. The company had an advantage on our group because it had better insight into how a high-volume factory would approach the problem. Thus, I was quite surprised when he told me that their next-generation product would continue to use core technology. My company had already decided to begin shifting to semiconductor memory.

At the end of the tour, he wanted to show me why the company was going to stay (for at least one more cycle) with core technology. In the lab, when I looked through the microscope, I was startled beyond belief. Inside the CDC 6600 machine's core hole was the core from a 7600 machine (the current processor). And inside the hole of the 7600 core was the core that they intended to use in either the 8600 or the STAR 100.

This was unbelievable; the company had learned to make the cores so small that the new core would fit into the hole of the previous generation. But the revelations did not stop there. The company had also figured out how to string the wires through the center of the core. The company had solved this problem, according to the display demonstration card, by developing a system whereby it would shake the cores onto a substrate-like platter. Then the cores would fall into little slots and the wires would be inserted not by a human but by an operator who would operate a device that would thread the wires through the cores along a path defined by a stream of air. This would center the wire in the core and keep the wire away from the core's inner wall.

As a developer, you cannot underestimate the abilities of your factory or the personnel to innovate and keep your technologies in place for an extended production run. Further, once you get your first product out the door, you have set down the face of a wave and you will have to live with the wave that you picked for a long time. Once the first product is released, you have to service and maintain that product. This will force you to create all kinds of new and ingenious solutions to problems that arise over the years.

Let's not forget about old plated wire and cores. It took forever, but eventually the semiconductor memory took over the market, although there are still uses for nonsemiconductor memories.

A couple of my friends eventually left the company and formed another where they adapted some of their lessons learned in the plated-wire business to make other forms of nonvolatile electronic devices.

The ability of an existing system provider to make any radical change to its technology or processes is very limited in the short term. This provides an advantage to the start-up company because it can pick out a bigger, or at least a different, wave to ride. But once you make your choices, you too have to innovate, as the wave starts to break, to keep your technology in the top spot.

This problem existing suppliers face in keeping new technology out of the market is not unique to the computer business. In the medical market, the time it takes to get a new product approved is legendary. In the energy field, fossil fuel facilities have a distinct advantage over other energy facilities. In the late 1950s, solar energy had its proponents and promise. It never materialized, and now you can hear the same arguments that you heard then. I heard the ethanol story in the late 1970s and again today. If you are in energy technology, do not underestimate the ability of the current fossil fuel companies to hang on.

White Rabbit

Sometimes technology development will feel like things are dropping out of a cartoon. In particular, the total environment will feel like a fanciful place that is not connected to reality. To be effective, the development team is generally disconnected from the real world. In some cases, the development will be totally sequestered from all other members of the company. This idea is not substantially different from how critical developments are run in large companies when they are actually trying to get a specific job done. In such cases, the development team is placed into a skunk works environment. I prefer to think of the environment as Wonderland from *Alice's Adventures in Wonderland*.

In a sense, your development environment will feel like Wonderland, a place populated by all types of fanciful characters who have specific skills and attributes that allow them to perform different tasks and behave in specific manners. Some of these characters are key members of your development team.

You will always have a couple of characters on the team who never contradict each other, but neither can they seem to get along. These characters are always threatening each other over some type of supercilious argument, but nothing ever seems to come of their escapades. These characters are very similar to Tweedledum and Tweedledee in that they will never really get along with each other, but when push comes to shove, they never contradict each other. They just like to argue. As long as it does not get out of control, they are harmless.

The key to a successful development is to avoid having a lead developer who exhibits the traits of the White Rabbit. The White Rabbit is bombastic and condescending toward underlings and does not support them. The White Rabbit sucks up to the queen and others above his station. Even worse, the White Rabbit sometimes seems to be in panic mode. The White Rabbit is nervous and seems always to note that he is late for a very important date. This is similar to the engineer who always has a project that is behind schedule. The engineer claims it's impossible to perform adequately given the limited resources that have been provided until somehow a miracle occurs at the very last minute. In some people's world, this happens all of the time on every project until the manager figures this out and puts a stop to it.

Big wave surfers must be confident and recognize the worth of their associates. Otherwise, they will never get the most out of their teams at the critical juncture in the development. The big wave surfers cannot exhibit any of the traits of the White Rabbit if they are to be successful.

Unless you have a lead developer who can act as an effective buffer among management, investors, marketing, and product development, the project will fail due to oversupervision and conflicting pressures that are not effectively buffered from the development team. Lead developers must exhibit the characteristics of peacemaker. They will continuously need to remind the development team what they signed up to accomplish and to remind the other groups that we can't continuously make project changes and expect that the development teams will ever accomplish anything.

When thinking about how the development will work, you need to think about the trials and tribulations that Alice encountered after she fell down the hole into Wonderland. The difference is that the lead developer will keep the other competing groups in check and the development moving out of the underground hole.

Big Company Innovation

At one time, big companies were the innovators in the technology business. Now they are the antithesis of innovation. They are the anti–big wave surfers of the industry. Because of economics, generally you will not find big wave surfers in big companies.

The costs of research and development (R&D) have escalated. At about the same time, the financial pressures on the companies began to escalate. The result was that a lot of large companies believe that their solutions to innovation were and still are to buy the technology that they need. The advantage is that they do not sustain the costs associated with developing technologies. Big companies believe that they do not have to innovate. They believe that they can buy any innovation any time they need innovation. This is called the no-risk advantage. The risk is minimized by having other companies take the development risk.

Running an advanced R&D shop is not a science. The types of people who you find in this arena are truly interesting. In Minnesota, the term *interesting* has a variety of connotations that could range in meaning from stupid people to unmanageable people. This wide range of people in an R&D environment is foreign to the management of a large company who expect to have all of the details of the process of engineering fall into distinct, highly transparent, and predictable categories of engineering work. They expect that development and advanced engineering can be managed down to the smallest detail.

The lack of predictability of the design and implementation process tends to drive people mad when they are responsible for the day-to-day financial results. If the product cannot be implemented on a predictable schedule, there is no way to accurately monetize the revenue stream.

The dual problems of difficult people and the lack of predictability cause the management of big companies to avoid any risk in development.

The solution to this problem from a big company's point of view is to minimize the number of difficult people to deal with by cutting the size of any R&D department to a bare minimum. The current standard for a company that wants an image as an industry leader is to have a small advanced technology lab that spends half of its time trying to monitor or incrementally advance technologies. The other half of its time is spent trying to help the product division transition its existing technology into new products. This fixes the problem of dealing with very difficult and unusual people.

The problem of predictability is also easily solved. If you do not develop any advanced technologies, but you adopt technologies that other companies have developed and proven, you minimize your development time and risk. Further, you do not have much risk. If the technology is proven, patented, and understood by the group or company that you are acquiring, you can maximize the results of your investments.

The risk that you take if you adopt this approach is that you must be able to really understand and correctly evaluate the technologies that are being procured. Further, the people that you acquire with the technology acquisition may have been living in a unique corporate culture and may have no chance to fit into a product culture. Thus, the management challenge will be to make sure that you get the technology transferred into the product line as fast as possible before the inevitable culture clashes begin.

The idea and the demonstrated ability to buy the technologies necessary to drive a product line forward have caused many large companies to completely rid themselves of any real advanced technology development capability.

In many cases, large companies are procurement organizations that buy technology from subcontractors and integrate the technology. This is particularly true with large prime contractors. This is the reason many large companies miss major opportunities.

Companies such as Cisco and Microsoft did not grow to the size they are today without spending huge amounts of money on R&D. There are many large companies that, although they have grown very well, completely missed the new technology transition because they decided they could get by without any large spending on R&D.

Look at the growth rates of many big companies such as Lockheed Martin, Boeing, Cisco, Google, Microsoft, and Oracle. Look at the length of time they have been in existence. That will give you a good feel about the growth rates that can be achieved by different companies at different times based on their spending on R&D.

Customer Intimacy

One big advantage of developers with current products is that they have access to a customer base. This allows them to have an understanding of the customers' potential future needs. This understanding is not from a theoretical basis; it is from operational observations. This is a huge advantage particularly if the vendor is a key supplier or has equipment installed at a customer site where the customer is happy.

If the customer is happy, the customer will not tend to be very receptive to other vendors' solutions. This is due to inertia. Even if you bring in a new product that has very advanced functions and the customer is happy, he may ask the current vendors if they can bring into the system the functions that you are proposing. This request is probably not going to include your equipment; it's more likely a request to see if the existing vendors can provide their own versions of your functions.

If the customer is not happy with its current vendors, you will face the hurdle of how much risk there is in changing vendors. Even when the customer is unhappy, the customer may not like your approach because it is risk averse. The question for the customer is, How bad is the current vendor? If the customer is willing to change its vendor and its systems, then the customer is usually truly dissatisfied.

This problem is a direct reflection of customer intimacy. The current vendors have relationships and trust established with the customer. Even if the customer is dissatisfied, there is the issue of the devil you know versus the devil you don't. In many cases, the vendor whose equipment you are trying to displace may actually be operating the systems you are trying to enhance or displace.

The fact is the customer and the existing vendors are in bed with each other. The major marketing strategy that established vendors use is customer intimacy.

If you are developing technology that is going to be put out into the world, you must make sure that it is fully functional, works well, and is easy to install and integrate. Otherwise, you do not stand a chance of getting your product into the system and keeping it in the system. The existing vendor and customer have a clear bias of keeping other new and varied vendors out. You are trying to swim upstream. The only chance you have to penetrate this environment is with a superior product that is easy to use and install. Just providing more and better functionality is not enough. You will have to overcome customer intimacy, and the product is the engine that will drive that car.

To get your chance, you must have a great product. The product can't become your albatross if marketing is to overcome customer intimacy.

Three Concerns

There I was having dinner with a couple of my friends and employees. The occasion was a going-away dinner for one of the employees. He did not want a big celebration for his departure, so a small number of us were taking him out to dinner. Such dinners are always a challenge because you usually have mixed feelings. And in this case, I was quite happy that the employee was moving on to what he considered a major new position.

As dinner went along, we were laughing and joking when the conversation got very serious. The departing employee suddenly took out a notebook and pen and asked me the following question: "What are your three big concerns?" This threw me for a loop.

Think about the question. I am primarily a product-type guy. In general, my concerns are performance, cost, and function. Is there anything else to be concerned about as long as you are on schedule? Is there more than that? Your job as a developer is to get the product ready. It is really that simple!

But there was the big question: What are your three big concerns? Is this a cosmic question? Is this a product question? Or, is it simply an inane question asked by an obsessive compulsive ex-employee?

I was completely thrown for a loop. Later, I realized this was a typical question a shrink would ask. But at the time, I had no knowledge of the situation and was completely thrown by it.

The question brings up our current concerns. As a developer trying to get a new product out in a hurry to catch a window of opportunity to get up onto a trend of new products or product category, what are your three big concerns? As the manager of a high-risk and fast-paced development, what are your concerns?

The single biggest issue is getting a development specification agreed upon by management, marketing, and development. Only with such an agreement can you move forward. And without a product, there will be nothing to be sold and the company will go under. Further, you must then get a realistic schedule for the development process, and because you tend to be optimistic, you need to be very careful in setting the time frame for the development. Lastly, you need the management team to buy in to make sure that you are able to hold the line on requirements creep.

Those are the three big concerns: a development specification, a realistic schedule, and a lack of requirements creep.

Unless you can get agreement on the fundamental product, you will never converge on an actual product. At some point, you must draw a line and say this is what the product looks like. Then you must develop a realistic schedule for all other activities necessary to commercialize the product and hang on the release date, and you must not miss that date. All of the adjacent costs are being geared around the product functions and the release date, and it is critical that you hit both of these targets.

Lastly, as word of the product leaks out, there will be a push to begin making changes. In setting your schedule, you need to account for some amount of requirements creep and schedule slippage. But at some point you must draw the line at trade-offs or additions to the product that will cause it to slip and not have a cohesive set of features.

Interestingly, the three big concerns of the development team are not necessarily technical issues. The technical issues should be accounted for in the product definition and schedule. Instead, the big concerns are actually people issues.

Giant Corporations

There are really only two manufacturers of large jet aircraft: Boeing and Airbus. They are so big that in an average week they each need to book about a billion dollars of new business. There are several companies of similar size, like Northrop Grumman, Lockheed Martin, Oracle, Microsoft, and Cisco, that have specific markets they dominate. But Boeing is one of the best examples of a big company that shows a variety of important features of business success and failure.

Big companies tend to become mindless, slow, low-innovation environments. They can never be truly innovative. At one point, they were innovative and nimble. But as they got big, they became risk averse and not innovative. This is part of the natural life cycle of successful companies. The problem is that if you need to bring in a huge amount of money, then you have no time to look to the future. Thus, Boeing (and it would protest this view) will never be able to be innovative. It has really two businesses: commercial aircraft and command and control for the U.S. Department of Defense.

If you look at Boeing from the point of view of a big wave company, it will never again meet the criteria. At one point in its history, it was a nimble high-tech company, but at this point, the commercial aircraft business is just not an innovative part of any business. The commercial aircraft business is about engineering and manufacturing products to build big airplanes that are fuel efficient. This part of Boeing's business is not very innovative and, in fact, is hopelessly mired in the constant churn as the waves slap on the beach. The military aerospace portion of the Boeing business is also hopelessly mired in a relatively low-profit engineering business that, due to its size, cannot afford to take large risks. It's basically a large program manager, not a supplier of innovative parts.

Companies such as Boeing are too large to get into the fast-growing portion of the wave. We are looking for a company or product that has the characteristics that put us on the face of a large wave. We are not looking for a company that will put us on the churn that is moving onto the beach. If a company such as Boeing is going to be evaluated, you need to see it as an investor would—a large blue-chip company and not a rapidly growing company.

Three examples will illustrate the problem with size and innovation: HAC (Huge Aerospace Company), AHAC (Another Huge Aerospace Company), and IBM (in terms of fairness, IBM can be identified; we will not jinx it with this discussion).

HAC wanted my company as a supplier in its bid. In due time,

HAC discovered that we planned to bid on the same contract. The discussions broke down. A short time later, HAC decided that it did not really have the technology to bid the job and asked us if it could be on our team. We were open to this overture because we were looking for a large hardware manufacturer to perform the volume production for our product. However, HAC felt that it should dictate the solution because it had an algorithm it felt was an important part of the product. We had a different approach to the product and could not get HAC to move off of its algorithm focus. Finally, in exasperation we asked HAC what value it was adding to the product. HAC stated that its value added was that it was HAC. It had no technology value added!

We did not add HAC to our product team. What we needed to add to our team was a company that could integrate and test more than 45,000 units containing our software if we won the bid. We did not need some little algorithm or some subcontractor whose vision of its value added was that it was HAC. In this bid, the stakes were high. The potential revenue stream for this product was (by year) $3 million for Rand D, $3 million for technical transition, and up to 45,000 units at an average price of $50,000 over a two-year period. Clearly, this was a high-risk development and it may or may not ever come to fruition.

In another case, we had a bid into AHAC and we were being evaluated along with seven other vendors. The other vendors were multibillion-dollar companies. Clearly, AHAC was trying its best to eliminate us; the irony was that at the time our company had less than forty people and we were bidding a job that was worth over $250 million. We eventually got through the procurement wickets to the point that we were one of the few finalists and we had to get through our oral presentation before submitting our final price.

The orals were quite instructive. There were one or two minor technical questions about the product. Then we got the stuffing kicked out of us for several hours about what AHAC viewed as our cavalier attitude about how we would manage subcontracts, finance, etc. At one point, one of the leaders of the evaluation team got so upset over our approach to subcontract management that he jumped up and started screaming that subcontracts were his life and we were making a mockery of his profession with our cavalier attitude to this critical problem. That was the problem with AHAC: It was so big that its technology was doing the paperwork associated with system integration rather than doing real work to develop products.

We ended up losing the sale, but AHAC could only eliminate us on the basis of soft criteria—its perceived notion about our capabilities to manage the program, not our solution. We had used very innovative technology to leverage us into the position of being in a place where we could modify our existing technology and not have to develop from scratch. This put us in position of being able to deliver in a rapid, cost-effective fashion compared to the other vendors and let us be competitive to many large ($10 billion) competitors. In the end, the winning vendor was not able to deliver on time and the success of the product is now in doubt.

Eventually, a successful company will get so big it will end up in the churn trying to evolve its products and stave off the competition. The company will not be innovative even though it is still successful. If you want to be in the big wave technology development business, you must be with a small company that is nimble and can take risks.

You would never buy a jet airliner from a start-up, but similarly you should not assume that a large company is able to innovate.

Huge Costs

It is difficult to understand the size of a company. When I first started in business, there were big companies, but now there are behemoth companies. Some companies are so large that they do not understand their own size. Take a company such as Boeing or Lockheed Martin. They are household names, but very few people understand how truly large these companies are. Look at companies like Microsoft and Cisco. They were small companies not long ago. When companies get large, they tend to modify their culture and enter a period in which there are large cost barriers to entry for any company that wants to compete in the product space. They may no longer have technology advantages, but they end up with size barriers that one would find difficult to overcome in a development sense.

Boeing has a revenue base of $63 billion a year. After the financial crisis created in 2008–09, a few billion may not seem like a big deal, but we do know that Boeing needs to bring in about $1.2 billion each week. To do that, it has to sell a lot of stuff and airplanes each week.

When you think about it, that is a big task. If you are in charge, you have to be looking for big opportunities. You do not really care about little technology changes. In fact, if I brought you a technology that had potential to go from $0 to $100 million in revenue by year four, but I needed one of your best engineers and sales guys to accomplish this task, you are probably not interested. Sales of $100 million in year four only amount to about $2 million per week, which is only a rounding error on the nut you must crack each and every week.

Thus, a lot of large companies forgo the small high-growth, high-potential markets that are available to the big wave surfers. Instead of riding the seldom-found big wave, they deploy themselves across a lot of beaches where there are a lot of smaller but more frequent waves. Big companies have huge cost numbers, which means they do not take risks.

Once I was giving a seminar where there were a lot of IBM employees. I had known some of them from other venues and found them to be an interesting and pleasant group. In the question-and-answer portion of the session, we were discussing growth rates in the computer industry. One of the IBM people spoke up and noted that IBM was going to grow about 15 percent a year for the foreseeable future. This seemed like a reasonable thing to say, and no one in the seminar challenged the assertion.

I knew a couple of the IBM strategic planners who were in the seminar and at the break stopped to chat with them on the subject of growth. At this point, IBM had been putting up stellar numbers each quarter and each year. It had a four- or six-year growth track record that was the envy of the industry. But the company had become pretty big. When talking with one of the planners, I noted that I had not felt like arguing with the other attendee, but the assertion seemed bogus. He asked me why I could doubt IBM, and my response was pretty simple: "Forget about percentages. IBM was so big that to grow 15 percent the next year was the equivalent of creating a company the size of Digital Equipment Corporation (DEC), which at the time was the world's largest minicomputer manufacturer." I thought that was going to be a difficult task. Further, if you claimed that you could do that for a number of years, you would take on the task of creating a new DEC each year.

At lunch, my friend cornered me and stated that he had never thought about the problem that way. Inside of IBM, they just threw around the percentage growth number without really thinking about the magnitude of the task they were setting out to accomplish. His conclusion was that although the upper management wanted that level of growth, they did not really understand the ramifications.

We are not trying to accomplish such lofty goals. We, as developers, are trying to figure out a new product that can achieve a very high growth rate for a short period of time. We need to leave the long-term problems to some other group of people as the technology matures.

Compatibility Curse

Compatibility is interesting because it is both a curse and a blessing. One of the key factors in developing new technologies that can grow into highly successful products is the issue and curse of compatibility. One aspect of compatibility is the result of user inertia. Once users understand and feel good about a product, they become attached to the product and do not want to learn a new product.

If you have a successful product, the customer base will want any new products that you bring out to be compatible with the old product. In the software business, this is especially true. The customers want to run their old software on any new hardware platforms. This made the Y2K problem really interesting because the number of old solutions and the strategies that were being used to run them were really ingenious. Trying to get them all converted was a major task because the management of the user corporations had no knowledge of what the information technology departments had wrought.

But the issue is even more ubiquitous than simply old software running on new platforms. People learn and do not want to change the familiar interface. Over time, people become comfortable with shortcuts and particular sequences of processes in performing a task. They want to continue that process indefinitely. You constantly run into the problem that people are not willing to change or have difficulty changing. Unless you provide a compelling argument about the new product, you cannot make significant changes to an installed base of products.

You can, however, easily introduce a new product if that product is built by adding features to an existing product. If the new product can be envisioned as an extension of an existing product, then the sale to the end user is greatly simplified. Further, the more that the new product looks and feels like the old product, the easier it is to sell the new product. In many cases, the producer of the product has in place maintenance agreements and it is easy to slip the new product into the market as an upgrade of an existing product under these agreements.

The curse part of compatibility is that if your new product is substantially different than the existing product, you have opened up the market for the user to consider other similar products by other vendors. A variation on this theme is that if the customers decide that the existing product is good enough, they will not buy any new products to replace the existing products until they absolutely have to get the new products. In some cases, the customers will sit with their existing product until the current products fail and are no longer repairable. The curse translates into a combination of good enough, no need for action, and opening up of the sales cycle.

The blessing is that if customers are unhappy with their current product, they tend to be open to change. They may be resistive to change, but they will not close you out of the sales process, and, in fact, they may be willing to listen to the arguments about the benefits of your new products. The blessing morphs into a mechanism that allows the sales department to move new products into the customer base with minimal effort.

Further, the more satisfied the customer is with your product, the easier it is to introduce new functions, particularly if the new product can be set as an upgrade and offers a way forward to new feature sets.

However, if you are the competition and are trying to break into an account with a new product, the bar gets set very high because purchasers of new technology will want to see quantifiable benefits before embarking on purchases of a new product.

It would be extremely difficult to replace or displace a running database system just to swap it out for another database system.

However, if you had a product that was completely different and provided an entirely new set of functions that worked in conjunction with existing databases, you have a chance to introduce and sell that product. If the new product also worked with a number of database systems, was an easy add-on, and provided a lot of new functions that the current products on the market did not have, then you have a chance of selling the customer on the new product because you have introduced new functions but maintained overall compatibility with the customer's critical applications.

Analysis Paralysis

One of the problems with trying to design and build a product is that there will be a large number of opinions about the product and what it should do. How do you know who is correct about the functions that should be included in the product? There are a number of questions that need to be answered.

However, if you have a core group of people who are highly skilled, they can narrow the choices at a very rapid rate. If you do not get the choices narrowed down and the base product defined rapidly, you run the risk of analysis paralysis. If you are Boeing and are designing the next-generation aircraft, you have a long lead time and a long product cycle. You can afford to conduct trade-off studies. You can afford to conduct user focus groups. Your management can afford to mull over the strategy, and your sales department can afford to show customers the new aircraft and get their feedback. However, if you are trying to be nimble and strike into the market with a completely new product and product approach, you do not have that luxury.

If you are a small software company and face nimble competition, then you are in a completely different position. You need to make rapid decisions and know how the product is positioned against the competition without spending a large amount of time doing detailed analysis. If you start doing analysis, a nimble competitor can get the jump on you.

Further, once you get into the analysis mode, you get into a situation where every decision is questioned by a member of the team, and you will spend all of your time justifying your decisions. This will only lead to more questions and analyses. This generates what is essentially a death spiral.

You can always make functional changes on the next version or model, and you can always accept feedback from the beta testers of your product or the early users of your product. What you cannot do is recoup lost time if you let a competitor control the introduction of products into a new sector. If you are about to create an entirely new product sector, you need to remember that others may be thinking of similar product ideas and you are not in a position to dilly dally while trying to define the perfect product that meets the needs (real or perceived) of arbitrary customers or design team members.

One of the single worst traps is to allow yourself to get sucked into an extended analysis cycle.

Little Company Innovation

A question I have often pondered is, What causes little company innovation? For some reason, little companies have a hidden factor that just makes them more innovative than large companies. The big company guys dispute this fact, but the majority of technology innovations are set into motion by individuals working in small technology companies.

There seems to be a number of reasons for this fact. A prevalent reason, based on my experience, is the issue of process. Big companies like to have in place processes that allow them to control their development processes. This is a good thing because some products are so complex that you need a massive organization to roll out the product. Further, you need massive manufacturing and distribution capabilities. But what comes with those large-scale capabilities is the need for formal methods of structuring your innovation. This is ridiculous. How can you structure or control innovation? Does this even make sense? What would cause anyone to think that you could create in a rigidly controlled environment? There is no way that you can structure a system in which innovation is institutionalized.

There are even colleges and higher-level educational institutions that think they can teach courses on innovation and entrepreneurship. Yet from my personal experience, you need to have unfettered individuals who have the mindset and ability to try new things. The cause of innovation is not institutionalized. In fact, the more structure, the more difficult it is to make anything happen.

The advantage of little technology companies is that, generally, they are formed by people who want to make something happen. Either they have or they develop a vision. They try to move their vision forward. They do not have to go to a committee to vet their idea and the resultant plan of action. They innovate!

In the innovation business, you need to see an idea and act upon it. If you have to go to a committee and vet the idea, you will never get anywhere.

A number of large companies have tried to put in place procedures that allow for individual initiative, but they can never get it right. In fact, some companies have an entrepreneur strategy for their research departments—an entrepreneur environment inside the large company. This will never work as a strategy. At some point, the researchers have to go back to the mother ship for final approval, and at that point, they get involved in the process arguments.

It is this lack of processes that frees the innovation and lets the little guy go forward.

Let me give you an example. A big company had won a bid to provide a major new system to a big customer. At stake were billions of dollars. The big company had to go outside of its capabilities and procure several parts that would complete the system. One part it needed was a capability that we had. However, based on one of the company's requirements, no one had a product that could meet the specifications. For some reason, the company decided that the product had to be able to run on Linux. A lot of people had products that could meet the specification if they could run on Windows, but no one had a Linux-based product. So the customer decided that the product had to be a custom development or modification of existing products to run on Linux. Because this product was in the sweet spot of our product set, we decided to bid. The stage was set for a classic shootout.

All of the big companies bid a product that was based on either a custom development or a new development. We bid a really innovative approach. We proposed to modify our product to enable it to run on virtual machines. Our strategy was to run Linux, on top of Linux run a Windows virtual machine, and on top of the virtual machine run our product. Thus, we would only need to slightly modify our product to account for some features that we did not normally provide. This would be a simple addition to the product and would be quite easily accomplished. The use of virtual machine technology would save hundreds of millions of dollars and in no way violate the specifications of the product procurement. But at the time we bid, the strategy was very new and considered risky. A small guy would take the risk; the question was whether a big company could see the logic and take some risk.

The procurement process grinded on with a lot of back and forth. At one point, we were eliminated due to the unconventional nature of our approach. Some of the technical evaluators just did not get it because they were not up to speed from a technology point of view. As the process wore on, we were in the position of being one of the last couple of products under consideration. Eventually we (and the other competitors) were allowed to present our approaches. The presentation was quite short, and we did very well. By now, some of the customers understood the innovation of our approach. But they rejected our approach as too risky.

Ten years later, the same big company proposed to purchase a product from us if it would run on top of a virtual machine. It goes to show that even big companies, given ten years of progress, can get close to an innovative solution. You can never tell where innovation comes from, but to get it executed, you need a highly dynamic environment, flexibility, and a driven team. You will never get that in a big company.

Performance Death

Resources is one of the big problems you'll face in trying to develop a product. In some cases, you will be working on a technology or product direction and will encounter a target-rich environment. This occurs when you have so many possibilities and potential products that you can pick and choose where you want to position your product. This is a good thing, but people will lose focus and try to diversify. If you can slightly modify the product and cover a large number of additional markets, why not?

If your product covers a particular market, then you will have to add features or capabilities to cover the additional opportunities. This will begin to constrain your development resources and increase your development cost and time to market. However, the counter argument is that the total marketplace will open up and the product will be more successful.

Those are all good arguments, but the real key is to get a product out, even if it is just a straw man product. You do not really know how long anything is going to take or what the customer really wants until you are in the marketplace. Nor do you know what the competition is up to until you get into the marketplace.

Thus, my predisposition is to get a basic product out, get it out quickly, and see what the market says. If you need more features or can capture other markets, you have the ability to build new models, build other product variations, or evolve the product in different directions.

If you divert your attention because you are trying to diversify the focus of your product to cover a larger audience, you will probably fail. You will end up defining a product that is, at best, a me-too product, i.e., a product that is not focused enough to be able to distinguish itself from potential competitive products.

In some cases, it becomes difficult to define a clearly focused product. You can't assume people will concentrate their efforts on a well-defined, narrowly scoped product. It's just against human nature.

A number of times, I had to referee the product definition. Sometimes, the team of developers was so disjointed I could not figure out what they thought the end product was. In such cases, I tried to get the developers to give me whatever product development information they had. I would describe the new product based on what I thought it should contain. The definition would then be turned over to the team to produce the final product definition within the constrained outline. Generally, they would come back with a very focused product description that would throw out some of the ideas that I had included. I never let this bother me. My personal feeling was that when we had to resort to this approach, we should have no invested ego in the result. We were trying to get a simple, coherent view of the initial product, and everything else was an issue of figuring out the product evolution so the product could evolve in the most judicious manner.

You should never view any product as an end result. Each product is just another step along a development line, and we need to stay focused and concentrate on getting the product out rather than having a highly diversified product that does everything.

Innovation Capability

In most examples of high-technology innovation, big companies are tiny in terms of innovation capabilities! Big companies are just not innovative because they have had their innovation driven out of them by processes that are designed to control risk. It is a very rare large company that is able to remain innovative as it gets larger.

In many cases, people admire and assume that big companies are where it's at in terms of making new and important developments. The big company has the resources and assets to make important contributions to the science and develop major products that are sold in high volume throughout the world. Yet it is clearly my premise that big companies are worthless in terms of innovation. There are a couple of exceptions, and we'll talk about them later in this chapter.

Big companies generally become process oriented, and that destroys the ability of the individual to make a serious contribution because the individual must go through a serious obstacle course that will destroy any innovative idea before it can get through the system.

If you go to any big company and talk about innovation and new product ideas, the company will trot out its vaunted research department. Wow! I am really impressed by these great capabilities all concentrated in one place generating great new product ideas and new technologies.

Periodically, big companies ask us to team with them to develop new products. Generally, I avoid such arrangements, but sometimes we have technology interchanges or mating dances as we try to pursue product opportunities. Sometimes we have discussions about why we had won a job that our prospective team-mate had lost. In most cases, when we bid a job or product we are going up against multibillion-dollar companies for small niche products that involve a large amount of risk. Due to the risk or size of the job or market, the job of winning the bid is relegated to the big company's "research" department so its product line groups are not involved. The vaunted R&D department is the group that we constantly face. Think of the problems if every time you go to market you face a number of multibillion-dollar companies throwing their best people at the job. And their job, if successful, is to keep you from making a living. It is, however, not personal.

A couple of times during these meetings, someone on the other side of the table has asked how we won a particular job that we both had bid. After encountering this question a number of times, I finally thought about the problems and came to the following conclusion. If we go to big system integrators or system product developers, they all have similar development structures. They have product lines that contain dedicated, hard-working people who are completely constrained by processes and product compatibility constraints, so I never have to face them. The vaunted R&D departments of all of these companies are very similar. Generally, they have 350 to 500 people. These people usually support five to seven technology areas so that the group supporting computer technologies tends to be less than seventy highly skilled researchers. Usually this group has to support four or five computer research areas, and only one of these areas encompasses the area where we compete (i.e., distributed systems), and that group probably contains ten to fifteen people.

Because of their product lines, the R&D department must usually spend 50 percent of its time working with the product lines to improve the corporate products. Thus, in the area that my company competes, the big companies generally can only dedicate six or seven people to a given project. And these people carry with them the baggage of corporate process and the big company mentality that requires even research groups not to accept risk.

Compare that group to my current company. At any time, my company is composed of between seventy-five and 100 professionals dedicated to development and implementation of advanced products based upon the most risky and advanced distributed systems technology. How does the big company expect to compete? It had better hope that either we do not bid or it has customer intimacy, because given a straight-up competition, it's really not a fair fight. We embrace risk and try to take risky positions to see how far we can push the envelope of innovation and change. Although our markets are small and our total revenue is also small, if you want an advanced product you have to come to a company such as ours.

The phenomenon described above is not limited to my company. It is the norm in the industry. If you want a significant, new, and innovative product developed, you need to go to a small company.

Big companies are too cumbersome, risk averse, and process oriented to compete with innovative products. They are great at running a slug farm, so we must give them their due.

There are exceptions. I am a great admirer of Apple. I own some of their products. But the key to Apple is really Steve Jobs. If at the top of a corporation you have a person of vision, you can overcome the problems of large size. Another company that had the advantage of a strong, driven leader that overcame size issues was Microsoft. Gates understood that the PC software business was not about technology, but about marketing and persistence. Keep trying with a product strategy until you get a reasonable product implementation. Put out the best product you can, but realize that there are going to be problems. Get the customer involved so that if possible, you make the people who debug your products pay for the privilege. How the Microsoft softies will continue to innovate is uncertain now that the head visionary is no longer running the company. Probably they are on the way to becoming a big enterprise that suppresses innovation to continue compatibility and evolution of existing products.

Fortunately, our economic system is such that the principals of small companies have a lot of opportunity to make their fortunes, and thus, our system will continue to perpetuate itself as long as we continue to reward innovation.

NIH Issues

Not invented here (NIH) is the kiss of death to a technology.

One of the big problems with developers is that they tend to fall into ruts. They have prior experience, and because that experience biases their facts and designs, they will try to correlate the current design problem back to design problems they have previously solved.

This goes all the way back to parts selection. In many cases, the developers will not want to add new functions to a new product that is similar to a product they previously designed because they have in mind a design that is quick and simple.

To counter this effect, the development team must build a solid specification of what functions are critical to the new product. You cannot afford to allow previous design experience to water down your new product efforts just because the designers knew how to design the previous product and do not feel comfortable in designing the new product.

If you bring to the project these new requirements, concepts, or parts, the designers will quickly move into a mode where they are trying to claim that the new functions are not necessary. What you are really doing is playing a game of NIH. Generally, this is a game of laziness—I do not want to do a huge amount of work and I do not know how to perform the required work without doing a lot of studying.

It is difficult to get past this game because you do not necessarily have an independent way to measure the amount of NIH versus the difficulty of the work to be performed. Whether the problem is hard or the design team (or one of the designers) does not want to address your issues is the question that you must answer.

The best way to figure this out is to get one of the less experienced designers and have that person do an independent estimate of the entire project. This junior designer will not have built up the NIH that years of experience bring to the project. With this independent estimate, you can then go over every detail of the implementation and get an independent estimate of what is really required. Further, you can get a feel for the reasonableness of the overall design.

Once you have such an estimate, you need to determine the choke points that will cause the implementation project to fail. You must determine if you have any designers who are going into obstructionist mode due to their adaptation of the NIH factor.

Any time you are trying to develop a new product, there will be a large amount of inertia if the design or product is unique. It is difficult to convince people of the importance of new features because people tend to be comfortable with what they know. Thus, most people will not see the importance of a new feature, concept, or product until the wave is starting to break and the cycle has overcome the need for other new entrants. You must find a way around this process.

Another is to develop trade-off matrices that isolate the context of these new functions to see if they are really alternatives that lead us to a truly unique product.

The last technique is to personally build scenarios to determine what new functions are not currently available and determine if the new features really can open up new system strategies. Then I try to determine how difficult it will be to implement these new strategies. If all else fails, you need to lay out the design yourself. Try to get the designers to critique the design so they will figure out better ways to implement your choices. They will take ownership of these strategies and designs. In this case, as the project goes forward, the alternatives to your design that were developed in the design review process will become the new NIH. The designers will not want to admit that the design review process revealed the existence of possible solutions and that the solutions are really not difficult. Thus, the design will make progress.

Correct Facts

One of the big problems with development is that in today's environment, there is not necessarily a right way to build a product. With the advent of modern digital electronics, a lot of products that were originally developed as electronic systems are now built as a computer system, where there is a basic processor and the system functions are now programmed into the processor to provide the required product functions.

But the problem is that there is really no good way to test computer programs over the wide range of applications that a product will be deployed in its life cycle. We need to understand that development of products on top of digital electronic platforms is really the simplest and least expensive way to develop the product, but may not be the best way to field a product. Programming tends to have bugs, and if you are not developing a large number of copies of a program and testing it through a very large number of environments, you may not be able to find and eliminate failure modes that are implicit in the design.

One of the issues you need to think about when you build new computer technology is the design. How much time have you put into the design? How new and untested are the parts that you are choosing for the implementation? How skilled are your programmers, and have they developed similar applications?

You need to understand the facts and the realities of your design. You do not want to unleash a system when it has not been fully tested. There is one level of testing concern if you are a fighter pilot. If you are piloting a high-performance jet airplane that was built to run at design limits, you know that it will occasionally fail. You know going in that there is a substantial amount of risk. Anytime you have a fly-by-wire system that has been in limited production, you have only a small number of real test results before you can decide if your product is ready. However, if you are designing cars that use a drive-by-wire throttle system, you need to have a completely different criteria in the design and testing to ensure that the system will work as specified. You do not want to be the manufacturer who ships defective systems to large population segments.

You need to have a mechanism that will allow you to quantify the risks you are taking with the design.

We used to joke about the idea of just releasing the design with minimal testing and letting the end user debug our system for us. You would be surprised at the number of designs that are released upon the public that are not thoroughly tested.

In some cases, you cannot actually test a system because it is one of a kind. There is no basis for testing until the system is fielded. However, if your technology is for end users, it is incumbent on the design team to ensure proper testing to make sure that not only the design meets the design specifications, but also the implementation is complete and bug free by testing and collecting a lot of test samples and statistics before releasing the product.

Relative Positioning

When we are developing a product, we must be aware of other products. Our product does not exist in a vacuum. Even if our product is unique, we need to understand how the product relates to other products, how our product can be explained in the context of other products, and what we believe is the position of our product in the overall product space.

We are in a dynamic environment, and we need to figure out how our product does and will relate to other products both today and over time. As the environment changes, we need to adapt and modify our product's position. We may have to add or alter features of our product to counter movement in the marketplace or in the strategies of other competitive products.

Thus, we will need to develop and document a set of design features that highlight our product, but in the context of how our product relates to other products. The start of this process is to develop a trade-off chart that will highlight the main features that distinguish our product as unique from a competitive point of view. In general, no product is unique, and we're trying to put the vision of our product in the best light. We will be trying to develop design positioning for our product that lets us emphasize and control the image of the uniqueness of our product.

If we have a feature that is unique, we will want to anchor the product position around that particular feature. We will want to build a complete category of information around this unique aspect of our product. When competitive or similar products are compared to our product, we will have a large number of unique features that show how we are different.

In developing the comparison, we will want to be aggressive in interpreting the special features of our product. We want not only to stack the deck in terms of how we view our product relative to other products, but also to create comparisons that highlight where we want the battleground to be when we are compared to other products.

We want to control the arena in which our product is compared to other products. If necessary, we may have to invent new concepts that allow us to define the product comparisons. If there is a product that is similar to our product, we will want to try to position our product as having more advanced or more relevant product features—features that other products do not have! On any directly comparable feature, we will need to define and illustrate the ways in which our product is superior.

The goal is to develop a complete product features chart that allows us to compare our product to any product that customers feel might be competitive. On this chart, we will be trying to illustrate all of our unique product features and the deficiencies of perceived competitive products. We will want to group the features so that we are shown in the best possible advantage.

We will need to have built this feature chart as we developed the product, and we want to make sure every time we present the product to any group we provide our product positioning chart and its clearly (un)biased set of important features.

Generally, people are lazy, and if we get potential customers and product evaluators imprinted with our product vision, we can set the playing field. It is not good enough to develop a relative product positioning strategy. We must own the comparison space for every feature and concept of our new product.

Bunched Waves

One of the problems with development is that waves come in bunches. Usually when you have started on an effort, others have started on similar efforts. You cannot believe the number of times that someone has come up with a "truly unique concept" only to find out that there were other people with similar concepts and a lot of variations on the concept.

This is because we can grade technology into types such as enabling technology or end user application technology. One is seen, one is not. And you must be able to distinguish between the types of technology.

Take, for example, enabling technologies. These are the fundamental underpinnings of technology and are what people use to support their developments and applications. Generally, these technologies are not the type of technologies that are highly visible to the general public. They are at the bottom of the technology product field.

At the other extreme is the idea of an application that revolutionizes a space. This is a technology that is highly visible to the end users or purchasers of a system.

Examples of these variations exist all around us. A cell phone contains enabling technologies that provide the wireless mechanisms that are necessary to provide for the cellular connectivity. But the users tend to see how the phone works and how to use the phone. Unless they are on a trip to Europe with a U.S. cell phone of an old vintage, they will not understand or care about the underlying technology.

Another example is game systems. There is a lot of underlying technology that is used to provide the user experience, but the users do not care about the technology. They care about the game. The game developers need to know and understand the underpinnings because it enables them to make more realistic games.

Lately, the markets have become so big for applications due to the ability to push out the applications to mass markets. Now the user has become aware of companies that provide the underpinning of applications. An example of such a company is Cisco, which is trying to make itself front and center in the user space by emphasizing applications that its equipment can provide to end users.

Because much of the technology underpinnings are the same or very similar, as new capabilities come to the fore, many people start to have ideas that are the same or similar because a given fundamental technology enables a certain level of new applications.

Once a new capability becomes available, it is a race to get onto the big wave and to try to implement a new set of applications of enabling products so that you can catch the next big wave.

Constant innovation in the enabling technologies provides a lot of opportunities for new and novel products. But once a new capability has come to the front of the line, time is sliding away. If you have not been appraised by the manufacturers of the enabling technologies about the forthcoming products and are not an early adopter or beta tester, you are already behind the power curve. If you are in the in crowd and have a good head start, you cannot underestimate the need to run extremely fast because the clock has started to tick and a lot of smart guys are looking at what ideas can be enabled by the new capabilities.

When the ocean sensors provide an alert of a storm that can generate big waves, surfers will congregate. Similarly, a new capability in the underlying hardware draws an immediate crowd. And any first-mover advantages are quickly dissipated.

Unintended Consequences

One of the basic design strategies is to try breaking up the work into individual-oriented work packages. Next, we will want to model these packages into layers or some other structure to manage the design complexity. During this process, we will have to make assumptions about how subsystems interface and relate to each other. By its very nature, this process is imprecise. So we'll need a framework for rules, interfaces, work breakdown structures, and schedules. This will allow us to manage the product's complexity.

This entire strategy is fraught with problems because we can't even begin to understand the potential problems we face. Between every set of modules, there are interfaces that need to be designed, and they must be precise and completely specified. However, even a simple-sounding task like defining an interface between two modules is not simple because any ambiguity will propagate throughout the entire system.

As the decomposition of the total system occurs, the dependencies of the modules can multiply rapidly. Throw in a large number of developers who will be working on the system and have to communicate with each other, and we have a recipe for disaster.

Any time you have a set of rules or information that defines a process, you also have two other categories of information to consider: the set of rules that defines what is supposed to happen and the possible side effects (unintended consequences).

Things outside of the rules are defined as things that cannot happen. But sometimes there are side effects of rules that were not considered and are not covered in either the set of allowable or disallowed actions. These side effects can be the cause of consequences that we never considered or intended. Such effects are called *unintended consequences*, and they can occur any time people try to structure a set of rules. It is impossible to structure a set of rules that are comprehensive and not subject to unintended consequences. In the technology business, two things often happen: the development can occur over a long period of time and the product has to last for a long period of time. But as technology evolves, the potential occurrences of side effects continues to increase.

The big problem is not that we get the system's decomposition incorrect. It is that we do not know what side effects are going to happen. The basic information for development was interpreted by different developers. Add to that the changes that occur over time, and we end up with a system that has a lot of potential problems. We just do not know how to control the evolution of a system over time. So we need to make sure that the system is well defined and that we keep the initial system design simple.

In many cases, the best strategy is to design a set of functions and then go to extreme efforts to ensure that they are tight and well defined. In the operating system business, these functions are known as the kernel functions. The idea of the kernel is to ensure that the functions are so well defined and implemented that they are bulletproof and will never cause a side effect. Our goal is to compartmentalize the design so that the most important parts of the design have minimal opportunity for leakage of unintended consequences into the rest of the design and implementation process.

This is a laudable goal, and we need to try to minimize the side effects if we are to have a workable system.

Compatibility Issues

Compatibility does not imply interoperability!

One of the dirty secrets of product development is the issue of compatibility. In recent years, a lot of companies have begun to embrace the idea of standards and products that comply with industry standards. The companies claim to be compatible with the standard that is popular in the arena that encompasses their products. This gives buyers or users a sense of peace. Their new products comply with the appropriate standards, and therefore, the products should have all of the advantages that the users dream of from a standard product. The products should be interoperable with other standards-based products. They should be easily replaced if lower cost solutions come along, and they should interoperate with other standard products.

The concept of interoperability is at the heart of this argument. The basic idea is that if a product meets the standard it will work with other products that meet the standard, and thus, all of the advantages that one expects from the standards process will be available to the end user.

A classic example of a standard is the uniform dialing system used by a telephone. Phone calls connect based upon a technique that connects them to an infrastructure, and a dialing scheme allows them to interconnect together. In the United States, this scheme is an area code followed by seven digits. If you are calling long distance, you must place a 1 in front of the area code. If only it were that simple. On my Voice over IP (VoIP) phone, I do not have to enter the 1 because every call figures out the right route. If you have a PBX, you may have to dial 9 to get an outside line. But in general, the phone-dialing system presents a set of standards, which can be used to implement a phone system.

Consider the developers' position. Would you as a developer find it advantageous to develop a product that is so standardized that it can be replaced by the end user with a less costly product? Of course not! The solution lies in the committees that define the standards. In general, the committees are composed of manufacturers because they are defining the industry standards that the manufacturers will be building their products to meet. There may be some users involved in the process, but they are at a severe disadvantage because they have no real idea how anything is or can be built. Thus, their inputs will usually have no effect on the overall process.

The manufacturers must get a standard that a large group of manufacturers can live with. The solution is to specify a set of capabilities that are useful to a large group, but leave a large niche available for manufacturers to innovate and develop value on top of the standard. This leaves areas in which interoperability may be impossible because another group may not understand how your product works outside of the basic functions specified by the standards.

It may be possible to take two products that meet a standard and not be able to have the products interoperate. A simple case is again drawn from the phone system world. You cannot take a PBX from one manufacturer and connect it directly to the PBX of another manufacturer. The manufacturers use the same line conventions and dialing mechanisms, but they are not compatible unless you place a set of phone lines between them. That is, you could not connect them together directly, but by connecting them to the phone system, you can get them to talk to each other. Another example is televisions and DVD/CD/Blue Ray players. There is no single standard for how the remote controls work. Yet all televisions can get and decode signals to display picture and sound. The signaling systems are very standard, but the control and features of the television set differ from manufacturer to manufacturer.

The classic example of this phenomenon is products built by Microsoft. Microsoft had (and still probably has) a nasty habit of only publishing part of the necessary application programming interfaces (APIs) to be able to build add-on products to its operating system. Now due to court settlements, Microsoft has to be better behaved. It is supposed to publish all of the APIs and let you know how to connect and add functions.

Yet at points in its product maturity, it may be adding things to its products that allow it to do things or add features that you as a user or competitive developer would not have been made aware of. Its intent is to keep you behind the power curve so that you are always playing catchup.

Low Bidders

A bad sign if you are trying to get a new product launched and gain momentum quickly is to get into a price shootout. If you are in a price shootout, there is probably another similar product and you may be on a crowded wave or not on a big wave.

Price is a sales and marketing function. Engineering does not get involved in sales, so why is this section in this chapter? In selling an innovative product and positioning the marketing and sales department to get us down the face of a big steep wave and get the growth that we want, the key responsibility is on engineering not sales.

To get the product launched rapidly, everyone in the company needs to be in sales. And not just in an abstract sense, but in an evangelist sense. We need to get the entire company involved! We need to get things done correctly and on time, but we also need to give marketing and management an edge that only engineering can bestow. But if we are in a price shootout, marketing has not done its job and we have a problem that has now backed up into the development department. To get a rapid product launch, we need a collaborative customer that champions our product, as described in chapter 11.

We not only need to get everything right, but also must make the trade-offs that ensure that we can build the product at minimum cost. We must design a high-value product that has very high profit margins. We need to give marketing and sales a product that not only is unique and highly useful, but also has the margins that will allow the management to grow the company without dealing with outside capital sources on their terms. We need a product that has high profit margins.

In the case of a price shootout, the high profit margins allow the sales department to get the deal done and overcome any price objections. Although I do not like price shootouts, sometimes they are inevitable, and engineering has to have the product positioned so that sales can do what is necessary to win. Low bidders seldom lose. We do need to be a little careful here because the tendency of a sales guy will be to go to the lowest common denominator of sales, and that is price. So we must give them a good value-added story and an incentive plan that really does not incentivize the sales guy to start this nonsense of price cutting. But in case price cutting is necessary, we need to have the product, and thus the corporation, positioned to withstand the effect of price cutting.

If sales has its act together, then we need to have a product that is highly value engineered so that we generate the margins that management needs to be able to drive the corporation forward while minimizing the use of external capital. Accepting capital has a ton of strings attached, all of which are highly counterproductive and discussed in the section on investing. But the bottom line is that we want the product to generate our income so that we can stay focused on the issue of development and sales and not on the issue of reporting to a bunch of investors who only understand financial reports and do not have our interests at heart. We want to be in a position where we control the key product decisions.

When we are launched and are on the wave we need to concentrate on staying up, not on someone talking to us as we try to avoid getting crushed.

Enough said.

Low Cost

It is important for the development team to distinguish between cost and price.

Cost of a product is the money that will be required for the producer to build the product. This is a measure of the cost of components and labor that go into the development and production of each product unit.

Price is the amount of compensation that the company will receive when a product is sold.

Both price and cost are very difficult to quantify because they have complex structures. In the case of cost, you must not only measure the cost of the materials and the manufacturing, but also consider the cost of development. You will tend to amortize the development costs across a large number of production units. Interestingly, in a number of software-related businesses, you could make a case that a portion of the development cost for a particular version needs to be amortized across successive versions based upon reusability of the software modules. In other assumptions, you may choose to expense the cost basis of the product to the development costs associated with just one version of the product. It is incumbent on the development team to develop the product with a minimum of development expense and to figure out strategies to make the units producible so that the recurring production expenses are minimized.

No matter what the sales department gets for the product on the street or what type of convoluted deals it cuts with resellers, it is in everybody's business interest that the product be designed so that it is easy and cheap to manufacture. Further, it is important that the design team stay on top of the design and modifications. This is to ensure that the product does not evolve in a manner that makes it more difficult to manufacture or in a manner that lets production costs rise.

Price, however, is easy to quantify but not easy to understand. Price is what the manufacturer gets for the product, and price can be very different based on how the product is sold. In the case of price, what the end user of the product pays can vary considerably depending on how the end user procured the product. Further, how the end user got hold of the product can vary due to differences in the distribution channel.

One big problem with the issue of cost versus price is that the design team really does not want to involve itself in the issue of how cost translates into price. The design team needs to stay focused on the issue of the cost of the design and the designed product. It is the design team's sole responsibility to make sure that it provides a quality product that can be produced at a low cost. The fact that the price to the end user is potentially variable does not affect the design team's sense of self-worth or what it thinks the product should cost. The design team does not have the responsibility to make the company profitable or set the product's price. It has the responsibility to build a quality product in a timely fashion.

This can be a problem for the designer, particularly in regards to original equipment manufacturer (OEM) price arrangements. I have seen deals cut that would amount to a 95 percent discount from the product's retail list price. And this was a good deal for the manufacturer.

Consider the case that the manufacturer was about to bring out a new version of the software and there was an OEM customer willing to pay 5 percent of retail list for the previous version that it would then issue as part of a larger suite of products under its private-label brand. If the volume of purchased product licenses was high enough, the discounts for this type of arrangement would be very extensive and could get into the 95 percent range.

This could be a really good deal for the manufacturer. It is essentially picking up free money because there is no production cost.

Life Cycle Cost

A big issue that you need to address as a designer is the cost of ownership for your product. You may not think this is your problem, but as a designer in a small company that is trying to take a rapid step forward, you may be in a position to influence this issue more than anyone else in your corporation. This problem is commonly known as life cycle cost. If your customers are concerned about life cycle and maintenance costs, then you are in the running to sell your product. However, if you have a new product, the customer must get over the hurdle of justifying the life cycle of your product before it can purchase the product. Typically, life cycle costs are associated with products that have already had a life span and may be going into an extended area, or the churn of the wave. If, however, you are just bringing out the new product, you can demonstrate the effectiveness of your product and actually use this argument to accelerate your product development as you lay out design scenarios that illustrate the superiority of your product.

As the designer, you have the real ability to influence this system issue. For example, what is your philosophy for maintenance? How does one replace a failed unit? What are the lowest replaceable modules in the system? How do you perform (and how often do you offer) software upgrades? What constitutes your recall strategy and upgrade to new model philosophy?

All of these questions are a function of design goals, product philosophy, parts selection, module decomposition, fault tolerance, and hooks for future product upgrades that you chose to design into the product.

In launching a new product, you will find that usually the design is complete and the product is in test before anyone understands that someone needs to address these issues. By that time, you have already made all of the fateful decisions that ensure a cohesive plan is in place for the future customer base. In a large company, there are groups of people dedicated to ensuring that these issues are considered. But due to the type of company we are trying to develop and the growth rate we are trying to achieve, you end up making the critical decisions without anyone really thinking abut the process.

In reality, you may not care about any of these issues, but if the product is successful, you will have to live with the end results so you might as well get the issues settled in the design so that you can live with the results over an extended time.

In some groups, like the military, who have long development cycles, the idea of life cycle cost is a critical aspect of the purchasing decision so that ill-conceived design decisions can have a profound effect on the merchantability of the product.

However, if you are an aggressive big wave surfer, you will remember that you are on just one wave and there will be other waves. So whatever compromises you make in the development that affect life cycle cost will be someone else's problem down the road, and you really only need to get the product out the door fast.

It is a rare designer who can balance these two positions.

Boundary Values

One problem that is a real concern to new product developers is the boundary value. Boundary values are the problems that occur when your product has to fit into a context and has to be initialized in some manner. The time when your product undergoes a major change or an installation or upgrade really reflects a discontinuity in the process of usage. You need to understand and provide easy measures to ensure customer continuity and satisfaction.

This problem also occurs when the product reaches a time period at which point some event occurs. A simple example is when the maintenance contract runs out on your product. Marketing must figure out how to get the customer to buy a new maintenance contract, and the development team (which probably includes the technical support team) has to decide what to do if a customer calls in with a recently expired maintenance contract.

If you have a new product or concept and it depends upon any other technologies, there is a cost for the integration of the two products. The product that will have to underwrite the integration is the new product. The current system is already installed and operating, and you will have to prove your value and make the installation of the product simple and easy.

At the time of your product's installation, you will have to decide how your product needs to be installed into the new system. Unless your product is so expensive that you can send an engineer to do every new installation, you must devise a bulletproof strategy for the installation and integration of your new product.

These examples are all relatively benign examples of boundary value problems. Other more difficult problems include what happens if you own or run a major system and it has to be shut down and restored. How do you actually accomplish this goal? An even more difficult problem is how to get everything ready to go if the system was inadvertently shut down or how to operate your system if it begins to overload.

These events do occur. The shutdown of the air traffic control system after 9/11 and how to bring the airline industry back up after the safety procedures were refined is an extreme example of a system that was brought down inadvertently. There was a lot of work before it could be restarted. Attacks on the Internet due to nation states trying to bring down either government or financial sites are another example of artificially induced boundary-value problems.

One of the challenges designers face is trying to figure out in advance what type of problems can occur with your product that could cause the product's installation or operation to create a severe operational discontinuity.

If you are providing a brand-new product, you may have no idea about possible operational discontinuities, but you need to think carefully about the subject prior to shipping the product. Further, at a minimum, you must design the installation and integration strategy so that it is robust enough that you do not get a large number of technical support calls.

Mechanical Engineers

Early in my career, I began to take pity on mechanical engineers. As near as I could tell, they had the toughest job in the world. When we were working on a new processor or system design, we would periodically have to present portions of the design and its status to upper management.

Marketing and our general manager would be there. They were all concerned with the status and progress of the design. None of them wanted to seem like they did not understand the design or that they were not engaged with the project, regardless of the design or the state of the project. They had to seem engaged. The preferred mode of engagement was to ask a question or get involved in some discussion about project issues.

Consider the design issues that are in play. As a manager, do you want to begin a discussion of how the drivers work that allow the I/O system to work with unique peripherals? Do you want to start a discussion of the alternative software strategies that can be used to speed up the systems applications? Or would you rather discuss the way the mechanical engineers suggest that the printed circuit cards are packaged? Pity the poor mechanical engineer! Everyone has an opinion on the mechanical aspects of the design or can ask a question on the mechanical design.

How big should the cards in the box be? How should the cards be attached to the rack? What is the overall form factor of the system? These are the questions that get the most play as the design is reviewed at higher and higher corporate levels. How easily the I/O drivers associated with the operating system can be modified quickly falls off the table if it ever gets on the table in the first place. Generally, if we can get the mechanical engineer scheduled early in the review, we will have nothing to do other than to simply give a summary of the software and assure the management that we are on track.

Marketing would always be satisfied with a one-liner, i.e., a one-sentence summary that assures we are on track. Some managers might, based on their backgrounds, be interested in some aspect of the design to assist the designers if they start to stumble in the review, but everyone really gets into the mechanical design. At first, this process was interesting to watch. Then, it became frustrating as the groups that I was associated with never got to explain our work in-depth or get any real feedback. Eventually, it got to be a joke as the mechanical engineers prepared for these reviews with incredible back-up analyses. They practiced their arguments while the software and architecture groups just worked on our take-away sentences. The best of all worlds would be that we never even got to present because we ran out of time as the managers argued over the mechanical design.

As the computer industry has advanced, standards for many aspects of the design have become important, including packaging. Yet, the design of the package is still an easy thing to talk about.

I was discussing with my group the design of a new system that we were thinking about introducing to our customer base. We were building a number of demo units that could be provided to the large systems integrators for their testing. The system was a piece of special software that we were putting on standard rack-mounted hardware. I could not resist tweaking my guys as we talked about the box we were building. The test units are built in a form factor known as 2U. This means it is a standard two rack units high (as an approximation, view a U as about an inch).

As the discussion ended, I was complaining that one of the issues we needed to address was making sure the second set of production units were 1U in size. In my mind, a 1U would be so much cooler than a 2U. As the conversations ended, no one could figure out why I wanted to discuss the size of the box. It is fun to poke the designers over the mechanical aspects of the design. Among other things, when you have faith in the designers and you just want to chat, it is easy to discuss the mechanical design. Also, a 1U box is so much cooler to show the customer than a crummy 2U box.

This goes back to the time our company and another company were both providing equipment to large system integrators for evaluation purposes. The functions provided by the equipment were the same, but we used a simpler and more primitive software approach. In our case, we were really trying to sell a software license and the competition was trying to sell a box. Because its box was a 12U form factor and ours was either a 1U or 2U box, I was pushing hard for the demo box to be a 1U. I loved the fact that if we could get into a side-by-side comparison, we would show up with a little tiny box that would be compared to a big fat box. And based upon my big company experience, I could see the management trying to figure out what was wrong with the competition that it needed such a fat box. I was trying to place the idea in the minds of the people making the selection that if we could perform the required functions in a 1U box and the competition required a 12U box, then their box had to be stupid. Otherwise it would have been as small as our box!

The disadvantage of a mechanical system is that you can see it and draw inferences based upon what you see. In the case of a computer system, you do not have any feel for the reality of what's inside the package.

Chapter Summary

To be an effective developer and to get our product or company started down a big wave, we must have a vision and keep the vision on track. This is a difficult process, as there is a wide and varying set of constraints and problems that need to be solved. Each individual problem or constraint will place demands on the design that need to be traded off.

A good developer will combine vision with a singular focus on making the concept a reality. You must stay focused and on top of the design process. The designers must understand that they are the first line of defense and have the responsibility to get a real product completed and into the field in a timely fashion. Once the first product is complete, other functions and capabilities can begin to be put into the product.

Chapter 10

Extreme Technology Management

This chapter examines the sweet science of technology management. In this chapter, the big wave surfer is the development manager. Generally, the management in a technology company consists of people who have grown up through the ranks of development and have successfully performed development tasks in the past.

It is with this background that they are deemed qualified to lead a new product development. However, the ability to successfully perform a development task is not the same as leading a development team. In particular, the keys to leading a development team are keeping the product in focus and keeping the team on track. Even the slightest slip in keeping the team forging ahead will have the potential to kill the development and derail the company like a major train wreck.

The key issue is to keep management from thinking that a miracle will bail them out or that they can engineer a great leap forward. Chairman Mao of China could not make a great leap forward happen. As the manager, you should not expect to be any more successful than he was. You might think that you will be able to leap over a tall building in a single bound, but leave that to Superman.

On the face of the wave trying to get development done quickly, we are trying to achieve success. One of the truly critical issues is to keep our focus on the target of completion. We are seeking to optimize our return on investment and the future potential of our product sales. We must remain focused and keep our product (and our surfboard) pointed in the direction of the bottom of the wave. Speed is the return on our investment.

One sign that the wave may be ending or starting to turn over is when you see the need for more staff to perform competitive analyses of other products. Another sign will be marketing looking to bring a compatible model of the product to market with specific features. And finally, there will be more engineering support needed for sales calls that need to differentiate the technical aspects of the product.

Principle: Big Wave Management Must Be Proactive

You must be proactive. Most every management that I have seen is reactive. Their goal is to milk their current products for high growth until they are able to get better jobs. Thus, they want to evolve their current product at the lowest investment cost possible. They become vulnerable to innovative, agile start-up companies with unique products. Big wave management must be proactive. To survive and prosper, you must seize the moment and get your product to the market in the front of the product cycle. If you are riding a big wave, you must anticipate and be aggressive.

A classic example of reactive management was Blockbuster Video. For years, they watched while upstart Netflix offered more titles, delivery by mail, and no late fees. In September 2010, Blockbuster filed for bankruptcy. After almost twenty-three years in business, Blockbuster may yet reinvent itself. Time will tell. Blockbuster's management must seize the moment and get their product to the market in front of the product cycle. Riding a big wave means you must anticipate and be aggressive at all times. You must ride the product cycle proactively.

Slug Farms

One of the big issues in trying to nimbly run a high-technology company is the issue of interfaces. **Figure 10-1** illustrates your position as a manager on the wave. After the basic concept is laid out, you must assemble and manage the team until marketing and investors are on board.

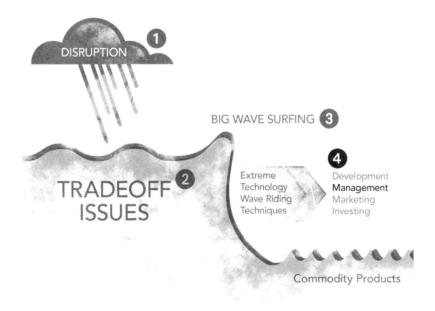

Fig. 10-1: Technology Big Wave Structure—Management

Building a group to provide such information is the first step to climbing on the wave. You can spend your time managing a wide variety of interfaces with no visible improvements to your project. However, all you'll end up with is a pretty set of slides.

You will constantly be running into requests to provide information to various groups ranging from investors to potential customers. You will also be pushed to keep up the design while trying to keep various internal constituencies satisfied. A typical example is your quarterly board of directors meeting. If you are not careful, this entire process can degenerate into a situation where you spend more time dealing with processes and reporting than creating and managing. At that point, you have degenerated into running what is commonly called a slug farm.

The problem is that you will be tempted to add staff to accommodate requests. This is a mistake. You really need to develop a succinct message that can be delivered in a cohesive fashion. Otherwise, you fall into the trap of developing an entire series of management status reports and briefings. These become an end item in and of themselves. This will lead into creating complicated slides where everything needs to be perfect. You will either fall into the analysis paralysis trap or into augmenting your staff to keep up with the requests that are not directly important to the development effort.

This is how large bureaucracies are formed. In fact, as the organization grows, the first group that I have seen formed is what I call the viewgraph engineers (also known as PowerPoint engineers). These are people who make sure that briefing charts and reports contain factually correct information and pretty pictures about the new product. They make sure that the charts and reports contain pretty pictures and wonderful prose. Their wonderful prose meets every little detail and management philosophy that is taught in management books in every graduate management program around the world. Of course none of this has anything to do with your ability to deliver a quality product.

As these organizations and reporting requirements grow, they actually cause the growth of slug farms. These organizations don't actually do any work, rather they support the reporting requirements of the organization and its insistence that it be constantly involved in the design, implementation, and management of the new product. If you are really trying to develop a new and innovative product, you do not have the time and energy to deal with the slugs. One alternative is to hire your own slug whose job is to satisfy the other slugs, but this just puts you into the slug farm business.

The way to deal with the impending slug farms is to remind everyone of the need to keep the organization lean and mean so that you actually get things accomplished.

I have had many experiences with slug farms. The best experience was with the slug farm of a large company that wanted us to develop a software product. But the company not only wanted the product, but also wanted us to provide specialized documentation to a specific international standard and format that required us to have a specific certification. The solution was that we would strive to develop the software to the standard, but we would not be certified. The customer would provide the slug farm that took our work and would, based upon the real code we were building, provide all of the specialized documentation and information necessary to document the process to the extent that the slug farm required. That all seemed reasonable because it satisfied the criteria that the client wanted. However, within weeks of the project start, the major firm had a problem.

We were working on the system design and requirements, laying it out in detail. The company suddenly decided that it needed code—not in a week or in a month—tomorrow. This meant that the company did not want the requirements and design before the coding. What it wanted was just a variation of one of our existing products. This product would not satisfy the system requirements (or the portion specified so far). And this methodology would violate the sacrosanct process the company had required. Further, this would cause us to have to build the code twice: once to satisfy this demand and once to build the correct code. Thus, the cost would go way up. No matter how much we talked, the firm insisted that we violate its own process and standards and deliver code that everyone agreed was going to be completely thrown away—the company just wanted to show the end customer how efficient it was.

If we had been wise guys, we could have had monkeys sit at typewriters and type out the code because it never got used and no one cared whether it actually worked. They just wanted to show the customer x lines of code.

This is the ultimate version of a slug farm. Get an army of slugs, and you can produce all kinds of good things that impede the actual design of the system.

Development Teams

Sometimes we're faced with a huge dilemma. We are running the company, and things are going well. We suddenly find out the next-generation product we are developing is behind schedule. What are we going to do about this small problem?

The management team usually picks the obvious solution, which is to add staff to the development team. Management may also change the team's management structure. This is the wrong thing to do. My solution is that you need to fire half the staff. You need to focus on the product development and not politics and people's feelings.

Let's think about this problem.

We are developing a product. It is behind schedule, and we are going to increase the development team. Thus, we have to take time from the current developers to bring the new developers up to speed. In working to bring the new developers up to speed, we will have a series of design reviews, briefings, and analysis meetings to make sure that the new designers are on board with the project. All of this effort takes resources away from the design team and will put the team further behind schedule. This will be justified because the theory is as new designers come up to speed, they will become productive and the schedule will accelerate.

Another issue to consider is that the new designers may have a fresher take on the technologies that are available to implement the new product. This is an internal form of requirements creep. We want to stay lean and mean.

The management may decide that the best thing to do is to ensure that the product has the best current technology available to ensure its success. As the new designers are brought up to speed, they will want to put some of their own ideas into the product and they will lobby for adding or modifying the base product. What we really need is a focused design team and a defined and implemented product. Adding features will delay the end product further. We are behind, and the last thing we need is to change the design. Yet the addition of new people will have just that effect. The theory is that all of this interaction will make the product better. If the product has problems, I will fix those problems in a future product release, but my goal is to get a product out.

An important aspect of adding new people is that the number of people trying to carve up the work has increased, and thus the number of paths of communications has increased. This means that more communication is taking place and more cooks have their hands in the pie. We have just increased the number of opinions of the product that we will be getting. What we need to do is get focused on the product and forget everything else. But the lead designers and implementers have just been saddled with an increased number of distractions. The amount of design time has just increased. This is not what we need if we truly want to get a product out.

Increasing the staff is fine if we don't care about getting a product out the door. If we are concerned about getting the product out, we have to adopt a different strategy. The most reasonable strategy is to fire half of the staff. Why do I want to fire half of the staff? On any given project, we have a team and half of that team is below the median in terms of capabilities, and that half will drag down the better half. A chain is only as strong as its weakest link. If we really want to get the product out, we need to unburden the top performers from the weight of the lower performers. We need to get our people focused and committed to getting the product out in a timely manner, not listening to people who should not be on the project in the first place.

We need to get a focused team that can make decisions and get the product out the door. But, at this point, I seem oriented to putting out a bad product. I am unwilling to allow for new ideas and updated technology and am taking people's careers lightly. If you believe that, you are wrong. My only goal is to get a product that we can sell. The first thing I want is a product that I can turn over to marketing. If we are really at the bleeding edge of technology in a high-growth market, it is important to have a product. If we have the only product in the high-growth space, we have the best product. We will then have to run hard to bring out our next version of the product. As we grow and are successful, we will have the money and time to put in all of the new technologies that people want added. Plus, we will have the advantages of market feedback helping us set the product's direction. Failure to get the product out the door will doom us to mediocrity at best. At worst, we will not generate revenue and may not have a good cash flow.

Firing half the staff makes the remaining staff understand that we are serious and committed. It also frees them up from all of the noise that is being generated in the corporate environment that hinders their efforts. A side effect is that it also cuts our costs while potentially accelerating the product development.

If you are in a high-growth market, early product shipments are key to your survival.

Reactive Development

The management team tends to be reactive in stressful situations. It may want to increase staff, bring in consultants, or fret about the way things should be in the development. But you can be assured that it will have extreme reactions to any setbacks and problems that are encountered.

Even though management signed on to the potential risks that the development team is undertaking, they will immediately forget the assumptions used when the details of the development were negotiated.

The management team has to gain perspective and understand that the development process was set up under a set of assumptions that were at best informed guesses. Thus, when something goes wrong, management needs to remain calm and try to gain perspective on how to make up for the miscues and get the development back on track rather than wringing its hands and complaining about how it may not make the goals. The management team must be proactive and try to anticipate problems and solve them before they get out of control.

The above advice seems simple and straightforward, but it is difficult to implement. There are a number of problems in the development process because people tend to be optimistic, and thus, inexperienced management fails to take into account the actual difficulties of completing the development. Second, it is human nature to try to fix things when you conceive that something is broken. In the case of a high-risk development, there may not actually be anything wrong when something in the development process breaks. It may just be that we underestimated the difficulty of a specific element of the development.

Hopefully, we will have as many successes as failures in the development process and we will on average be able to complete the development within the allotted time and budget.

This situation is a true test of how the development management reacts to crisis. If you are undertaking a high-risk development effort, you will probably always be in crisis. But it is the job of the management team to guide the development in an informed and professional manner, taking each problem as it comes and making sure that no particular problem derails the effort.

One of the problems, if the management team overreacts, is that soon the development team and its management could fall into the trap where every pebble becomes a mountain to climb and then the entire development goes south.

You need to have enough experience to differentiate between serious development problems and a small problem that one developer can fix. You need to avoid panic; otherwise, you should be in a different job.

Opportunity Windows

One of the key issues in technology big wave surfing is getting into the window of opportunity and making a splash before the window starts to close. Because the time to catch the wave is very short, you must be able to launch your product quickly and easily differentiate it from the competition.

One of the big problems is differentiating between technologies that are really research and development curiosities. Some technologies will eventually become products, and some technologies will never become viable enough to let you field a product.

There are some technologies that you are never able to put into production. The reasons for this are varied, but usually involve whether you can scale up the production of the technology. Many technologies look good on paper but are never able to be viably produced because you are not able to develop viable production processes. It is one problem to build a couple of prototypes and another problem to actually produce the technology in high volume.

Consider a large software system. It may be possible to build a prototype, but very difficult to get reasonable performance over a large system application. An example of such a problem is backup systems. It is one problem to be able to back up a simple personal computer (PC), but a completely different problem to back up a server farm. If the overall system requires a lot of database accesses and the queries are complex, then the system might not be able to process the queries over a large database even though it could perform well on a small system. A similar problem is how you replace a failed server in a large server farm when the server farm must run twenty-four hours a day.

When you are doing your development, you are dependent on your team and its choices. If the team picks technologies that can't be put into production, your product will fail. You can avoid this problem by picking a majority of the technologies in your product out of technologies that are proven in production. It is not too risky to have one or two technologies in your product that are risky, but you need to control both the number of risky technologies as well as the level of risk in each technology.

Every time you accept a risky technology, you have to solve problems involving not only the technology but also its interactions with other technologies. You may also have to solve problems about how the technologies relate to each other in terms of production incompatibilities. It is important to understand the risks; otherwise, you may end up being just another research study on the path of technology advancement.

A classic example of an area that is continually fraught with problems of converting technology into product is memory technologies. There are a lot of schemes that have been proposed over the years to solve the need for large amounts of high-speed, low-cost memory. Some of the schemes involve organizing memory into various high-speed structured hierarchies. Other schemes involve uses of different types of memory technologies to ensure that little-used data are stored in low-cost storage technologies.

Today, even with very cheap, large memories available, there is still difficulty meeting the demands for large, cheap memory systems. Social networks and the digitizing of data continue the need for ever larger memories. Yet some of the data that might be stored forever has no need to be accessed in any time-sensitive manner (if ever), and thus, you need to figure out how to keep the data really cheaply.

Memory is one of those technologies that frequent breakthroughs cause a lot of excitement, yet the ability to move the technology from the lab into high-volume, cost-effective production is very difficult.

Recurring Costs

Recurring costs are the costs that are incurred when you have your product in production. These costs are what you have to pay for each product unit that you produce. Generally, these costs reflect the cost of your materials, the operation of your factory, and the cost of your labor. These costs also include your sales and distribution expenses. When all costs are added up, this determines your total manufacturing costs, including any sums of money that are available for product-improvement or cost-reduction strategies. Before we deal with recurring costs, we need to talk about nonrecurring costs.

Nonrecurring costs are the one-time costs that you incur to develop the product. In the simplest form, these costs are your engineering costs and can be assumed to not be relevant to the cost of the end product if you can amortize these costs over a large enough number of units. However, in today's fast-changing product environment, you may not have the luxury of assuming that these costs do not affect your recurring cost basis. You may not be able to generate enough unit sales to ensure that the value of these costs is so negligible that they have no effect on the cost of a product.

When new companies start, they have a large amount of non-recurring costs to get their product launched. Generally, these costs will be funded from the capital that is provided by the founders and initial investors. Usually the investors do not want to fund the company fully until they see progress, so it is critical that the development managers accurately estimate what needs to be accomplished and how long it will take. Further, the development will have to be in stages that allow for more monies to arrive so the development can continue. It is extremely dangerous to underestimate either the difficulty or the time necessary to get to your milestones because you have no control over outside events. If you are using outside funding for the development, you have no control over the stock market and thus are at risk. If your development occurs when there is a market crash and if you are not fully funded, your funding may dry up through no fault of your own.

Many times, companies that are about to go public have a tremendous loss carry-forward from the expenditures of these start-up funds.

It is very important to keep the recurring costs low. This is the source of your continuing revenue stream. However, you need to decide how to price your product based upon what the market will bear. This pricing exercise will determine what margins the product can sustain on an ongoing basis. If you set the price too high, you may not be able to get rapid and sustainable revenue growth. As a result, you may end up letting in competitors at a time when you really need to dominate the market.

If you set the price too low, you risk your ability to generate enough funds to keep your product moving at the rate you need to capture the market. It is very tricky to set the price point for the product that will keep everything in balance. If you are going to err, it is the job of the development team to try to get the price set on the high side, because the tendency of marketing and sales will be to cut the price at the first sign of any pushback or delay in purchasing by a customer so that prices will always end up being lower than you expect. If you priced a little high, it still allows room for price reductions while keeping sales and money flowing.

Another trick to include in the pricing strategy is a maintenance charge that can be used to service product problems and provide funds to evolve the product. Another example of a nonrecurring revenue stream would be an original equipment manufacturer (OEM) licensing agreement.

The issue of maintenance or training funds is that they have very high margins, and you need to ensure that the funds are used properly. You do not want to waste such funds.

In the end, you need to be able to generate income as soon as possible, whether from recurring or nonrecurring revenue streams such as OEM agreements (nonrecurring) or sales (recurring). Either revenue source will be very useful.

When thinking about the type of income you have possible, you need to think broadly and you need to consider the ways in which you can slice and dice your product so that you can maximize your income. In the same way, you need to consider every possible way to minimize your development and your unit production costs.

OEM Arrangements

Developing a big wave product and getting traction on the wave is expensive. One of the ways that you can raise money rapidly and also get your product into the sales stream fast is to leverage others capabilities. As long as there are partners out there who do not compete with you, but need similar capabilities, you may want to embrace them.

One of the ways that you can increase your sales is to find partners who can incorporate your product into their more complex product. Another variation of this strategy is to use component parts of your product to enhance other companies' products. A third variation of this strategy is to provide a private-label product to another company.

All of these product strategies are designed to provide a means of gathering cash flow from what are essentially wholesale sales of your product or portions of your product. The key to this strategy is to make sure that you do not allow these sales to cannibalize sales of your product to the actual end users of your product. This can be accomplished by selling into vertical markets that you are not targeting or selling special versions of your product.

One advantage of OEM arrangements is that you can derive significant income while maintaining your competitive position. A strategy that we used was to keep the private-label deals one full product version behind our product. This worked because the inclusion of our product was not necessary for the competitive position of the private-label product. Our product was simply an add-on feature for the other company, and if the feature it provided was not state of the art, it was not a big deal. Our product was simply another feature in the overall product.

Another advantage to these arrangements is that we build a much larger user base for our product. This can help us ensure that we have the highest volumes we can achieve (and, therefore, the lowest possible production cost) and the attendant benefits, such as a larger user base, to make sure that we catch all possible design flaws during product operation. This will help us improve future products.

In some cases, the products we build may all be private-label products. There are many companies, especially in the auto industry, that supply products to a number of auto manufacturers. In some cases, there are manufacturers who totally design their products so that they can be built as much as possible from readily available parts. In the case of the PC industry, manufacturers primarily are in the packaging and marketing business. Every part they need can be procured from a source outside the company that sells the final product.

The more you make a product from off-the-shelf parts, the harder it will be to figure out how to make your product unique. If you have a unique product, you need to figure out ways to use your components to increase your cash flow without giving up your basic competitive advantages.

Product Versions

One of the big problems with technical personnel is that they become invested in their designs. As the design progresses, the designers begin to take ownership of the design and will eventually put on blinders to any possibility of design changes.

If a competitor suddenly shows up with a similar product, instead of thinking about how to reposition or modify the product, the designers will take a defensive approach. They will try to put down the competitor's product without thinking seriously about the realities of the new competitive situation.

There are variations of this problem, but the best solution is to try to avoid designing and conceptualizing a point source solution. Managing a rapid product development means that you must have a lean and mean design. You must couple that with flexibility and the ability to change. You must create an environment that provides for open-minded creativity with a focus on getting the product out fast.

This is accomplished by trying to design a family of solutions, also known as spreading out the design. You want to define not only the basic design, but also the future or follow-on products. The family should include possible products that have less and more functionality. You will need to define the product in such a manner that you can add or delete features as you get to the point of product launch.

If the competition is light or nonexistent when you get ready to introduce your product, you might want to introduce a product with less capability than originally planned. This would allow you to have a second product in the shadows waiting to be quickly introduced if needed. You might also have to introduce a more functional product, and this creates issues with the timing of the product launch. If the competition forces us to introduce a more functional product, then we have big problems, as we may have lost our product leadership.

This problem is similar to what car dealers face when they have a variety of models at different price levels. If we are truly a new and unique product, we may choose to introduce a set of products with different capabilities and phase them in as a set of product introductions.

The advantage of various product models is that we can adjust our pricing structure to provide a total income without relying on the total success of any given model. Also, we can adjust the price of any given model to try to boost sales. Car manufacturers do this by providing specific car models with fixed packages of options and features. By bundling the features, the manufacturer can set the model's price to achieve a specific objective.

Additionally, you need to think about not only the relative set of functions in versions, but also what future versions will look like. The features that could be put into future versions of the product need to be developed for these future products. Keeping a perspective on the variety of models and solutions will keep us on track and keep the designers from focusing on a single-point solution that they feel they have to defend to the death. Version strategy also allows us the ability to more easily adapt to the possibility of competition.

The downside of this strategy is that we must build a solid set of fundamental functions that we can use to build our upper-level functions. However, this problem also presents an opportunity, because we can get our best designers to focus on the critical portions of the product and we will develop a significant reusable base for future products.

Products/Upgrades

It is important to think of the product that we are developing in a high-volume context. Unless you get the volume up to massive levels, you have no way to amortize the nonrecurring costs and no way to get economy of scale in production. However, you have the problem of maintaining and upgrading the product.

In the case of televisions and radios, you have a situation where the product lasts until it breaks down. The stability of specifications allowed for televisions to last for a long time. The technology that you bought does not have to be updated unless you choose to get a better set. The set gets the same channels that it got when it was first bought. (This is true with the exception of the change-over to digital high-definition television when the government made obsolete a massive amount of older televisions in the drive to bring about higher quality television and free up some frequencies for first responders.) The same is true of radios. Generally, a radio will work forever.

However, some other systems become obsolete due to rapid technological change and the end user expectations to be able to easily update the product. An example is the operating systems that run on PCs. First, there are periodic updates of the whole system due to major new functions that are introduced. Then there are the constant barrage of little updates that occur almost weekly to fix little bugs that appear in the overall system. When you have hundreds of millions of customers using slightly different application configurations, there will be lots of errors that need to be fixed and updates that need to be pushed often and rapidly to the user base.

When you are developing your product, you need to think about how and when you intend to upgrade your product. This is a big problem because there are not only technology issues, but also financial issues.

If you have a software product, how do you charge to fix bugs? When do you put out a totally new release? In the software business, you need to think that after a rapid product growth phase, you may actually be in a maintenance and upgrade business. In the case of Microsoft, the company long ago shifted into a business that is primarily based on product upgrades and incremental product improvements.

Development of an upgrade strategy is key to getting your product launched and sustained. You may want to give away maintenance contracts with an initial purchase, or you may want to give away all product upgrades for a period of time to initial purchasers.

When thinking strategically, you need to place some constraints on the upgrades and maintenance contracts. In some cases, you may want to constrain the product upgrades and contracts to the original purchasers. As a general rule, you should consider allowing only one upgrade per product. If someone has product version one and upgrades that product to version two, when version three comes out, you need to have enough bookkeeping capability that you do not allow anyone to upgrade version one again.

Another trick to consider in positioning the product is the competitive upgrade program. In this program, you will upgrade any person using a competitor's product (or category of competitive products) to your product for the same price that you will upgrade your own users if they turn in the competitor's product. This strategy was used in the PC software industry in the mid- to late 1980s and was quite successful.

A further issue is whether you can get the users to provide a credit or debit card agreement tailored to your product and upgrade cycle; this is a way to automatically keep extending and collecting the revenues from future product releases.

Another strategy that can be employed in the upgrade business is changing prices and functions. If you have a set of functions that are sold as one product and you are beginning to see a lack of revenues from upgrades, you can always modify the product and bring out a newly renamed and priced product while over time discontinuing your current product. A further variation on this is used by a lot of retailers. In this case, the retailers offer price guarantees and they claim they will never be undersold because they will match the price on any model that is the same. The problem with this guarantee is that they have their own models that can only be bought at that chain of stores so you will never find a lower price.

Introduction of a new product or category of products provides a number of opportunities for the building of advanced revenue streams. One of the key issues is how you can become innovative in the packaging and selling of upgrade and maintenance packages.

Seminar Guy

There are a lot of people who believe in Murphy's Law. Essentially, Murphy's Law is a statement that if anything can go wrong, it will. This is a staple in the engineering business. It can only be better if you consider Murphy an optimist. Things just do not go wrong. In many cases, they go wrong in spades and compound themselves.

The problem when things go wrong is that often you cannot figure out how they went wrong in the first place.

The key to not being wiped out by Murphy's Law is risk management. You must anticipate and mange the risk in your development. The example below illustrates how everything can go wrong along with some explanation of possible risk-management techniques.

We were once giving a seminar on local area network technology. We had been putting these seminars on for years and thought we knew exactly what we were doing. We had statistics for everything. We knew how many brochures to send out to get a specific result like the number of attendees. We had rented out a great facility, and everything had fallen into place.

Our statistics were so accurate that we would know the attendance to an accuracy of 1.5 percent. We had tuned the product offering until we could predict the result that precisely.

The morning of the seminar, everything started out fine. Everything was going well for the first fifteen minutes of the registration period. We would have 100 attendees and had prepared for up to 102. Fifteen minutes into the course registration period, we began to see attendees arrive who had not preregistered. This was not usually a problem because we were confident in our statistics. We felt that we could cover the overage. However, we soon found ourselves at an overage of eleven students. Then we went to fifteen over. This was both not possible and unheard of. We were in big trouble. But we figured we could solve the problem, and in any case, it could not possibly get worse.

Then, disaster struck. Seminar Guy arrived. A pleasant guy walked up and wanted to register. We were out of whack, and he was upset that we were not aware of his preregistration. A fit of anger began to swell up. He insisted that he had preregistered and would not accept that he was not preregistered, and he said that he would not attend the seminar if he was not on our preregistered list. (We charge more money for nonpreregistered students, and he did not want to agree to the extra charges.) We offered to let him have the preregistration price, but to no avail.

Our suggestion was to take the seminar, and we would get it straightened out later. Seminar Guy went postal. He described how incompetent we were and how he was not going to put up with our lack of competence. A lot of things could have gone wrong: Our people could have misplaced the registration, the registration could have gotten lost in our mail room, the U.S. mail service could have lost his letter, his mail room could have lost the registration, his purchasing department may not have sent in the order, etc. At this point, Seminar Guy went nuclear. It was just simply not his fault. The registrants in line were now in a state of fear. They were clearly uncomfortable. Seminar Guy finally decided to call his administrative people and get the information necessary to prove that we were wrong.

Our position had not changed. Do not worry about it, just take the seminar and over the next two days your people and our people will work out the details and figure out what happened. That strategy works if you do not get yourself into the position of having to prove that you are right and we are wrong.

Seminar Guy went to the phones, and our statistics went into the dump. We had ten no shows and fifteen nonpreregistered attendees giving us a total of 105. Plus we had Seminar Guy. Seminar Guy came back to collect his briefcase that he had left with us while he went to get his people on the phone. The issue turned out to be that his administrative assistant had forgotten to send in his registration, and now he felt too embarrassed to attend the seminar.

No matter how much you think you know about any given situation, you will never know all the ways things can go wrong. Something as simple as registering for a seminar has many actions, and they all have to happen in concert to be correct. Unless everything happens correctly, the result will not be correct. In a complex project, the number of steps is so large that the management must have a detailed contingency plan that accounts for large numbers of categories of problems that will be encountered. If anything can go wrong, it will. If anything can be forgotten, it will. If someone can get sick, or a snow storm can happen when you are trying to get to the customer site, it will happen. Murphy was an optimist.

A good technology manager understands these potential problems, tries to compensate for them, tries to anticipate the problems, and carefully tries to recover from them. Good technology managers understand that no solution will solve all problems at the beginning and allow for a level of contingency planning that they hope will cover the unforeseen.

The issue is risk management. What can we do to foresee the potential problems? What do we do to plan for unforeseen problems? How do we cope with the unforeseen? Panic is not a good solution because we will not know what caused the problem. To be successful, we must act in a rational and prudent fashion. As we try to develop an early stage product, and get it into the market early, we will increase our risk profile. It is in this environment that we must really be able to look at the goal and where we can get a solution that can move us forward. When the swamp is filling up there seems to be no solution. It is instructive to remember Seminar Guy for two reasons. First, do not panic and get upset. Second, remember the number of things that can go wrong on something as simple as registering for a seminar.

Monkey Movement

Time is the enemy of any development project. Once you get the basic product prototyped, you need to go to product test. In product test, you need to find out what changes are needed to the product to get any user concerns satisfied. Every second counts because there are many other smart guys thinking about similar ideas. You can easily get off track, but one of the easiest ways to create a problem is to accept responsibility for someone else's problem.

As the technology manager, you need to be sensitive to the variety of trade-offs and problems that the designers are facing. But you should not be accepting of problems that are not of your team's making. Your goal is to complete the development. It is not to accept a lot of changes or modifications of the product. At the same time, you need to be sensitive to the realities of the marketplace. What if halfway through your development some other group puts out a similar but better product? You will have to address the issue. But you need to decide just what the competition is really providing. As you begin to get your product through test, you need to ensure that a complete list of development priorities are assigned and made.

You do not want to get into a situation where you are fighting vaporware—imaginary features or capabilities that are claimed to be in a competitor's product. When your product goes out for actual testing, you will get a lot of feedback and you need to address any open issues. However, you need to have a strategy to parcel out the work and get it done in a timely fashion.

There are really two problems that the manager needs to be concerned about near the development's end. The first issue is what actually needs to be done to complete the product. The second issue is who needs to do the work. As time starts to run out, decision making is a key element of success.

The immediate problem is to decide what actually needs to be done and in what order. You need to make a realistic list of changes, feature enhancements, and product problems that must be fixed. This list needs to be adjusted so that you meet not only your original design specification, but also what may have been occurring in the marketplace during your development time.

Then you need to figure out how you intend to complete the product. In this process, you need a lot of judgment to ensure that you have not included unnecessary features or accepted any changes or redefinition of the project unless there is a good reason to change the product. You face the trade-off of how much function to provide.

One of the problems that you face as the development manager is that you need to be careful accepting monkeys that other people try to put on your back. You need to understand what has to be done to make sure that the product is completely functional and competitive. You need to know who has the capabilities in the development team to quickly and accurately finish the product.

You need to take each monkey that gets placed on your back during the last of the development process and move that monkey onto someone else's back—someone who is capable of putting the monkey back onto the shelf from whence it came.

You decide what monkeys get accepted and then parcel them out.

This is a critical stage of the development process. Upon completion of a test phase, you should be able to go to sales. Because we want to work fast, we will have to complete the project in parallel with the other final aspects necessary to get the product on the market. You are at a critical stage, and you need to ensure that the people who have accepted the monkeys are people who can be depended on to accept the monkey and move it back onto the shelf.

Irrational Consensus

Obtaining consensus in a technical environment is a difficult process. There are not necessarily any guidelines on what a product should cost, what it should do, or how it should be sold. This is particularly true of new products. There is no proven track record of what will sell or how to sell the new product. It is all conjecture.

Further, it is emotional and difficult for people to think about all of the ramifications and possibilities. How do you know if a new product will actually go? Will it sell? Can you create buzz and thus minimize advertising?

If you are trying to develop a new product that you are hoping will really take off and grow rapidly, and if you are a small company hoping to capitalize on the strategy, your company is probably populated by a relatively large number of people who may be described as strong willed, opinionated, aggressive, and actively engaged in the entire process.

How to navigate through the morass is difficult to figure out.

In a large company, the bureaucracy is dominated by process or some number of people who are just trying to serve out their time. This overall process will dictate the resolution of issues that stand in the way of the product introduction. You may encounter the occasional ideologue, but in general, there is someone who can override their objections, and we can get on with the slow and painstaking process of getting our product out the door.

In the small company where a lot is at stake and there is no proven record for the type of product that we are introducing, there is no real way to *a priori* determine if the correct decisions are being made.

It is like trying to guess which set of swells will really turn into the big wave. Now mix in a volatile set of personalities, and you will find extensive irrationality. Some participants will get really upset about some of the smallest issues and will become irrational because you would not participate in such a project if you did not believe in it. Add to that the potential financial stakes, and you have the beginnings of a serious set of strongly held beliefs about how to proceed. It falls on management who don't have any really established processes to sort out the mess. You get to straighten out irrationality and get consensus.

Typically, you will be faced with problems like, "This guy is a really important customer and we need to treat him with kid gloves." Or "Can't you just tell development to add this one little feature?" Or "Why can't development (marketing) be more responsive to the potential customer base and let me have a sample (early prototype)?"

No amount of emotional outbursts or garbage should stop you from delivering a timely, well-defined product. You need to learn how to deal with these issues, and the best way is to make the requestors understand that they need to understand the larger corporate perspective.

In the specific cases above, the answers are simple. Every customer or potential customer is important, and not one customer is more important than any other. Even if the customer claims to be an industry influencer, can you bend the rules? Then everyone will have such a story, and you will suddenly find that all customers are again equal.

In the case of just adding the one little feature, what you may think is easy may be quite difficult. So just take it under advisement and see what you can do, but remember that your job is to get the base product out in a timely fashion. Extra features are just a bonus.

The most difficult request is the issue of early release products. This is a really difficult problem. Some companies like Microsoft make a career of this by selling development kits that contain products that are about to be released, hoping to get a lot of buzz and a quick launch when the product is actually released. Other companies are quite secretive. In the case of a new start-up and a really unique product, you need to be very careful. You need to understand what you are doing and then go with the flow.

At times, things are going to be difficult, and there will probably be a lot of finger pointing and shouting, but you must be on top of your game and understand that you are really in the business of herding cats and they all happen to be wild tigers. If you stay consistent and push back, you can get the situation resolved, but during the process it may look like a mess.

I was faced with four phone calls, all explaining how either I or some other person other than the caller was screwing up the sales, distribution, or development of a small software product that we were about to introduce. Yet, we managed to sell the product, it was introduced in a timely fashion, and it made money for our corporation. But the process will never satisfy the people who know for a fact that I have again screwed up the product introduction and yell at me on the phone as if I did not hear their position. I did hear it; I just rejected it! There are days when you have no friends and you will need to stay the course. All people have reasons why their customers deserve special treatment!

Big Trucks

Eighteen-wheelers are massive trucks that ply the highways of many countries. But particularly in the United States, the highways have a large number of eighteen-wheelers. These big trucks can carry huge loads, and they can move at very high speeds. Look out if you get in an accident with one of these giant trucks. Whatever type of vehicle you are in, the result will not be pretty.

If you are on foot and you collide with an eighteen-wheeler, you are probably best described as a spot in the road.

Your problem as a high-technology manager is that you will become attached to the skills and capabilities of your team. Whether it is the lead developer or the person in quality, you will eventually begin to believe that the people are critical to your success. And they are! Without good people, you will not be in a position to succeed. The better the quality of your people, in general, the better your results. In terms of getting your product done correctly with a minimum of rework and in a timely fashion, you need good people.

The people on a project will build on each others' skills and set a pecking order. Eventually, they will all fit into a set of relationships that will make the project run smoothly. That does not mean there will not be friction, but over time the team will sort out its roles and function in a fashion that should get your project done if the project is scoped out in a manner that will allow it to succeed.

Now comes the hard part. What if, for whatever reason, you are now faced with the prospect that someone is going to have to leave the project?

This can happen for a number of reasons: people quit performing and you have to fire them, people take other jobs, or people have family problems. In all of these cases, you are about to become short staffed and have to figure out a new game plan.

This process can be extremely difficult if the people who are no longer going to be part of your team were key players. Maybe even one of the founders quit. The worst case is if the person was your lead developer, because you are now in a position of having to replace your key player. In the old days, the employee would usually give you a couple of weeks' notice and you could do what was necessary to assure continuity of the project.

When I was working in product development, I was on a project that had a critical lead logic designer assigned to the project, and this designer quit. I was extremely upset and was having a discussion about the effect (which I viewed as massive) with my boss when he turned the discussion to pizza. He wanted to know if John and I were going to the pizza shop across the street for lunch. I responded that yes, that was our plan. He pointed out that the street we were to cross was a major highway and usually had a large number of eighteen-wheelers on it. Then he made a comment that I will never forget. He said that someone quitting for whatever reason was better than if they got run over by an eighteen-wheeler.

This was a lesson in folk wisdom that I will never forget.

No matter how important people are, if they were to get hit by the eighteen-wheeler going to lunch, life and the rest of the world would go on. You will have to make adjustments, and things will work out slightly differently, but projects will go forward, and you will find that in a short time the project will be back to normal. Yes, it will be difficult if the person quits at the wrong time, but you will adjust. Further, if the person goes out and forms a competitor, you will have to work a lot harder.

Sometimes you may have to drive the eighteen-wheeler. There are cases when the project gets off the track. There are a number of ways this can happen. What if in the middle of the project someone decides that the project should start over because it should be going in a different direction? Or what if there is a person on the project who is counterproductive and divisive? In these cases, you must make a change to the project staff. Two cases I personally encountered involved one of the key designers who decided after the product was in checkout that the product was no good and we should not introduce it. In fact, we should kill the project.

In this case, the designer was told that the product would go out and if he did not like it he should find his own alternative project, which he promptly did.

A more amazing experience was a project that was a large service contract. It employed nearly half the company. Because we had the project for a number of years, it could be reasonably assumed that we were in that particular business for the long term. However, the customer decided to redo the contract to where his bosses felt that the costs were in line. During the process of the re-complete, one of the lead proposal writers decided that we did not have to work very hard on the proposal because there would be no other bidders, and if there were the customer would make sure that we won. However, whenever any service or product is up for a competitive bid, you can never be sure that you have the inside track on the result. In this case, we had to change out the entire proposal team to get the proposal completed. As the proposal team was changed out, I made sure the participants understood my concerns. I also made sure they understood that we would have to deal with these issues when the proposal was complete. Everyone thought that there would be no consequences.

The first sign of trouble came when (on the day I was to leave for Europe for a month) the lead proposal writer came to see me and said there were other bidders. One of them was a company that had beaten us in the past, and he wanted to apologize for his attitude and performance. At that point and for the rest of the day, there was a steady string of contrite proposal writers. When I got back from Europe, we started a major overhaul of that division of the company. The result was that we tied for the best technical score on the proposal, and to keep the job we had to reduce our price severely. There were ten writers on the proposal that were relieved of their duties during the proposal effort. Every Friday, we terminated two of these people and on the next Monday replaced them with two new hires. As this process went along, there was a severe case of contrition and panic. Sometimes you just have to drive the eighteen-wheeler because there is no other choice.

Debriefing is a critical aspect of any resignation. If someone resigns from your company or project, you need to make sure that you find out as much as possible from them as fast as possible. Once they have resigned, their interests and yours have just reached a dramatic fork in the road. As soon as they are debriefed, they can leave. You should pay them for their complete notice term. The biggest decision at this point is who should take over their functions, and that person should do the debrief.

The worst thing you can do if someone has been terminated is to rehire. No matter why the two of you parted ways, if you rehire that reason is still there. If you are in a new company and a completely different situation, you can hire anyone, even someone who has previously departed from your employment, but rehiring back into the same firm will only result in another termination.

These views may seem harsh, but we are in a high-performance, high-stress environment. We only want people who want to be in our company and who perform. Just think of it in this context. If you are screaming down the front of a monster wave and you expect the watercraft operator to pick you up at a certain point, you must trust the operators, and they have to show up at the right time. No exceptions. When you are trying to rapidly build a company or product, you cannot afford to have people who do not perform or do not want to move in the right direction.

Big wave surfing is not a game. It is a responsible discipline, and you must focus to ensure that everyone gets and stays involved.

Seven Numbers

In the early days of the development of the phone system, the scientists of Bell Labs did a large number of studies on the subject of dialing system strategies. The big issue was how to organize a phone system. A less important issue was how many numbers should be included in a phone number.

Today the question of how many numbers should be included in a phone number is not interesting. Because of digitally stored phone books, you can look up the person by putting their name into your phone's contact list. There is no reason for any person to have to remember a telephone number.

But the conclusions of the phone company from the early days are of interest if you are trying to manage a complex project. Generally, a person can easily remember a sequence of seven numbers. There are tricks you can use so that you can remember more items, but generally a person seems to easily remember seven items.

There are many schools that teach presentation techniques. When developing a presentation, many strategies talk about how to limit the content of a slide to ensure that the people receiving the information can adequately understand and process the information. Most strategies try to limit the number of points that are going to be made on a slide to between four and six. These numbers were derived from experience or studies that measured how to make sure the receiver understands and remembers your points.

In managing a complex project, you need to think carefully about your ability to manage complexity. How much complexity can you handle? If you are in charge of the project, you probably are highly skilled and can deal with a lot of issues. But how much complexity is too much? Every time a new issue gets added to the list of problems, you need to deal with that problem. Adding another issue may provide a connection to another problem.

Problems are not isolated singularities in space. There is usually some level of interconnection or overlap. You need to get the product built, and you need to get it built before you begin fiddling with the project. Concentrate your efforts on a small set of critical problems, and then if you get those problems solved, you can add other features or related capabilities into the situation.

Many times you hear of technology people who designed their products on cocktail napkins in restaurants or bars. There are numerous successful companies that started in this fashion. How much information do you think was detailed on that napkin? The people who designed their systems in this manner clearly emphasized the most important aspects of their products.

The question to address as a development manger is how much complexity can you accept and explain. If you are trying to introduce a new concept into an existing field based upon a new technology innovation, you will want to focus on one or two benefits and capabilities. If you are creating an entirely new area of technology, you may want to concentrate on four or five key issues, but it seems to be a stretch to expect sales and customers to make sense of a large series of new capabilities. If you talk about large numbers of new capabilities, the end user will not have the ability to discern what is important. You must be able to guide the product development and set up the message for sales and marketing. To do this, you need to be focused.

Based upon the ideas of the phone company and people who design effective presentations, you should at most have seven new capabilities that you try to implement, explain, and sell. Four seems to be the number that works best in my experience.

Big Programs

Lean and mean projects with rapid development schedules that push the state of the art and have high payoffs are what the big wave surfer looks for in a product management environment. If you have a product that requires lots of specifications and a huge team of designers, you are not on a big wave. Big programs are anti-big wave.

One of the key issues is that the larger the project, the more screwed up the project will be or will appear to be. The problem is the larger the project, the more the corporate management does not want any one person to control the overall result. Thus, the project has to deal with a large number of issues that may not have anything to do with the real success of the project.

The real problem with big programs, products, or technologies is that at some point someone in corporate management may decide that the product must have "ilities." Ilities are sets of capabilities that the management wants the product to have. An example is reliability. Everyone wants their product to be reliable. But some genius may decide they want to have a certain level of reliability in a new product and may specify that level without an understanding of the mathematics necessary to achieve this certain level of reliability. This puts a huge stress on the design team. Now they have to try to meet a hypothetical level of reliability, which could put a huge constraint on the product's design without providing any real benefit.

One of the problems of design is institutionalized groups within the corporate structure. These groups have responsibilities that cause them to lay down the law on how the design should proceed. However, they are not accountable for any part of the design or any part of the success or failure of the product.

One area where this problem is particularly acute is performance.

You cannot believe the number of times I have been associated with a new product that performs a really important new function. The first thing out of everyone's mouth is that the performance is inadequate. The reality is that the current state of the art does not solve the problem in an automated manner. We have just given you an automated solution, and you are complaining because the solution does not meet some preconceived notion of how fast the product should work.

The current problem is not solved, is solved manually, or is on someone's wish list. We bring you a solution, and you do not like the solution because of some preconceived notion of what you expect the product to do (how fast, how reliable or flexible it should be, or how we should have structured the interfaces to the product, etc.). Some people are just never satisfied.

If you are trying to design a product that solves a critical problem that is currently not solved, you can't allow the design to get encumbered by a lot of wishful thinking and get off track. Yet, if the product is going to be built by a big corporation (which has processes) or solves a large problem (creates a lot of overview and oversight), it will become a big development. What will happen is that a lot of extraneous requirements will get placed on the product, and suddenly, you have a big program, and from there it goes down the drain.

The bigger the development effort, the bigger the number of participants, the larger the management oversight, the more the project will be hosed.

Classic examples are big military and government programs. The military and government are very good at figuring out what new technologies should be developed to support their missions. They are terrible at putting such technologies into new systems and products because as soon as they try to deploy a technology, the ilities start to arrive and the program starts to grow and will eventually collapse from its own weight.

Big programs can succeed, but they will cost more than they should and they will always be late and over budget.

Let there be no misunderstanding. If a product development gets large, it is by definition hosed. This will never change.

Everybody's Ax

One of the big problems development managers face is finding the idiosyncrasies of the development team.

You would like to think that you have a well-oiled machine for product development. What you have is a team of different capabilities, characteristics, work ethics, and intellectual capabilities. You would be truly surprised at the different capabilities between the best and worst developers in a ten-person team. One of the developers may be able to do three or four times the amount of work as another team member. But the capability that I found most fascinating was the ability to grasp and lay out the project or a portion of the project. There are some developers who are extremely hardworking and capable if the project is laid out in detail for them.

One big problem that managers face is that the lower the overall capability of a developer, the higher the probability the developer will have an ax. Something in their background becomes some sort of hot button. Try to move them off this issue and there will be hell to pay.

My first encounter with this was in software development. One of the developers hated to admit that he could produce software that contained bugs. So he set up a process to quickly create new versions of the software that would correct any newly found bug. This became an interesting problem that we had to solve. As the software was developed, the designer would go around the test group and build a new version every time a bug was found. The result was that there was no real long-term configuration control of the software. If the developer heard that tests had found a new bug, he would immediately correct it and submit a new version to test. The problem was that he would bypass the configuration control system. So he might introduce bugs that had been previously corrected back into the system. The ax carried by this developer was that he prided himself on not only the quality of his code, but also the speed at which he could crank out code. Eventually the problem got fixed, but it was difficult.

There are many other examples of these ax-carrying problems. One example is the logic designer who did not understand a set of functions, but rather than admit a lack of understanding, he deleted the functions in every new version of the design. Another example is the secretary who did not understand the functions of a word processor and corrected every document by the page instead of correcting the exact word or phrase that needed to be corrected. More examples are easy to come up with, but as long as the ax is not destructive, the issues can be dealt with by simply correcting behavior. In some cases, the axes can sabotage the project. You need to watch for extremely bad behavior patterns that can dramatically affect the project.

One big problem the development manager faces is what happens when two opposites attack. In such a case, one person's ax will become another person's ox and the two will get locked in an intense struggle over who is correct and in charge of the important functions. In this case, it is incumbent on the management to step in and resolve the problem quickly. If we are trying to get a product out, we do not have the time to referee a fight between two developers. In this case, there will be a winner and a loser and we should not be concerned about the result as long as the project moves forward.

In many cases, I have had to watch over or supervise a disparate set of personalities. In a lot of cases, you will find that the worst performer is the guy who thinks he is the best performer. You will never be able to convince that person that he is wrong.

Some of the worst cases I have seen involved a mismatch of such expectations. I have actually seen developers quit a company and assume that the company would fail because they left. At the same time, the development team has been trying to get rid of the ax carried by such a developer and move the project forward. In the most extreme case I have seen, the developer was in the process of having his code isolated as it kept diverging from the development direction and the team was trying to grasp what the code actually did and its worth before firing the person.

Just because you carry an ax does not mean that anyone else cares. Just because someone sets an ax up to be an ox does not mean you should ignore it. Just get rid of the problem developer. Keep your team tight, and do not let your focus shift from the end goal.

Big Cards

Technology management is a funny business. You can never tell what will cause a change in a product or development direction. It could be trivial, or it could be monumental. You never know what the issues are that create and sustain a big wave of technology. Yet, you will encounter all types of issues that have to be resolved. In chapter 9, we discussed the problem of being a mechanical engineer because everyone is an expert in mechanical design. It gets worse than that. The classic story is that of big boards versus little boards.

How you build and package a system is of critical importance. However, it is not really the most important issue in the system

EXTREME TECHNOLOGY MANAGEMENT

design. Generally, you will spend a lot of money on the hardware, but the real costs will eventually be software costs. For the moment, let's ignore that issue and concentrate on hardware.

In the early 1970s, one of the big issues designers faced was how to partition a system. This was a serious problem. You have a fixed area, and you need to implement as many functions as possible in that area. This is similar to being on a big wave with a bag of tricks you can use in a competition. You have to choose the required tricks you want to display as you ride the wave into shore.

You need to pull out a similar required bag of tricks to solve the partitioning problem to set up the blocks of hardware and how they interconnect. This problem becomes particularly tricky because the hardware needs more than one printed circuit board with which to implement the function. In this case, you must figure out how to package the hardware, how to get the heat out of the product, and how to build what is called a backplane.

This leads to design decisions about the size of the hardware and how the hardware is partitioned into cards or boards.

There are two really disparate views of this problem. One is to make the product with very large boards that can contain a lot of function and minimize the communications between functions on the boards. The other approach is to make the boards relatively small and make the communications between the boards very robust.

There is no real correct answer to this problem because both solutions will work and let you have a functional design that works well. The decision will affect the overall product package aesthetics and how it looks to the end user. In smaller systems, partitioning is done on a single chip, but in large systems partitioning is still a critical issue. In general, partitioning and packaging is a constant battle and a battle that needs to be faced early in the design process. Further, this is an area in which many people assume they are experts.

One of the most classic cases occurred in the early 1970s. At Digital Equipment Corporation (DEC), the design team had been very successful at using small cards and modules to build its systems and components. After one particularly difficult set of design meetings, some of the staff members became obsessed with the issue of the size of the board being considered for use in the newest computer. The fundamental question was whether to use a small board (a DEC tradition) or to use a new packaging scheme that would use large cards and thus have a high amount of function on each board.

The answer by clear-thinking individuals and management was obvious. DEC stayed with small boards. A group of engineers left to form Data General. There they built minicomputers to compete with DEC and used large boards. Something as simple as an argument over small or big boards can quickly become a sticking point even though no one can really prove which approach is definitively better.

Multiple Heads

One of the realities of managing a major development project that is on a tight schedule is that the serpent you are trying to slay will evolve over time and the serpent will create new and unforeseen problems.

There is no way to foresee how many ways you can manage to get the team in trouble. It might be something simple like a developer gets sick for a week at a critical time. It might be that halfway through the development, an unknown and unforeseen competitor comes out of the woodwork and you have to stop and recast the entire development process. It is like dealing with a serpent with multiple heads: Cut one off and another appears.

You need to look at the development process as if it were a multiheaded serpent that can regrow one or more heads if and when you manage to cut a head off. You have embarked upon a risky venture. The stakes are high, and you should not expect that the process and journey will be easy or straightforward.

In a sense, it is like playing Whack-a-Mole. You have a hammer, and you stand in front of a board full of holes. Every time a head pops out and you hit it, more heads pop out. These little moles that pop out come at an increasing rate the more successful you become.

This will become the norm if you are trying to develop new, high-risk products in an intense, rapid-development environment. This entire effect is compounded because of the basic financial effects of success. As time goes on and you are successful, the potential for a high return on capital will make the scrutiny of the project huge. You need to understand that once the development gets on track and looks like it will be highly successful, you will need to bring into the fold all of the people associated with making the product launch a success.

This process will actually create the multiple heads on the serpent for the development process. You will be faced with a constantly changing environment, and the changes will be unexpected and follow in a highly unstructured fashion. You will have to be highly adaptive, but not too optimistic. If you set your time and contingency budgets reasonably, you should be able to weather the storm and deliver what you promised.

End Direction

Keep your eye on the end point. You must run hard and get your tasks accomplished in a timely fashion. You need to keep your product pointed in the direction of completion, just like big wave surfers must keep their boards pointed in the direction they want to go.

Let us assume that you are a really smart person with a great idea. Somehow that idea was formed, and you were able to articulate the idea, describe the idea, and get other people on board. Unfortunately, no matter how smart you are, there are other smart people who are also thinking about good ideas. The probability is that at least one other person has also thought about similar ideas. Thus, once you have your idea you must drive hard to the end product. There are a number of reasons for this sense of urgency.

First, if you have a truly unique idea, you can be sure that others are really close behind. No matter how smart you are, there are a lot of other smart people who are close behind.

Second, if you are really the first with the idea, unless you move quickly, you may not be the first to market. The first person to conceive an idea is not necessarily the first to get the product to market. It is not enough to have the idea; you must act on the idea and make that product and get it into the marketplace. Otherwise, all you have is a very good idea.

Third, you do not know how long it will take to implement the idea and put in place all of the trappings that are necessary for the launch of a successful product. You need to start product implementation right away.

Fourth, you do not really know what problems you will run into when you are trying to build the product. Therefore, you need to get started to give yourself time to recover from any potential setbacks.

Assuming you get started and have everything in place, you need to avoid distractions.

Think of this in terms of a series of analogies. A lot of technology people think of the problem like a window opening and closing. The window of opportunity opens up, and then it closes. Either you got through the window or you didn't, and if you did not get through, if your product is late to market, you will have a tremendous hill to climb. You must get through the window. You must catch the wave. Otherwise, find another wave or window.

The big wave is the best analogy. The waves keep coming into shore, and they are all different sizes. But when you see a series of big waves breaking on shore, you will notice that every now and then one of the waves is a little larger than the others. In fact, there may actually be a series of slightly larger waves that come into shore in succession. If you have one of those ideas, you do not want to miss these larger waves. Like an unsold airline seat when the plane takes off, the seat is now worthless. If you miss the biggest wave in a series of big waves, you will never have an opportunity to catch that wave again, so time is of the essence. You must keep your eye on the ball and keep the project moving forward with intensity.

Any time you have a team of people there will be a lot of opportunity for distractions. This may range from a particularly nice sunny day to someone leaving to go see a child in a school event. None of these issues can be allowed to derail your schedules, or you will have your product introduction miss its timeline. You can get up on the wave too late to catch the rapid growth of your market.

I used to marvel at a television commercial that was on late at night when I would be working. It was for a local car dealer and featured his son who was a professional wrestler extolling the virtues of how easy it was to buy a car from his dad's dealership. The ad basically said that if you had no credit, there were no worries. If you had bad credit, there were no worries. But if you missed a payment, there was a problem. At that point, the wrestler threw the salesperson through the car's front window. This ad became a cult favorite in our local area.

The attitude of the development manager must be similar. You've got kids, I do not care. You've got a wife, I do not care. You miss a deadline, I care! I do not promote throwing the offending developer through the window of a car, but when you are doing a new product development, the team must sign up and meet the schedule. It is management's responsibility to hold the line on the time frame. The wave is starting to break, and we must get onto the slope to be successful.

Scope Change

One of the big problems in managing development is called change in scope. This is where, as the development proceeds, someone makes a good case for a design change to accommodate another customer requirement, a cool new feature, etc. This process is a problem.

In some circles, this is called requirements creep. This is where a small set of incremental changes morphs into a major new set of design features that must be implemented. This process is very common in military systems. The company building the system may encounter major design changes required by the customer because the system as originally specified did not cover all of the required functions and the customer wants to make the system completely functional. In many cases, the customer adds new features, and the system then balloons in cost. I have heard of bidders trying to win such jobs who bid the original system below cost because they believe that they will make their profits off of change orders. Once you lock into a vendor, if you change anything, the cost of the change order is not very negotiable if it is negotiable at all.

This is a problem if you are managing the development of a system where there are slight changes to the basic features and capabilities of the system. In fact, you should expect that there will be changes because during the development period, everything is in flux and changing. But the question you must address is, How much change have you accounted for in your development process?

There are changes that are easy to make and characterize. If you have a software product that you are developing, changing the background color of the product is probably trivial. However, changing the product so that it will run on Linux as well as Windows is not an easy change depending upon your initial design.

The big problem for management is change in scope. Change in scope is the point at which you must go in and say enough is enough. We either need more time or more money to complete the product. Actually, what you should be doing all along is deciding, with a critical eye, what changes you are willing to accept.

There may be very good reasons for making a change in the product or its capabilities. But your development process and its attendant costs and schedule are based upon a design. Changes to the product design can and will cause problems in meeting the agreed-upon result. For each and every design point, you need to decide what, if anything, you need to do to maintain your product's schedule.

Once you start on the development process, you should not allow any changes to the product specification without attendant consideration to key elements like schedule and cost of the development. You are being judged by the need to get the product out in a timely fashion.

Further, you need to understand that the process of changing the product will come from a variety of sources. You will get requests from not only marketing and sales but also developers to add features. They see all kinds of new features that could be "easily" added to the product. You need to make sure that the totality of these requests does not destroy your product's deployment into the sales arena.

You can always improve the product, but you can never recover its momentum if it fails to catch the wave.

Arbitrary Changes

One of the big challenges of technology management is that the second you make a decision you are wrong and your product is obsolete. Thus, you are immediately subject to criticism about the inadequacy of your approach and what your competitors are perceived to be doing or are actually doing. From the beach, surfing the big wave looks easy. On the wave, it is not an easy task and you must remain focused at all times to avoid wiping out. Managing a development requires a lot of focus, or the development can get off track quickly.

These problems are really a result of the inability of technical people to make a commitment. The number of people who can actually make a commitment is very small. The result is that when you make a commitment or decision, you will hear all kinds of reasons why it was the wrong decision. This goes beyond system decisions that have actually been made, and it's the basic problem of not wanting to be the person responsible for any decision. In fact, it underscores the quote, "Success has many fathers, while failure is an orphan."

The tendency of an inexperienced leader is to fold under the pressure of continual criticism and to fiddle with the design. This must be avoided at all costs, or the system will never get built because the system and its specifications will continually change.

I have seen this occur many times. It is an easy trap to fall into. One way to avoid this trap is to simply say that we can reconsider some of these issues once we get the first prototype finished. Then, based upon changes in the marketplace, we can decide if we need to make further functional changes or if we need to modify our approach. But it is critical to get a stable implementation before fiddling with the product regardless of the amount of criticism that you are receiving.

In estimating the work required to implement a function, it is typical to estimate the time it would take a programmer to develop a function. This is measured in man months. The problem is that all programmers are not created equal and what one person can achieve in a month is different than what another person can achieve. A better way to make assignments is to create functions that each individual programmer can implement during an allot-ted time. Some programmers will have a larger workload under this system. The trade-off is a more accurate time estimate for a specific project with a given group of programmers.

Once the product is "done," then you know how long it takes to build a specific function. It is now no longer a secret what your programmers can accomplish and who's your best programmer. You have a real production benchmark. In fact, you have a real benchmark on not only your programmers' capabilities but also how well they can do the type of functions that were encountered and how well they manage complexity. In fact, it is important for future implementations that you use this information to calibrate your best practices.

There I was on the phone talking about a new product that we had developed and were in the process of selling. The customer was an interesting person who claimed to have great ideas for new product functions and features that should be included in future products. Some of his ideas we were implementing and testing, and we knew the exact cost of implementation. During the discussion, the potential customer began to tell us what new functions should be added to the product. Then, he said he could extend our code to include all of the new functions he was suggesting. He claimed that he was an expert programmer and that he could get the job done quickly. Out of curiosity, I asked him how long it would take to implement the functions he was suggesting, and he replied a couple of weeks. We had spent a couple of million dollars to implement the functions that he claimed to be able to implement in a couple of weeks. In fact, our quality-control process (our regression-testing procedure) for the base product alone took longer than his product implementation estimate. Fortunately for him, I was able to suppress massive amounts of derisive laughter.

We were working on another product when one of the designers decided that a potential competitive product had better (more interesting) architecture that would make the product far superior. Clearly, because he had the idea it was logical that he was right. Unfortunately for him, he was right about the other product, but what he failed to understand was that the other product had an architecture that was not able to be implemented with comparable performance. The competitive product, although comparable in function, was not able to perform satisfactorily, and thus it never got off the ground in terms of sales. It was elegant and seemed to provide interesting functions, but it never achieved any type of acceptable performance levels.

Chapter Summary

Management of a rapidly growing product or company is a real challenge. You are subjected to a variety of forces with limited control. Everyone will be second guessing you, and you will be faced with myriad decisions and decision points. You must stay focused because your responsibility is to get the product completed in a timely fashion.

Someone is responsible to make the tough decisions because everyone else believes they can do a better job. Yet they have no overview of the total problem. You are caught between a visionary developer who has strong ideas about the product and marketing that will want every decision to go their way. Just like a big wave surfer coming down the steep wave, you are constrained. It is the same as trying to take a brief ride in the curl. On the one hand you have the face of the wave that you are shooting down. On the other hand, you have the curl breaking over you. You must shoot out of the pipe and make sure you keep your product firmly launched down the steep part of the wave. Price, performance, and function are the key issues that you must keep in focus. Selection of the route down the front of the wave will always be changing, but you can succeed by keeping your singular focus. Get the product done!

Chapter 11

Extreme Technology Marketing

There are many types of big wave surfers in start-up companies, including people in marketing, sales, and business development. We will generally refer to all these people as the marketing people. Marketing technology is a very tricky business. It requires a set of skills that are beyond the normal skill set of a salesperson. In this chapter, the big wave surfer is the product sales guy. If the sale is a new technology, it often requires a paradigm shift. The salesperson has to convince the user that not only is this new paradigm advantageous, but also that the customer should procure the product from him. However, really, the customer may be ready to procure its technology from a large system vendor.

In many cases, the sale is really a process improvement, and that may be disruptive to the entire organization. The salesperson is in search of the decision maker. But the improvements the technology promises may cross several disciplines and there may not be a clear decision maker.

Finding early adopters who need the new paradigm is the key problem. After the customer is identified, the issue is describing the product's value. Getting a number of early adopters creates the marketing buzz necessary to launch the product.

The single most important sign that the wave and its cycle may be coming to an end is when the customer asks, during a sales call, for clarification of your product's capabilities against another product.

Principle: Marketing Requires Early Adopter Buzz

To really launch a new product, it is incumbent that you create a marketing buzz. This requires identifying and selling to key individuals who are early adopters. You must identify a champion at the customer site who has the purchasing authority or ability to determine what product to purchase. Preferably, the early adopter will not only be able to assess risk and accept risk, but also will champion your new product for deployment in a system.

The key to creating a big wave is to find a unique concept in a research and development lab. Nurture the idea until you get a unique product so that you can create a distinct value for this product. You then need to find an early adopter who can see the unique value in adopting the capabilities that you have created. Getting a number of early adopters pushing the product into their respective organizations will create the buzz necessary to launch the product into the market in a big way. If the product has a broad market, you will be riding a big wave, but watch out because the competition is not far behind. The wave may start to break soon, and you may drown as the competition floods in.

Figure 11-1 illustrates our position on the wave. At this point, we have started down the wave and our management strategy and team has begun to form. As we try to push our product into the mainstream of product sales, we need to add a full complement of sales and marketing resources. This chapter will examine how we go about selling our breakthrough product.

Fig. 11-1: Technology Big Wave Structure—Marketing

Blue Screen of Death

Marketing can't make your product really unique, but you can do a really unique job marketing your product.

Take Microsoft. It is probably the only company that has mastered the art of selling software that does not work all of the time. The blue screen of death (BSOD) periodically appeared in Microsoft products, completely demolishing the user's entire system and causing a hard reboot of the machine to occur with its attendant loss of data or work product. Lately, the BSOD has been replaced with a program asking you if it can be ended because it is nonresponsive. Then the program wants you to tell it if it should report its bugs back to Microsoft.

I am not knocking Microsoft because the company has done an unbelievable job. Its software has to work in all configurations that the user demands with a wide variety of independently provided software products and do it correctly. Sometimes the products just do not work, and Microsoft will get blamed for the failure. Further, it has the Linux boys nipping at its heels as well as Google and a batch of other companies wanting to dethrone it. In the midst of this morass, it has prevailed over the competition. It is by sheer marketing strategy that the company has been able to advance its products. Even though the Justice Department does not like its strategies, you can learn from them.

What distinguished Microsoft were its attempts to make a simple and elegant user interface. Early on, the computer user had to deal with DOS- and CP/M-based machines. These machines were, to say the least, difficult to use and, in fact, essentially required that the user be a system administrator. Without going into the details, the design of the operating system memory layout was done in a fashion that even a first-year computer science student would not use. You would never place state information in the high-order bytes. You would always put them in the low-order bytes for expansion reasons. Yet this design was not of Microsoft's making because it bought and resold DOS when it bought the rights to the source code and later licensed the product to IBM on a per personal computer (PC) basis. By licensing the operating system software, Microsoft was free to license it to any other computer manufacturer. We should look at this transaction as a stroke of great marketing and possibly great luck. The urban myth is that Microsoft actually offered to sell the software to IBM. At the time IBM didn't see much future in "software" and particularly didn't see a future for operating system software for PCs. Hardware was where the money was!

Eventually, depending on who you believe, Microsoft stole

from Apple (or Apple stole from Xerox and then Microsoft stole from Apple or Xerox) or Microsoft eventually decided to make a graphical interface. High-technology entrepreneurs borrow from each other all of the time. This can result in intellectual property lawsuits, but it also allows for rapid innovation. Further, depending on how you design and develop products, you may take a fundamental idea that has a long history and redesign it without infringing on anyone's property.

The big problem was that the idea was cool, but the execution was terrible. In fact, it took Microsoft a lot of tries to make the software work with any sense of reliability. Thus, we end up with the BSOD. It got to be such a joke in the industry that Microsoft eventually came up with a scheme where for a fee it provided a kit for software developers that contained the most recent version of the yet-to-be-released operating system. Plus, you also got tools to help you develop applications for that operating system. Lastly, you got a way to report back to the company any errors you found.

Bill Gates was a great sales guy. You pay a fee to get a developer's kit for software that may blow your brains out, and you are expected to report errors that you find.

Because users were enamored with the interface and it was being installed on the most popular types of PCs, this company ended up in the unique position of selling software that only kind of worked. Many programs that it developed would take two or three tries to even function. Yet, Microsoft was able to position itself as a leader and provider of high-function software. It is a story of a magnificent sales job.

Microsoft created a simple message and a great value statement. It was able to consistently embrace the early adopter and create product buzz. Eventually, it became the standard for corporate software at the desktop.

Blood Sport

In the technology area, there tends to be few winners. In fact, generally there will be one or two major companies created. As these companies become successful, they will leave unfulfilled niches that competitors will try to fill.

Generally it forms like a wave structure. As the basic technology starts to come of age, money will flow in at a fast and furious rate. The bigger the perceived wave, the more money that will flow into the particular technology area. Many companies will form and go after the gold at the end of the rainbow. These companies will generally make the mistake of trying to differentiate themselves by describing their product features. As the field starts to mature in terms of products, the products will not be differentiated and thus the lines between the products will blur. It will be very difficult for any product to stand out against other products. This is when the real marketing begins.

If an area of technology has attracted a lot of funds and is showing real potential, serious efforts to build real companies with multiple product lines will begin. This effort includes mergers, cross licensing of technologies, and leap frog strategies (knowing your competitors' strategies and trying to build a product that jumps over the competition's product in terms of functions).

Other strategies will occur as companies try to exaggerate the deficiencies of their competitors' products.

Almost anything will be allowed while trying to win because, if the technology is really a big wave technology, the stakes are high. Real money will begin to chase the technology. This is true for software as well as solar power, wind turbines, and medical technologies.

The problem in this high-stakes game is that it is difficult to sort out reality from fiction. You are not able to really tell what is fact and what is fiction because the technology is changing at a rapid rate and the developers may have difficulty meeting their goals in the allowed development time. Schedules and success will be defined not only by the company that is trying to defend its turf, but also by the rumors and competitors' disinformation.

Any time the stakes get large and the money starts to flow, management, marketing, and engineering will all get involved in a high-stakes set of bets, trying to ensure that the company is perceived as having the most advanced product with the best features.

Because of the money, the risk profile will become extremely large and the game will become a game of winner-takes-all high-stakes poker with hundreds of millions of dollars at stake. In many cases, billions of dollars will be at stake.

It will become difficult for one company to come out on top, unless drastic measures are undertaken, because technology can probably only support one or two major companies after the inevitable shakeout plus maybe one or two niche-oriented upstarts. Thus if you want to be a survivor, you need to roll up as many capabilities as fast as possible. At this point, the major players will try to dominate the industry.

The size of the stakes will dictate how fast the industry consolidates. Once consolidation starts, you have to either be the consolidator and win big or sell and find another wave. It is critical not to get crushed by the consolidation because the wave rolls over and turns into churn moving up onto the beach.

Money will make the most aggressive actors and most aggressive marketing strategies come to the fore. At some time, all-out war breaks out because a company's very survival is at stake. Discounting will become rampant as the war heats up.

Finally, blood will be spilled, the big winner will emerge, and the game will be over. The competitors will move onto other areas and try to play again.

Microsoft, Cisco, and Dell are all examples of companies that started small and survived the shakeout to become top companies. Google and eBay are companies that also survived such battles.

Money Tracks

Selling into an early adopter environment is conceptually a really simple task. So is big wave surfing! However, being out on a board on a seventy-foot wave is not simple. Both disciplines require precision, guts, extensive training, and nerves of steel.

First, understand that the stakes are really high. There is no room for error. We are trying to create a rapidly growing earnings stream, and as such, there is little room for error. If we are riding a real wave, we need to avoid a wipeout.

Never forget the first rule of marketing: only follow the qualified leads. You need to follow the money. Any customer can be interested in your new product, but you can only do so much work; thus, you must make sure that any lead is really qualified, and that means that they have control of the budget.

You cannot go into the organization and deal with people who do not have control of a budget for the type of product you are selling. It is critically important that you identify the person who controls the budget so that you can make your value proposition to the right level of the organization.

If you go in at the wrong level, you will have to fight up the organization. Some other person will carry your message up the chain to the person who is in charge. In such a case, even if the person you are dealing with is well intentioned and motivated, there are a number of problems that can arise. It is critically important that you get to the person with the budget. Even if you do not end up dealing with that person directly, you need the backing of that person in the forthcoming negotiations.

Trying to find the right person can be a trying proposition. It may require an extensive network both outside and inside the target company. You need help to find the right person and qualify that lead. In some cases, the decision maker may not even be in the company that you are trying to sell to.

In some cases of information technology groups, the entire function is outsourced to an independent company and the internal software group only acts in a supervisory manner. Unless this outside group wants and decides to add your functions, you are not going to sell your product no matter how much the internal software guys want your product! That is the bad news.

The good news is that if you find the decision maker in the external group and you can sell him, then you have completed a sale to all the customers of that third-party supplier.

One last piece of bad news: In many cases the vendor may also be a supplier of the system, so they have no reason to consider your solution. They will convince the customer that they can provide a similar product and you will not get the business.

Even a third-party supplier situation can be overcome if the person controlling the purse strings to the third party stands up and says thou shall implement this set of functions.

Budgets may be hierarchical, so it is not sufficient to find the lowest-level person with a budget authority. You must find someone who has not only a budget, but also a budget with contingency funds that allow the person to implement new things. That person must have complete authority to find, define, and implement new functions. Further, the person who has such authority must also have the contingency funds and authority to roll out that functional capability throughout the organization. Anyone in the organization who does not have such authority cannot make the purchase you need to get a steep rise on your sales curve!

Golden Rule

We all know the golden rule: "He who has the gold rules." It is simple but important to any salesperson. Unless you get to the guy with the money, you do not get the business. This is central to the sales process. No matter how much we discuss the idea of champions, and other ideas, it all boils down to the golden rule. In the end, the guy with the money has the responsibility. We discuss in length the sales process, but it all boils down to the golden rule. Ignore it at your own risk because no one ever gets the sale by forgetting the golden rule!

The golden rule also works great in life. There are slight variations to the golden rule, but one of these variations is the rule of compromise. This one works best with a wife. On any decision, you discuss all of the issues, and then your wife makes the decision. This is called compromise. In the end, the correct decision was made and harmony remains. The sales cycle is the same. You can discuss and discuss, but in the end, the customers' wishes always will prevail because the customer controls the gold. The easiest way to extract the gold is to create a unique and compelling product. Technology allows you to do this in the event of a disruption. But you must convince the customers that they cannot live without your new product. You must have a compelling argument or product and then convince them that it is their idea.

Another variation in the same vein is the process of managing children. This one is the rule of two. When faced with a difficult problem child, an easy strategy is to give the child a choice of two alternatives, both of which are acceptable to you. The child can then make a decision and feel good about the situation, but you will control the process and get a solution that is acceptable to you. The number of sales situations that boil down to needing this strategy is unbelievable. Many sales guys view this as providing the customer options, but the reality is just like a child. This gets the customers into a position that they can make their choices, which is acceptable to the salesperson. If the champion has detractors that are causing problems in the organization, this gives the champion a way to give the detractors some feeling of self-esteem and ownership by letting them make a choice. You need to position a unique product in such a way that the customers can select one of two possible variations of the product. Do they want a trial solution, or do they want to buy the special sales price that you have available on the current product this month? Do they want a crippleware (crippleware is usually a free product that has not been enabled to provide full capability until you purchase a product registration key or pay when the next version comes out) test product, or do they want to buy the entire product with a 90-day, satisfaction, money-back guarantee? You want to give the customer an easy choice!

If these sound like strategies to herd cats, the sales process for a new high-technology process is very much like that. The best sales guys can herd cats and manage more than one herd at a time. There are some recent areas of technology application where the cats herd themselves. In some areas, like social networking, companies spring out of nowhere on buzz and go from zero to near infinity in a single step. This is a great result because the wave being ridden goes so quickly. The guy with the best idea wins almost every time. But the life span of the company may be small.

Value Pricing

Pricing is always a problem with a new concept product. No one is really sure what its value is. Is it cost savings? Is it new capabilities? What is the cost of disruption? But you want to sell your product based upon its value. Value pricing, not time and materials pricing, is the key to generating profits.

There are really two parts to the sale. One part is the product itself, and the other part is the service, installations, training, and support. There is real money in service, installation, training, and support. These areas also get you into the application development and other service business.

The product business is a clean business. You have a product price. If the product is unique, then you set a very high but justifiable price and stick to your guns. You have analysis that supports your rationale, and the customer buys the function. You make profits at a rapid rate, and things can ramp as fast as your factory gets the product out the door. If the product is software, it is easy to replicate and distribute the software with high profit margins.

Now the services issue comes to the fore. This is a good business for a small part of the market, but a bummer business for the most part. Almost every product needs these support facilities. The problem is that most people know in detail what human services cost. A Java programmer costs X. When Java was first introduced, there was a limited number of programmers and the cost was high. Now the cost has come down, and the cost is very quantifiable. If your product needs a Java programmer for support, the customer will know how much this will cost. As technology becomes better understood, there will be a large number of suppliers and your margins will be squeezed down to the industry norm.

This will not get it done if you are trying to grow the business rapidly.

The way you play this game is to have a cadre of highly skilled personnel who provide the initial services and train service groups to do this mundane work at normal industry rates and margins while you take the smaller, higher-margin work that is involved in the front end. By approaching the problem this way, you can get a number of large companies pushing your product because they know that they will pick up the service business that is important to them to sustain their large army of employees that compete in the service industry. You cannot grow rapidly unless you get these service groups on board. They are so used to this model that they forget that you are getting high growth and high profits because you are taking the product and the cream of the services business. They are truly happy to take the large mundane work and skim a meager living off thousands of employees.

Yes, with disdain, big wave surfers know their place. They are trying to get big sales and make it happen. They will be polite and, in a sense, will go out of their way to court the big service groups. In the vernacular, they will court the slug farms (SFs). The big guys like to think they are superior and you cannot succeed without them, but the reverse is true. The SF needs new products to keep the slugs farming, but they have lost the ability to really develop such capabilities.

Thus, the upper management of the SFs and the big wave surfers have divided the pie. Each party gets value.

As a sales guy, you need the slugs. Don't hire them. Partner. Price for value. Feed your local slug farm. Better yet, feed several at a time. Time and material services pricing is anti–big wave surfing. The big wave surfers need product sales and pricing so that they can grow rapidly. Otherwise, they just deteriorate into regular surfers.

Unfair Advantage

When you are trying to get the sale, there are so many factors over which you have no control. Until the check clears you cannot figure out how to actually get the sale. Many times in the sales process, I have seen everything done right, only to have the sale fall apart for no apparent reason.

How does this happen? It is all about people. Somewhere along the sales cycle, you must find the unfair advantage. Remember that at the end of the sale, someone is going to sign off on the purchase order and until that actually occurs you cannot count on the sale. At the end of the day, the key to getting the sale is to get an unfair advantage that no competitor can ever overcome. This will allow the buyer to sign off on that purchase order.

This key idea is the unfair advantage; it may be as simple as getting the support of all of the technical staff. Or it may be something as simple as your wife's conversation with the buyer's wife at a charity function where your wife reiterates how committed your company is to the success of the buyer's company.

The environment is competitive, and if the area that you are trying to bring your new product into is really hot, competition will develop very quickly, so you must get all of your sales closed quickly to get the buzz and market momentum that you need. Anything that you can do to stop the competition from closing in on your sale is key. This search should get you an unfair advantage. One advantage that I always liked is a true understanding of the competitor's position. What does any potential competitor really do? What is the state of its product? What development problems is it having? When was the last time that it delivered a product on time?

Create the unfair advantage!

Comical Spies

Because we are trying to get our product uniquely positioned, we will be subjected to an unwitting game of cat and mouse. The idea that we will create buzz means that the idea becomes exposed quickly to other people. These people may want to copy your idea, modify your idea, or claim that they have similar products or services. Once you have let your idea out of the bag, many people will become aware of the idea and your first-mover advantage will become difficult to defend. Consider how small the world is. If you are truly only six or seven levels away from any other person, that means your idea is only a few levels away from all of your friends, associates, and competitors. Thus, once your idea is out, it is really a game of spy versus spy. You must move very fast or risk being crushed by the flock of others trying to jump into your ocean. Just like in *MAD* magazine where the little spies were always trying to counter each other's moves, you now face the same problem. Move fast.

FUD Strategy

FUD (fear, uncertainty, and doubt) was the strategy popularized by IBM for mainframe sales in the 1960s. IBM did not own the concept, but it was the best at applying the strategy. When trying to make a sale, IBM created an environment that did not allow the customer a choice as to when or how to buy a product.

Developing such a strategy is really pretty simple. If you do not have our specific capability, then your company will be behind the competition. If your company does not implement the new technology, then it will be seen as backward. If your company does not buy from IBM, then your company will not be seen as a progressive company by your customers. Fear! You will be backward, not up to date, less capable than your competition, etc. You are being put into a position where you have no way of evaluating the claims of the salesperson because you cannot actually measure the effect of the technology.

Any new technology will probably require that the adopting organization make changes to its operations to realize the benefits of the technology. Yet, the actual costs and savings may or may not be measurable. If a technology enables a function that has not been performed before or saves time on a labor-intensive process, the cost trade-offs are simple and convincing. Other large, functional changes may not be so obvious.

The big problem in setting up a sale is what to do when the sale involves a technology that is so new that the big guys do not have such technology. Then the big guy strategy is to dismiss the technology as a toy, not well developed, produced by a small company, and not a technology that integrates well with the mainstream technologies that are currently in use in your company. This is one set of arguments that is used within the context of uncertainty. The salesperson has a vested interest in preserving the status quo until the user can be enticed into buying the new technology from the large mainstream provider. Uncertainty. You need the solution that the big provider has and not the technology that can be provided by the new technology vendor. If the technology were significant enough to be used (or could be used with low risk) in your business, then the mainstream provider would have the technology because, in fact, we are investigating just such technologies for use by our user base.

Further, the technology provided by the vendor is not fully up to the standards that a company such as yours needs to operate its plant, office, or distribution channel. If the technology were really significant, then we the serious system provider would be offering the technology. Doubt. If our corporation, which has been your long-term supplier, really felt that the technology were important, then we would be providing the technology to our customers. Another way that the sales guys approach the problem is to note that we are working on an integrated solution but feel the state of the art is such that the implementation of the technology is premature and you do not want to implement the inferior technology when, if you just wait for a few months, we will have a superior technology that can really make a difference in your operations.

When the vendor fails to deliver on time, the arguments are that the technology was and is still premature, because if we cannot provide the correct functionality, then no one can. After all, no one ever got fired because they bought an IBM solution, because if we (IBM) cannot provide the solution, then the solution is not mature and could cause problems in your company and that could cost you your job. Watch out for the risk factors that are hidden by taking that other company's solution.

Thank heaven for early adopters.

The reality is that the big companies do not generally have the types of advanced technology that will give you a technology edge. You need to seek such technologies from companies that are nimble. The big companies have developed niches that allow them to dominate markets that can easily be production intensive. Consider Boeing—one of only two large airplane makers. It has developed a process for developing large planes (or in its view, systems). From its perspective, it is then able to apply those same processes to other large, complex jobs.

Yes, many companies such as Boeing say that their main technology capability is the ability to manage the process of large jobs. This is the classic case of FUD. Your system is so complex that you need a special firm that knows how to manage large jobs.

This concept of sales is prevalent in many large organizations because no one in the customer base wants to take any risk. The customer is susceptible to the FUD sales strategy if it is unwilling to consider new and innovative solutions. This may occur because the customer does not have a well-developed process of implementation that will allow for the introduction of new technology.

Coopetition Concept

An important concept for the technology marketer is coopetition: cooperative competition. You should not always look at your competitors as your competition. There may be days when they are competitors, but there may be days when you need to cooperate because the real enemies are the groups that have a solution that is detrimental to both you and your competition's sales position. I first heard about this idea from Ray Noorda of Novell. He was a master at using coopetition to get a significant advantage for his products.

In the airline industry (one of the most competitive industries), the competing airlines would cut each other's throats to get an additional passenger, but let a foreign carrier try to enter the market and the airlines rally together to stop the intruder. The same goes for high-speed rail service. There is nothing that the airline industry wants less than high-speed rail connections available across the United States.

A clear strategy for coopetition was found in the local area network (LAN) business at its onset in the early 1980s. In this case, several groups, all of whom would have liked to eliminate the other, joined forces in various standards-producing groups that were trying to eliminate (euphemistically speaking) the old-line mainframe and minicomputer manufacturers by causing the adaptation of workstations on a LAN. Yet, various groups within this paradigm-changing group were at each other's throats. The proponents of Token Ring would like to eliminate the Ethernet group, and the proponents of mainframe-interconnection LANs could do without the workstation LAN crowd. Yet, all of these groups could band together to pitch the idea that modern systems should be built out of high-performance servers and workstations connected on a high-speed transport and not by terminals connected to mainframes.

This idea is both complex and simple. There have been various sayings and jokes that simplify the concept. The enemy of my enemy is my friend. The reason the scorpion stung his transport going across the river was because he was, after all, a scorpion. Amazing alliances can be formed when necessary.

Yet coopetition is more complex. Consider a high-tech product. It is probably built out of a number of components, each of which compete with other components made by other manufacturers. It is within this global context that groups of friends can be formed and groups of enemies are singled out. In some cases, it may be a third party that provides the coopetition. In the game console market, it may be the development of a game for a specific console that leads to development deals by the competition. For example, a particular game developed for a specific console may dramatically affect the console wars due to the game's popularity.

This is a multiple choice game. Mergers, cross-licensing of technology, and development (or the withholding of development) of software for a specific platform are all strategies that tend to create groups of coopetiting companies. The consortium could be your early adopter.

In fact, in big businesses, like government contracting, the large primes might be trying to kill a competitor on one bid while teaming up with the same contractor on a different bid. You just never can know or tell who your friends are, but it is a very small world.

Because of the size of large companies such as a Lockheed Martin or General Dynamics, parts of a company may be in competition with itself, causing the upper management to have to referee. Further complicating the issue may be that different parts of the company may want to use outside vendors to provide services to help a team that is being constructed to win a bid. This makes teaming a difficult mating dance with a lot of people both inside and outside the major company unhappy.

Critical Decision

In developing a product, the designers will run into the same problem: make or buy? Do you get a competitor's (or near competitor's) component, or do you develop it yourself? A big problem in this decision is, How do you get the license? Another question is, Can you get the license? Using it or building it is a true test of coopetition.

Time changes everything! The enemy today is not necessarily the enemy tomorrow. Over time, your enemy will be both your friend and your enemy. One of the most used and abused relationships that illustrates this point is the relationship between Apple and Microsoft. When, if, and under what circumstances Apple products can run Microsoft software has changed since the early 1980s so many times. In the early days, Microsoft built boards that were add-on functions to the Apple II system. Today, Microsoft is trying to compete with Apple in the music business. This relationship is a classic case of my enemy, my friend, my enemy. Enemies and friends are made by convenience!

Copycat technologies are a result of coopetition. Marketing sets out to develop a product. It obtains a license or other type of agreement, and the next thing the developers know a product emerges that contains technology developed by another company. Engineering then leap frogs the competition and introduces new technology that makes the licensed technology unnecessary. Suddenly that competitor leap frogs its purchaser and the marketing department wants to relicense. Life can be very complex. If the interfaces are correctly developed, technology is interchangeable.

Acquisition is one of the last great acts of defiance. If the engineering department is not getting things done fast enough, then marketing may decide that the easiest way to solve the problem is to buy the technology! In this case the purchase may be to leap frog the competition or to take the competition off the street. If nothing else, the simplest solution to a lack of technology is to buy the competitor. Having multiple technology alternatives within a large company is like diversifying one's portfolio. It can smooth the technology development cycle so that your products do not go through a top-bottom-top cycle.

Competitive Intelligence

A simple marketing tool that many people forget is to talk to your competitors. Even if you're not out to cut a deal or in a life-or-death struggle, you want to a least know your competitors. (Face it, at some point you may want a new job.) There are several advantages: You can swap old war stories, you can get an overall sense of the problems they are encountering, you can get a feel for what directions they may be going, and you can swap customer horror stories so you may both save some time. If both of you are having the same problems with the same customers, you can either adjust your strategy or move on to other customers.

This talk will curl the toes of your lawyer. Antitrust concerns are dancing in your lawyer's head. But as long as you are not fixing prices, conspiring to create a monopoly, or engaging in unfair business practices, you have no worries. Look at Microsoft; it beat up the Justice Department. All I am suggesting is a little conversation. This type of conversation goes on all of the time. Your technical people presenting at a conference about your technical products' strengths and weaknesses will talk to a lot of people. Your members on a standards committee who are arguing for your position will talk to a lot of people. Clearly, in both cases you are discussing your technical position with the competition. Just do not fix prices! Big companies actually conspire to divide up markets. Whenever two big companies team up to go after a bid or project, they effectively take out some of the competition. This is completely legal. Teaming is not only legal, but also encouraged. The problem arises when you get together with a competitor and set minimum prices.

A favorite strategy of people who like to know the competition is to march right into their trade show booth and announce their presence. Ask to meet the vice president of sales, and ask for two things: a demonstration of the company's product and a acceptance by this competitor of an invitation to visit your booth for a demonstration of your product. What's the worst that could happen? They could throw you out of their booth. But usually, the vice president of sales will be more than happy to demonstrate and see a demonstration. They may ask to do it at a later time when the show is closing down or just starting because they don't want to be distracted when potential customers are coming by the booth. In many cases, the vice president of sales will welcome your invitation because he really wants to see your product. An additional advantage of meeting this way is that sometimes the look on his face will make your day as he tries to figure out if you are really serious. Are you really asking the vice president of sales to talk to you, a competitor? And asking for a demonstration while offering to reciprocate? After the initial shock of your request, most people will be curious enough that they will accept your request and offer.

The world is very small. People run into each other all of the time. You need to know your competitors so that if and when you encounter a situation where you need a partner, a business associate, or even a G-2 on a new entrant into the field and want to pick up the phone to talk to your counterpart, it will not be for the first time. You need to have a basis of trust or some understanding of what motivates your competitive counterparts.

Just like big wave surfers congregate at a beach to surf and to learn from each other about good locations, waves, techniques, and boards, salespeople can learn from each other by talking to a variety of other salespeople about strategies and product placement. Networking is a key part of the salesperson's tool kit.

Knowledge of others is a common ground. What are the competitions' interests? How do they conduct business? Do they have any technology that can be used or repackaged to enhance your product? What competitors are a possible merger or acquisition partner? Where do they see themselves going? These are all things that you should know about your competition, and the best way to find out is to ask them directly. Plus, you may actually like your competitor.

The previous section spoke of coopetition, but you want to know your competitors in a more personal way. You never know what the future brings and where your counterparts will be, so it is good practice to have a little knowledge of the person you compete with. You just never know when your interests will align. Having a wide and diverse network is important, but even more important is to have a network of people whose business interests are aligned with yours. It is within the inner circle of people with similar interests that people will do business together, form companies together, or simply share experiences.

You will find that a key group of people that you need to know and nurture is your competition. You can never tell when your interests will align and what will come of that alignment.

Product Positioning

If you have a product to sell and you want to close sales in a quick and efficient manner, you need to really understand your product. You need a complete product understanding, not just what your product does, but how it does what it does, how fast it works, and numerous other details. Further, you need to understand the competition. Not just at a superficial level, but at a detailed level. You need to understand not only how the competition's product works, but also their sales strategy. We will need to understand not only our product, but also our competition's product and other products and their features sets that may affect the sales and product space we're trying to sell to.

Lawyers call this preparation. One of the things I have learned from friends who are lawyers is the need to be completely prepared for any eventuality. If you are going to get a rapid sales penetration, you need the same level of preparation as a lawyer trying a big case. Some of the best lawyers and salespeople are grinders. They keep digging, researching, and practicing until they have all eventualities down pat. Now we know that you will never cover all bases, but you need to do your research.

In the product positioning area, we want to know everything about our product.

Who are the competitors? (There had better not be any if we are going to really get a rapid ramp.) What products exhibit some aspect of the technology of our product? (There may be a few products that have some aspect of our technology, but we hope that we can provide a real distinct list of benefits.)

To position our product, we need to go through a number of issues. The first issue is our intended application and market space. What area of user need do we expect to satisfy? With luck, we will find that there are no other solutions that are direct competitors. Included in this analysis, we need to generate a use case that provides an understanding of how the product is expected to be deployed and used.

At the second stage of analysis, we need to do two things to make ourselves comfortable with our product positioning. We need to make a list of all application areas that are similar to our primary application. We also need to make a list of other products that may have functions that could be applied in some way to part of our application space. Our product is made up of a set of functions. One use of our product would be to perform part of an application in a very closely allied space. Thus, we need to examine closely related applications. Microsoft has been known to sell products in packages that combine several functions. For example, when the company entered the server business it included a protocol analyzer tool with the server "for free," thus starting the demise of the pure protocol analyzer business. This is a common strategy for all kinds of manufacturers. Car manufacturers package options, and software vendors build extra functions into their base products.

Next, for all application spaces and all products, we need to make up use cases. Then, we can develop a comprehensive set of applicable features, product benefits, and value statements about what problems are solved by each product in each application space.

The lead salesperson must commit this information to memory and be ready at an instance to counter any arguments in the sales cycle.

In the analysis, the salesperson needs to develop a pricing strategy based upon the product position.

With the analysis complete, we can develop a positioning strategy. With luck, we will have developed a set of strategies that keep us positioned as a unique product solving a critical application.

Value Proposition

The key to being a successful salesperson is to offer the customer value. This is encapsulated in the value statement.

Technology provides the salesperson one of the best ways to work with customers. Technology can create major functional improvements for customers, offering them many ways to save money. If your company is the inventor of this technology, then the company has a great opportunity to expand and grow at a very rapid rate. This can be accomplished if you can get the product and technology positioned correctly.

The value proposition that I like best goes something like this: Our company has product XYZ that performs a completely new set of functions that will improve the productivity of your organization. The product is used in the following manner. Based on our life cycle cost model, this product will save your organization substantially more money than it will cost to buy and deploy. Because there is no other product like this on the market, you can get a jump on your competition and increase your profits.

If you have a unique product to sell, if you can get an audience with the decision makers, if you can show the cost-benefit of the product, and if you can invoke competitive pressure, then the product sale is a layup. You do not need forty motivational seminars and sophisticated sales strategies; all you have to do is clearly document the value and simply ask for the order. These ifs are the measure of good marketing and sales. If we don't have ifs, then we must create them. In the case of a disruptive product, there is a major opportunity to create the ifs. This is similar in concept to the creation of tow-in surfing. At some point, waves became so large that you could not catch them by paddling onto the wave. Thus, tow-in surf-ing was invented so a watercraft could sling shot the surfer onto the wave. The "if" was no longer an if once we proved we could catch larger waves by using the speed of a watercraft.

The value of the product is key. Use cases that illustrate value are important. Showing specifically how the new function works, saves money, and provides a competitive edge is key. Make the cus-tomers heroes within their organizations, and the sale will follow.

The key is to make a business case for the product. What are you trying to improve? Will the product save money in the manu-facturing process, will it enable manufacturing to turn around model changes quicker, or will it let the manufacturing process be more flexible, running multiple product lines? Depending on the product's functions, you will approach the customer in a different fashion. Before approaching the customer, you must determine the customer's needs. If the factory is fairly static in its production and has only one product line, it is not sufficient to propose a solution that allows for quick factory changeovers. You must approach the value proposition as a cost savings in that case. Study the customer. Know the customer. Tailor the value proposition.

One of the classic value propositions happened in a bar in Los Angeles in the 1970s. The Rock, a computer salesperson for a major company, had been working the coast. He had been selling ruggedized, highly reliable computers to major systems integrators in the San Diego and Los Angeles area. To work the coast was not the most pleasant thing if you were based in Minneapolis because you eventually had to either waste a day to get home or take the red eye. At this time in history, technology was not the great sav-ior. Thus, we would go to Los Angeles, make the pitches and sales calls, and then get back to LAX sometime around 9 P.M. and wait for the red eye. This left after midnight and got us back to Min-neapolis and work the next morning.

Things were simpler then, and there were no cell phones.

Phone calls were expensive, and no one had a PC. Thus, the normal strategy was to get back to the airport no later than about 9 P.M., go to the airport bar, which also sold food, have dinner and some beer, and then climb on the red eye.

People were also friendlier, and because of the space in the bar/restaurant, it was not uncommon to find yourself seated with a number of strangers who were going to the same place you were going.

The Rock was in a very good mood this particular night because we had several good sales calls and he felt certain of getting a number of nice-sized orders. We had gotten to the airport early and were settling in for a nice meal and a couple of beers. The bar was crowded so we were joined by some other people. Eventually everyone got acquainted, and the Rock and this manufacturer got into a deep discussion of problems in the computer industry. It turned out that the manufacturer did not own a computer system, but used a service for some data processing. His data would be typed onto punch cards and read into a computer. Programs would be run, and the results would be printed onto sheets of paper and onto additional punch cards.

The problem with punch cards was that over time, temperature and humidity would make them unreliable. The Rock was explaining solutions to the problem and really listening to the manufacturer's problem. One of the items that the Rock sold was a form of nonvolatile memory, a memory that would not lose data if the power went off. In particular, the Rock had some drum memories available, where a cylinder rotated and the information stored magnetically on circles on the outside of the cylinder. This was in contrast to a disk memory, which was shaped like a platter and stored its information in concentric circles. The big problem was that the manufacturer feared losing his data. Before long, the Rock was sketching out solutions to the problem.

As time passed, the solution emerged that we would pick up

the manufacturer's cards, bring them to the factory, read them into a computer, organize the data into files, and then write the files onto the drum. Then we'd return the cards and the drum memory to the manufacturer where he could now feel safe that his data had been stored reliably. As I sat in amazement, the Rock and the manufacturer got out some paper, wrote out a purchase contract, listed out the tasks to be performed, agreed on a price, and signed the document. The manufacturer then produced his checkbook, wrote a check for the agreed-upon price of slightly over $100,000, and the Rock completed the sale.

A few days later back in Minneapolis, the Rock arranged to perform the contract and delivered the drum memory to the manufacturer, who were now secure that his data was permanently stored on the nonvolatile drum.

The Rock had successfully sold a drum memory full of data to someone who did not even own a computer!

The Rock listened, had an advanced technological solution, articulated the value, and simply closed the sale. In discussing this sale, I was telling someone how amazed I was by this sale. Without so much as a pause, the salesman replied that it was a perfectly logical sale and that it was probably one of the first instances of a computer data backup and restore data recovery solution sold in the industry. In that context, the sale makes great sense and the value proposition stands the test of time.

Value Marketing

The value provided by your product is the key to successful marketing of products.

What is your value? In constructing your value statement, you need to understand your value. Not only do you need to understand your value, but also you must be able to articulate the value in different circumstances. Each customer will be a little different and will need a specific approach. You need a flexible tagline, a focused mission statement, and a three- or four-sentence elevator speech.

The tagline should be something very concise. It should delineate the main functional benefit of your technology. It needs to encapsulate the fundamental discriminator of your technology. What does your technology enable that has been missing before? Can you describe that in three or four words? In the case discussed above, the manufacturer had data that was stored in a manner that was making him nervous. He had a fear of losing his data due to deterioration of the cards. He was intrigued by the idea of storing the data in a fashion that ensured that it would not be lost. A simple important requirement was solved. Further, this requirement was simply stated. We will take your unreliable cards, read the data, and store the data permanently. You need not fear losing your data!

If it takes fifty viewgraphs to get the idea across, you will not get the sale, let alone even get close to the decision maker. You must have something that catches the eye. A new function that can be easily described is your best value statement.

Steve Jobs is a person who creates admirable value statements. The idea of the iPod is remarkable. You can store your music collection on this little device, easily carry the collection with you, and access it via this simple wheel-like interface that anyone can learn to use. When the iPod was introduced, it was unique, created a new class of applications, and quickly became a must-have status symbol.

Value Statements

The key is to determine what constitutes value. Is it cost, new functions, or just plain performance?

Early in the sales cycle, we must establish the value statement.

This can be as simple as one statement, or it may be a series of statements that make up the value proposition.

This decision will set up our strategy for the sales cycle. The value statement that I prefer is a simple one. Let's devise a set of functions that are truly new and then find the corresponding value statement. How do we do this? You can talk to users, and they will tell you about their problems. If you can come up with a solution to a user need or problem, then you can develop a product concept, value statement, etc.

My personal preference for a value statement is a statement based upon new functions. If you have new and useful functions, then it is easy to construct the value statement. In constructing the value statement, the functions must be not only new, but also easily understood. When constructing the value statement, it is important that the statement be clear and precise. There is a reason that contests sometimes ask the entrant to explain the concept, benefits, or advantages in twenty-five words or less. It makes you focus on the key elements of the proposition.

What we want to do is to construct an easily understood description of the product and its value in a clear and concise fashion that will make the user want to buy or implement the functions.

We can almost do this as a formula. We want to cover at least four points:

1. What is it?

2. Why is this important?

3. Give an example of how to use it.

4. How do we implement it?

Our goal is to set up and prove that the product will save time, money, or some other important and scarce resource that the customer is concerned about. Alternatively, if possible and if we have a really disruptive technology product, we want to show that we can enable a completely new capability.

This formula covers the basic elements of value. *Why* answers the question of value. *What* describes the product concept. The *example* gives us our use case, and *how* is the implementation strategy.

If we can explain why the customer should implement the function, then we are really on track.

At the start of this section, two other potential benefits listed were cost and performance. We could also build our value statement around these two issues. However, when we talk cost, we are not talking price. We do not want to compete on price, but are willing to compete on a cost-benefit basis or a performance-benefit basis. If you think about what happened to the auto industry or the airline industry, you can see why price is not a good competitive value statement.

Yet, even in the auto industry there are examples of specialty cars that command a value statement (even a cult following) that allows them to not be categorized in the same discount price strategy that is common for half-ton pickups. Think about the Chevrolet Corvette!

Sales Differentiation

A common problem in the sales cycle is trying to verbalize why the customer should buy your product. The biggest pitfall in this process is the issue of benefits versus features. You must differentiate between benefits and features.

A benefit is something that you will gain in the business process when you implement the proposed new functions. A feature is something associated with the product that you can describe. For example, a low price is a feature of the product. The size of the memory is a feature. The size of the code base and its maturity is a feature.

However, if the new product speeds up the transaction rate of a real-time transaction (think about the speed of your online banking experience) while lowering the cost of the transaction, then improved performance and an improved cost-benefit ratio is a benefit.

The ultimate benefit is a description of your product's ability to introduce new business functions that improve the flow of information and the quality of decisions made in a highly competitive environment. Sometimes the salesperson will want to tie benefits and features together.

If you have a completely new product, you may want to tie the features and benefits into a package of information. Make a list of new features, and then for each feature, derive a benefit. If you have a new product that is full of new functions, each function should be defined as a new set of capabilities (features) that can be used to derive a set of benefits to sell the product.

Trying to make a comprehensive list of benefits is difficult. You will have to go back and forth over a period of time to truly articulate benefits. The majority of people will tend to quickly gravitate to features because it is a lot easier. In particular, the feature that you do not want to discuss is price. If you have to get to a bottom-line price discussion, you are probably not going to be in a position to describe and close the sale on the basis of benefits. Once price becomes the discussion point, you are on thin ice to get the sale. If the product is truly new and we expect to get the sale, we do not want to get into a price shootout. In a price shootout, the users may decide that they can get by with less or different functions. Then, the price dictates the sale, and you will probably lose. Further, if the feature under discussion is price, we can run into a detailed discussion of the rationale for our price. We want to go at the problem by providing a value statement that encompasses the price as part of a cost-benefit analysis rather than a standalone element of a comparison matrix.

The benefits will drive the value statement. It is possible to construct a series of value statements based on the different benefits that are derived from the product. The various benefits and value statements can be tailored to each customer to maximize the possibility of a sale. Benefits must be built into the value proposition.

Product Commoditization

The good and bad news can be seen by thinking about the airline industry. The airline industry performs important functions. Instead of having to drive across the United States, you can get on an airplane and fly across the continent in about six hours. That is a miracle time-saving product. In addition, the cost is usually dirt cheap if you have any sort of advance planning.

Anyone who has driven across the United States knows how much time is saved, let alone wear and tear on your body, nerves, and sense of humor. There's also considerable cost savings when you don't have to drive your vehicle, stay in hotels, and buy food.

The good news is that the consumer gets a tremendous value: time savings and low cost. The bad news is that the consumer gets a tremendous value: time savings and low cost. Whether the news is good or bad is an issue of perspective. The airline industry has become such a commodity business that it is virtually impossible to make money in this business. This is bad news for the airlines. Yet the volumes of travelers are so high that, given a new cost model, a start-up airline can make large sums of money. Good news for parts of the industry.

Any time a product or service becomes a commodity, it loses

its product differentiation and value added. Thus, the value proposition becomes useless. In the airline industry, because most major cities are served by multiple airlines with multiple flights per day, the only difference is cost.

When your industry deteriorates to the point where the only difference is cost, the industry has been fully commoditized. This makes the industry completely suspect. Now the only way that you can expand your market is by lowering customer cost, and what if someone comes in and sells the product for less?

If you are a big wave surfer, and you want to keep surfing, you must be out of the wave before it becomes a commodity! There is no reason to try to ride the wave in to shore because the thrill is gone.

There is a tremendous value proposition for a flight across the United States. Yet the industry is so commoditized that there is no money to be made. Rates are so low that, in many cases, a full flight may yield the airline only a few hundred dollars of profit.

This is the type of business that must be avoided at all costs. There may be money to be made, but only by insiders, managers, and bankruptcy lawyers. The workforce and the middle management may find themselves on the wrong side of an economic spiral.

There is no intent to disparage the airline industry. The same circumstances can be seen in the tech industry. It has happened in the mainframe, minicomputer, PC, and calculator businesses. It has happened in disk storage. Office software applications suffered a similar fate. It is easy to make a list of fallen tech industries: modems, phone systems, input/output cards, and memory chips. The landscape is littered with demand destruction. Once an industry turns into a commodity industry, it generates little interest or wealth.

In these industries, there is still money to be made, but like the churn of the wave moving up on to the beach, the industry is of little interest to any surfer let alone a big wave surfer.

Customer Bias

There are going to be days when no matter how prepared and on target you feel, you are going to have a tough time in a sale. You may not even get to first base in contacting the decision maker. If you do get to see the decision makers, they may be hostile and nonresponsive.

Dealing with unknown customers can be very difficult.

The worst experience that I ever observed contains a number of valuable lessons.

In the late 1970s, I accompanied the Rock to a briefing with the Army. At the time, I was with product development and we wanted to sell the Army new tactical computers. The Army was about to come out with a procurement for a lot of computers and had invited all interested manufacturers to make a presentation. As the largest manufacturer of mil spec computers, we were there to discuss our product line. However, we primarily built the Naval Tactical Data System (NTDS) product set. Our slide set carefully discussed how we designed, built, and provided all necessary support for this product set.

We were all ready at the briefing. We had our title slide up on the vu-graph machine, and our handouts were ready. We were just waiting for the general to begin our briefing. The general arrived, and introductions were made. Then the general made his opening comment. Basically he said, I know that you guys sell the NTDS and are a big supplier to the Navy, but this is the Army. If you two clowns say the word Navy or NTDS once, this briefing is over, and you are out of here. This was definitely a biased sales environment. We were in hostile territory, and it was clear that our whole presentation was out the door.

Without skipping a beat, the Rock made the one-hour briefing using only the title slide and concluded the meeting by distributing the handout. Afterward, I asked him how he did it. His only comment was take your presentation, bring your handouts, but use a blackboard or flipchart because you need flexibility when giving your introductory presentation so that you can tailor the presentation in real time. This includes making sure that you do not initially offend any real decision makers. In some cases, you will only need the title slide.

After you deliver your tailored presentation to the audience, then you can leave the handouts.

Pit Bull Marketing

An aggressive strategy that can do wonders for any product or technology is what I call a pit bull sales and marketing strategy. The basic idea is simple, and in fact, this technique has worked successfully. Consider that the basic structure is the development of a new product or technology. Further assume that you want to succeed and evolve the capabilities of the product over an extended period of years. Then develop a simple, basic product that encompasses its most fundamental element. Introduce this product as a basic product in a set of products. Then evolve the product as fast as possible by building variations that alter its functions and combinations of functions, costs, and performance.

This pit bull strategy can be seen in the abstract.

Essentially the strategy is to develop a basic product. This product is designed to anchor your product set. This product can be considered a stake that you plant in the sand and intend to defend in the sense of controlling and defending turf. This basic product is forming the basis of an entire product strategy. An enhanced product is attached to the basic product by a module or some other option that allows us to sell both the enhanced and the basic product. The enhanced product can be seen as protection for the stake we have tried to establish. The extended product can be seen in the abstract as a pit bull that is attached by leash or chain to the basic product.

The types of pit bulls that can be attached to the basic product include optional modules, additional functions, patent protection, OEM deals, or technologies that add or integrate other companies' functions.

A classic example of this strategy has been employed in the sale of multiport cards. If the types of cards sold by your competitors contain two, four, or eight ports, you might introduce a product set that contains two- and four-port cards. That is the basic stake you drive into the ground. Your first pit bull product may be a six-port card that is cheaper than the competition and has fewer functions than an eight-port card. Another variation is a card with multiple types of ports. If competitors have cards that contain multiple types of ports, then you should put a different number of ports on your card. You could build cards that contain three types of ports. In fact, you could also build a system that provides ports and disks. As you can see, the number of variations is quite robust.

Essentially, we want to take the base technology, drive our stake in the ground, and begin to destroy our base product. We destroy the fundamental technology as fast as possible and try to create many new variations of the technology to keep the competition off balance as it defends against this "pacman" attack led by aggressive pit bulls.

The pit bull strategy has many dimensions. The primary strategy is the total number of pit bulls we can attach to the stake. The next bit of strategy is the length of the chains on which the pit bulls are attached (this can be seen as the different functions). Lastly is the speed at which we can put the pit bulls into action.

With this strategy, we are trying to develop a robust set of products based on our core product so that no other competitor can make significant inroads into our space. If a competitor tries to approach, the nearest pit bull can be moved into position to fend off the product attack.

If we are successful in implementing the strategy, we will control the space and establish ownership of the stake. At that point, we can begin to add other pit bull–type functions onto our stake. A simple example of this strategy is the evolution of Facebook to allow ads and to allow for purchases (for example, the ability to make airline reservations off the Delta Airlines Facebook page). This strategy not only protects Facebook but attacks Google's ad strategy.

This strategy works for both new and existing product space if we can catch the existing product developers by surprise. It works even better if a company can be caught napping. (Apple got the jump on Microsoft in the smart phone business recently.) Then, we can put into the market a superior product and establish market dominance. To do this, we need to redefine the product space to suit our needs. Further, we might have to make several attempts at the base product until we get the space defined in a manner that we deem defendable. A good example of this problem is that of tablet computers and eReaders, such as the Apple's iPad and Amazon's Kindle, where the space has yet to be completely defined and dominated.

The real downside to this strategy is that these actions taken may energize the entire space and make us as vulnerable as the competition. We will have created a rate of rapid change, and we will have essentially institutionalized a rate that now defines our own future.

Happy Calls, Talks, and Meetings

Meetings are a big part of any sale. You need to make a presentation that represents your product and its value proposition. However, there are some key rules about meetings if you are a big wave salesperson.

First, you do not need long meetings. You do not want to get sucked into detailed arguments about subtle product features. Your value statement must drive the sale forward so you don't have to spend hours and hours comparing your product to other products. Any meeting that does not have both the money person and the decision maker is a waste of time. If your goal is to get your picture on the cover of the most popular big wave surfing magazine, there is no need to get onto a big wave if the photographer is not on the beach taking pictures.

Your initial meetings should not last over an hour. There is nothing about a viable value statement that cannot be articulated in an hour. In fact, you should be able to articulate and sell the product in twenty-five words or less if it is unique enough and we think it's the start of a serious revenue ramp. In your initial meetings, you should go over the user system as you understand it, make sure you know all the players, and provide three or four charts that emphasize your value and unique benefits. Make sure that the meeting is attended by the decision maker or his deputies.

Once the hook is set, you must keep driving the sale forward. Each and every meeting must have a purpose and move the process forward. Do not get sucked into meetings with lower-level personnel who want to kibitz about all kinds of distracting points and silliness.

In many organizations, there are professional meeting attendees. They create meetings as their primary job. Attending a meeting and taking and distributing meeting notes is their job. Further, they practice a paradigm that is a form of irrational consensus. They try to make sure that everyone is on board and content with the purchase decision. Thus, nothing ever gets done because at least one person can never agree! It is the job of the salesperson to not let this happen and to keep driving the purchase forward.

Meetings where everyone sits around and talks about the decision and, at the end of the meeting, agrees to another meeting by the same cast of characters are called happy meetings. Everyone is working to resolve all of the issues. People discuss how well the meeting went. Everyone is happy, but nothing ever happens.

If you are trying to ramp sales, you cannot afford to be involved in these meetings. You need the attention of the decision maker, and you need to go around the happy meeting people and get a directed result that picks your technology and product as the solution. As the sale progresses, the meetings should become shorter and shorter and eventually the meetings should be turned over to your technical staff to begin the implementation planning.

Happy meetings are but one technique that is the kiss of death. Other examples are happy calls and happy talks. Happy calls usually end with a potential customer stating something like, "I will have to run your idea through our company process." Right away you are dealing at the wrong level. Happy talks are face-to-face versions of happy calls.

My assessment may seem harsh, but I have seen a lot of sales go south, and the thing that is the initial kiss of death is the advent of happy calls, talks, and meetings. If you are not able to control the direction of the sale and the process begins to get happy, you must ratchet up the level of management involvement, or you will lose the sale. If you are managing a sales force and the sale starts to turn happy, you must get it on track. Once we get to the happy point in a sales cycle, the sale will not turn into a big deal because we are talking to the wrong people.

Free Work

The biggest problem in technology marketing is that you, as a salesperson, are selling a highly intangible idea—an improvement of some sort. Generally, to make the sale it must be an improvement sale. You promise to improve productivity, quality, speed of job completion, etc. What is difficult to measure is the real benefit. Thus, there is a wide range of methods when trying to sell the high-technology product. Some methods try to measure quality, some speed, and some even try to measure the life-cycle cost or life-cycle improvement of a process or product.

The problem with these types of sales is that the buyer has a lot of power (or at least thinks so). In fact, assuming that the technology actually works, the buyer has two choices: adopt the new technology and take whatever process improvements the new technology promises, or persevere and attempt to get through with current capabilities. This creates two types of customers. The first is the early adopters, and the second is the customers who only buy once the technology has become a commodity.

You will hear a variety of answers from customers as to why they are not willing to buy a product. "You are too early in my deployment cycle." "You are too late in the deployment cycle." "We have outsourced the operation of that department." And then there is the kiss of death comment, "I would buy it if it just had XYZ."

That sentence is the bane of all technology sales people. The usual salesperson starts to slobber as that sentence comes to mind. They have a sale. All they have to do is to get the development department to make one little addition to the product, and then it is a vacation in Tahiti, a new BMW roadster, and easy street. The only problem is that the buyers have no intention of buying. If you press them, they will claim that they are going to buy, but the reality is that either they don't want the product or they are not the decision makers.

If you are dumb enough to make the product change, they will just add another item to your list the next time you come back with the "required" feature in your product.

In the military, this is called requirements creep. This is how you get a $400 hammer or toilet seat. Someone wants to buy a common device, and before you know it, a group of people have started to add "required" features to the procurement. Magically, the item has now become a major purchase and the costs have gone way up.

No product ever has all the functions and features that a customer wants. No product is ever complete. Start with a purchasing committee. Next, add in a diverse set of requirements. Now you have a divided committee that can't agree on a purchase. But most products that contain unique functions can be sold on the basis of need. The strategy is simple: This product contains the most advanced features available and it provides a set of benefits that will improve your productivity. The lack of one insignificant feature is not a detriment to the product and, thus should not stop the purchase of the product.

Marketing and sales get paid to sell a product, and if the only thing standing between them and a sale is one feature, they will try to get the development plan modified to incorporate that one feature. But that change will not get the product sold. If the technology is new and innovative, the fact that the user needs the extra feature means that either the user has not gotten approval or the user doesn't have the authority to buy the product.

Simply put, I am trying to sell a brand-new product. It does not have a direct competitor. It brings benefits that are quantifiable to the user of the product. What possible reason could there be not to buy the product? Only one: The customers cannot buy it for institutional reasons or they are not the decision maker. In either case, they will still have the same problem if you return with the modified product.

The correct approach to this situation is to collect customer feedback and develop an overall strategy on how the product is to evolve. When customers say they will buy if you just had this one feature, your response is that this request will go to the product development group and they'll put it on the development schedule. You can then get back to the customers with the estimated date at which the feature will be included. The customers then have to decide if that's satisfactory or admit that they really do not want or need the product.

Cultural Sensitivity

One of the most amazing discoveries of the sales cycle is that you can never tell what someone is about to say. This has truly amazing ramifications. After doing everything right, it is possible that a simple comment can completely kill a sale and ruin all of the hard work that has been done to get the sale. There is an incredible degree of polarization, and it is really difficult to stay out of trouble. One person's joke is another person's slur. How do you get around this mine field? It is simple: listen, stick to business, and really get to know the customer.

In fact, behavior that can lose a sale can be very subtle. You must always be on guard, and you cannot make any untoward comments or requests. Don't assume that you understand another culture. If there is any question, you need to ask, confirm, and validate any assumptions that you make. You must be sensitive to your environment. That includes culture, organization, users, management bias, and pace of movement. You need to be flexible and able to react quickly so that you do not get blindsided or flustered by strange happenings. Just like riding down the face of the wave, you need to be alert and flexible.

In a sales situation, you cannot carry any stereotypes or biases into the process or you stand to lose the sale. In particular, when you are trying to sell a big wave–type product based on new and potentially radical technology, you must be absolutely focused on the job and avoid any bias or comments that can be misconstrued.

It is easy to make a mistake and make people feel uncomfortable. Because I am from Montana, my view of food is that if it did not start with hoofs, it probably is not edible. At a sushi bar in the Bay Area, a friend was trying to convince one of his customers that my firm should be brought in to do some work. The potential customer was of Japanese descent and had picked this particular restaurant because it was his favorite. In fact, he had ordered all of us his favorite sushi sampler platter. I could eat everything, but I was having a real problem with the raw baby octopus. As we ate, it was being avoided. Clearly, my friend Tom was not having the same problem, as his baby octopus was gone right away. When I got to the baby octopus, Tom leaned over and said how much he liked the sushi platter, but in particular how good the baby octopus was. He wondered if he could have mine so that he didn't have to order another complete platter. That was a wish that was gladly granted, and everyone saved face.

Another subtle problem occurred in a steakhouse. The waitress brought out a large knife for each person at the table. She carefully placed each knife in a position that from her viewpoint was correct, but to our Japanese customers the knife placement indicated that they should consider suicide. The customers politely asked if we could rearrange the silverware. That was an easy request to grant.

These are all clearly easy things to be aware of, but some things can get very subtle. It is important to really listen and pay attention because something that can kill your sale is very easily done.

The most subtle example I recall was associated with a tie.

In the mid-1980s, I was in the product analysis business. The company worked in the area of technology analysis and projection. It offered product analysis and projected trends and used this information to design system updates and evolution strategies. In simple terms, we tried to keep up with state-of-the-art products and design systems using these products. There were a number of other companies that had similar offerings. Many of these other companies looked at the problem through market analysis. They tried to project what companies, technologies, and trends would be the leaders. Sometimes, they used this information to design a system.

In one case, we were invited to submit a bid on a system design job. The customer had already narrowed down the field to us and another group whom we will dub "the confederates." The confederates were a formidable foe and had a market analysis approach, whereas we had the aforementioned product approach. Eventually, we won the contract and set off to do the job.

Over the time with this particular job and later follow-on work, a number of interesting things were observed as we became close friends with the customers and their families. They were an interesting bunch. Between them, our families, and the children who spanned a variety of ages, it made for some interesting dinners and social events. One thing that always amazed me about this particular customer was the emphasis top executives placed on proper dress and grooming. Proper dress in the software business in the 1980s could be a ponytail, T-shirt, jeans, flip-flops, and a Mountain Dew. These customers were in the big pharma industry, and all of the executives dressed very well and had a very spectacular executive dining room. Unlike most companies, this company did not have the usual batch of corporate logo stuff hanging around. In most companies, there are coffee cups with logos, pens with logos, golf balls with logos, folders with logos, etc. You name it, logo stuff is everywhere. Not so in this company. You could go through the company offices, cafeteria, and executive dining room and nary a logo was to be found except for the signs indicating the company's name on the walls. Pretty unusual!

There was one serious anomaly in this whole equation. Periodically, you would see someone in the executive dining room and even a couple of times on the factory floor who was wearing a tie that was in the company colors and had a small company logo on it. In fact, numerous times when I saw both my customer and his associates in the dining room, I wondered if the people were color blind, because no matter what color their clothes, they always wore this one tie. In fact, I wondered if my client only owned one tie. But it was really none of my business, so I never bothered to ask. At the time we won the initial job, my customer quit wearing his logo tie and began wearing a wide variety of ties that were color coordinated.

Over time, we performed a couple of tasks for this company.

After the last task, we were at dinner and the customer asked whether we would like to know why we had won the job. Clearly, we wanted to know. This particular company was founded and run by a gentleman who viewed his company's logo as very important—so important that it should not be used or displayed without a specific and compelling business purpose. That accounted for the lack of logo material around the company. In fact, the only logo-bearing items were the ties. The ties were awarded each year to a very small number of employees. There may have been less than thirty ties in the company. This made ownership of a tie an incredible honor, and you would wear it every day of your work life so that everyone knew you were one of the high achievers.

When we were competing for our contract, the confederate salesperson, being a collector of corporate logo memorabilia, had asked about getting a logo item and had been told that there were no such items. Being an aggressive and observant salesperson, he had then asked the customer if he could have his tie because it had a logo on it. The customer looked over at his boss and simply took off his tie and gave it to the salesperson. The next day, they awarded us the contract. The customer had felt that the confederate group was not in tune, and by asking for the tie it had crossed a barrier, and the client would not do business with the confederates. The reason the customer then wore regular ties was that the president of the company only gave you a tie when you had earned it. If you gave it away, you did not get another until you again earned it.

In 1987 dollars, the tie was worth over $100,000.

Listen to the customer, stay focused on business, and be careful to not offend people.

Your Champion

The key to this technology marketing problem is to find the technology champion and get that potential champion on your side. The best and quickest way to sell a new technology product is to find an early adopter with vision and get the early adopter to champion your product.

To get a quick sale, we need to have a unique product, a great value story, and a champion. Actually, we need the early adopter to be a trinity man and function as the money guy, the champion, and the pusher. In many cases, in a small company, these functions will be held by one person, but in big organizations, the functions may be handled by three or more persons.

It is incumbent that we have the blessing and, in fact, that we have the insistence of the money guy that the product we are offering be purchased. The money guy has to buy into the product purchase and implementation. The money guy is the key. The money guy controls the system functions and the budget to pick what is implemented in the system. Once the money guy buys into the new functions, it is necessary to set the process in motion. The usual strategy is to have a phased rollout of the product into the system. We want to get a series of product rollouts. We start with an initial proof of concept demonstration and have that morph into the first product site before rolling across the total system enterprise.

Because of the amount of work involved in the process and the duties of the money guy, the money guy may make a decision to let someone else lead the day-to-day charge in implementing the product purchase. This person is our champion. This person knows that he is under the direction of the money guy to make the project happen. The champion reports to the money guy and acts on his behalf to ensure that the project moves ahead. There may be competing projects, products, etc., but the function of the champion is to overcome any arguments or obstacles put in front of the project. He is the agent of change and represents the money guy. The money guy probably doesn't have the time to personally shepherd the project through all of its hurdles, and the purpose of the champion is to push the project through. In general, the sales interface is to get the money guy on board and then interface with the champion to ensure that the project moves swiftly and successfully to completion. In helping to set up the champion, it is important to assist in finding the champion. You want a champion who wants to make the boss a hero rather than wanting to replace the boss.

Because of the issues and the personal relations necessary to push through a major project, a third function or person may become involved in the project on a day-to-day basis. This is the gopher (or pusher), and the function of the gopher is to push through the paperwork that is required by the bureaucracy to implement the project. It is the function of the salesperson to stay in contact with the gopher to push the paperwork through the system.

In some cases, the salesperson will have one contact, but in a large purchase, the salesperson will have to deal with different contacts, and that requires different personal skill sets.

We have now set up our first sale, but the real trick is to replicate this as fast as possible, because the way to really get the wave going is to set into motion a number of early adopters and get them all in a race to be first, biggest, most successful, etc. based upon implementing your new functions. If we can get enough of these early adopters in play, we can create a massive initial sales cycle and drive the product into a premier position in the market.

The downside is that in each organization there are a number of people involved in the sale. Some of these people have cozy relationships with existing vendors and salespeople. Because of this, the second that we have exposed our product to the potential customer, we must run hard. The existing vendors and other potential competitors know that we are in the process of a major sale. Suddenly, the entire competitive environment will become energized. The key to our success is that we have the money guy, champion, and gopher in our corner and the ball is already moving in an unstoppable way.

A good salesperson gets groups of early adopters energized at the same time and begins to drive the wave on to the shore.

Once a couple of early adopters pick up your product, the sales cycle will become easier. As the new functions become widely accepted, you will need to modify your value statement. But you will have reference accounts. Your position on the wave will be constantly changing, and you will need to make constant adjustments to your strategy.

Chapter Summary

As our product develops into a functional and salable system, we need to bring on a marketing big wave surfer. The key to success for the salesperson is the ability to articulate the uniqueness and benefits of our product. The salesperson must construct a solid value statement and be able to position the uniqueness of our product.

As we pick up momentum, competition will try to blunt our efforts, but a great marketing person will be able to adjust our product positioning, find early adopters, and close sales, keeping us firmly moving down the face of the wave.

Chapter 12

Extreme Technology Investing

I have been careful to state that this book is not primarily about money. There are many ways to achieve satisfaction in your life. Well, this chapter is all about the money. It is really only about the money. One absolute measure of things is how much money you have. In this chapter, the big wave surfer is an investor. Thus, it should be no surprise that people go for the jugular when money is involved. When possible, they will try to take your money. Many times, people will tell you how to deal with money guys such as venture capitalists, but if you assume they are anything but an adversary you are wrong.

When it comes down to measuring your ability as a big wave surfer, investors measure the size of the waves you ride. Then they look at your form and how well you ride the waves. Eventually, a champion is crowned at a competition. There are, however, many big wave surfers who are really good, but only a few who are really great. It seems that most of the big wave surfers ride the waves for the thrill and sensation of riding the big wave. But the great ones want to be the best at what they do.

In the technology business, one of the only ways we can measure the success of the big wave surfer is by money. How much did you make? How big was the contract win? How big was your commission? Did you get an initial public offering done? Who are your investors? There are many ways to measure the money factor. We will look at some of the issues associated with technology investments, and we'll see if we can understand how money is made in the technology business.

It is helpful to let you know about the Weasel. He was a very successful broker. In fact, he was the prototype of a very successful guy who always wanted to be more successful. He worked about six hours a day and left his work at the office all of the time. He played hard and had all of the requisite toys. He had boats, a fancy house on a lake, a deer hunting camp, a farm, etc.—all of the toys that make for the good life that hard-driving, very rich people should have in their lives. He enjoyed his life quite a lot.

The Weasel had an interesting reputation and sometimes had an interesting habit. It was said that he would go to any extreme to take your money on a stock trade. In fact, he claimed that he would smash your hand over a quarter. To prove his point, he would sometimes set a quarter on the table when you were talking to him. The running joke among his friends was that you did not want to pick up the quarter, or even reach for the quarter, because he would smash your hand to bits to keep the quarter from you. I never discovered if this was true because I never knew anyone who tried to pick up his quarter. But the type of personality that will be successful at technology investing would smash your hand!

In this chapter, we will be dealing with a different personality when dealing with moneymen and the investor community. Remember that the category of guys we will be talking about is the same quality group of people who brought us the savings and loan crisis, hedge fund firms such as Long-Term Capital Management, and the recent mortgage melt down. They also funded companies such as the Internet pet supply company whose only claim to fame was their stupid little advertising puppet who told you to buy pet food via the Internet rather than down at your local pet food store. Many of the people we may encounter have no real skills other than what they were taught in business school, and they may have a very naïve view of what it actually takes to make a company or a product a success. Corporate success does not necessarily equate to huge financial success (although it helps). Making matters worse is the fact that they may not be playing with their own money. When you play with someone else's money, you take on a fiduciary duty. You must put their interests first. This ethical situation can be a problem because what may be best for a customer may not be best for the investor in the short term. The fiduciary duty of a money manager is to maximize the return on investment regardless of the consequences. That goal may not be in the best interest of the company you are trying to build. I may not be kind to venture capitalists in this chapter, but they provide the same function as tow-in surfing where a personal watercraft is used to accelerate the surfer. In this case, the reason you should use venture capital, if you can get it, is to accelerate your growth.

In the end, I will give you one way to pick technology stocks from an investment point of view, and with a little luck, you will be able to understand why you can make money in some stocks and others turn into disasters. If you are a business school guy, when you get to the end of this chapter and have read about my strategy, you will be tempted to dismiss me as a hot money guy. I am not a hot money guy, and my strategy does not depend on being a hot money guy. I want to go where success is happening, and then I want to put in place a strategy of controlling my risk. Finally, if I get it right, I want to concentrate and leverage up. If I get up on a big wave, I want to ride it as long and hard as I possibly can because I never know if there will be another wave coming along. At the same time, I do not want to get killed, so I will take precautions to preserve my capital.

Principle: They'll Take Your Money

The finance industry has developed procedures that are aimed at managing corporate development and product risk. They also have developed a strategy that is designed to ensure that they move their risks to other people. Whether your technology has matured to the point of cashing out as a publicly traded company or is simply a promising emerging company, the money guys are not fools. Whenever possible, they are trying to take your money.

The single best way to tell if you should jump off the wave is when the rate of increase in profits drops below the rate of increase in revenue.

Investor Types

If we are to achieve real growth as we get our product into its marketing stage, we need to add a large amount of money to accelerate product development and sales. **Figure 12-1** illustrates our current position on the wave. We are now adding the last component, investors, to ensure a fast descent on a big wave.

There are two main categories of investors: accredited and nonaccredited. The real difference between these categories is that in one category we have rich guys. In the accredited category, there are usually investors who have either a high net worth or a high relative income over the past few years. They become accredited because they have the financial means to sustain losses on investments if that were to happen.

Fig. 12-1: Technology Big Wave Structure—Investing

Generally, accredited investors have access to different types of investments due to their ability to take on risk. Usually, the accredited investors deal with a wider array of financing vehicles. They can invest in hedge and venture capital funds. They are also allowed to be involved in private placements. The definition of an accredited investor changes over time as defined by the Securities and Exchange Commission. Other than noting that both categories exist and to simplify our discussion, we'll look at investors and investment strategies without regard to whether you need to be accredited.

There are many types of investors who tend to invest in high-technology stocks.

Typically, the investors specialize in different markets. Some invest primarily in private deals. Included in this category are angels and venture capitalists. Both of these groups like to invest in high-risk, early-stage deals that are in the formative stages. We will simply call this group of investors the initial investors. Generally, you are not going to be in the category of an initial investor unless you are an accredited investor. The way to be an initial investor without being an accredited investor is to be one of the founders. Otherwise, you must already have a lot of money and meet the criteria of an investor or group that can afford to lose all of your money if you want to invest in early-stage, high-technology deals. The advantage of this type of investing is that although you are taking high risks, you are hoping to (and in many cases you will) make a large profit. In investing, you will not make a large profit without taking large risks. There are different types of early-stage investors. In some cases, they are pools of investors, and in other cases, they are single investors or invest family money. In a large number of cases, this money is provided through institutional channels, and the actual investment comes from a liquid pool of investment capital that is contained in a limited partnership.

The next group of investors are the mezzanine players. Generally, these players are part of well-known financial institutions and they provide the capital after the company seems to be on its way to success. Generally, they fill in the gap until the company is able to go public.

Finally, if the company goes public, then the public shareholders will be allowed into the deal and the stock of the company will trade on an exchange.

Once ownership has passed to the public, there are a large number of "funny" investors that can come into play. That's why companies periodically go private if they get put into play by hedge funds and other types of institutional investors who are trading the companies and trying to figure out their value based on a variety of economic models.

We have ignored a critical yet vital form of investor in this discussion: the founders. In any new company, there are the founding investors, the people who cook up the basic idea and then try to get the funding to develop the ideas and build the companies that eventually go public or get acquired.

If a company is successful at developing a product and executing its business plan, the founders can be amply rewarded, but usually the founders are too aggressive and optimistic and end up aced out of their fair share of the results. In the technology investing business, money trumps technology. There are way more ideas than money to fund the ideas. The usual error of the founders is to have a business plan that is too aggressive. The founders sell the company concept through rose-colored glasses. When the plan is not met, the venture capitalists who provided part of the start-up capital take advantage of the overly optimistic founders by refinancing and equity dilution provisions. This ensures that the venture capitalists get extremely outsized gains if the company is successful. The founders no longer have a choice or a say in how the company is run due to missing their business plan goals (aka lacking proper cash flow).

If you are good and lucky and have a unique product, you might make a lot of money. In most cases, you will just make a lot of money for other people.

The success of a large number of high-profile, start-up technology companies keeps bringing them back to try again, but the Apples, Microsofts, and Oracles of the world are few and far between. The huge amounts of money that are made in these well-known names sets the stage for the need to try to ride that wave.

There are a near infinite supply of technology guys available to make a grab for the brass ring, and they keep getting chewed up. But the only way to ride the wave is to get up on it and take your shot. Unless you have your own money, you are really stuck trying to make it happen with other people's money and all the attendant risks, rewards, and constraints that go with taking another person's money. We have previously talked about the issues and techniques that are necessary to run a company. In this chapter, I will tell you how to hit it big as a technology investor.

Stopped Clocks

It is helpful to remember that even a stopped clock is right twice a day.

You will encounter many investors every day. With the advent of defined contribution pension plans (401(k)s and their equivalents) almost everyone is an investor in some way. The government encourages savings and investment in the stock market.

Investment talk is all the rage. There are entire television channels devoted to the stock market, and there are cult figures that have developed around these channels and their on-air personalities. Retirement talk is all the rage. Some of the personalities are wild and crazy but may actually have ideas that make sense. One of the wildest is Jim Cramer of CNBC's *Mad Money*. Cramer tells you how he thinks you can invest your mad money—your risk capital. He does not tell you what to do with your real savings and investment account. Is he right? Who knows. The market is a really neat animal. Even if you get the right answer, it may be an issue of the quality of your execution that determines the end result. Cramer has his fans and detractors, but no one can doubt his passion.

So how do we get to be rich or to retire rich? One way is to create a company. Be a successful big wave surfer!

"Too much work," you say. Another way is to work for a long time and pay attention to your money. I have no doubt that if you follow the conventional wisdom of working for a company, saving money in your retirement account, collecting the company matching funds in your retirement account, and watching your asset allocation over the years, you will have a large and ample retirement fund. However, that is not what this book is about and this chapter is about making the green stuff, and that is not a strategy that big wave surfers would embrace. They need risks, thrills, and big returns.

Another option is to be a conventional retirement-oriented investor and put aside a little mad money to see if you can get it done in the market—not an unreasonable strategy with a little upside, and it might even give you a little fun on the side.

What does the surfer think is a good strategy? A very successful broker that I knew had a saying: "The only way to preserve capital is to double it as fast as possible." Now that's got the makings of a big wave strategy! Let's go out and double our capital today. If we can do that, we are on a roll. If you are young, a big wave strategy is to make that mad money pool big and go for it. You do not have to worry. If you make a mistake, you will have a long time to compensate for errors. This is in contrast to the conventional wisdom that wants to have a consistent and prudent savings rate for the time of your working life.

The issue is whether you have the stomach and guts to go for it early. If you mess it up, you will always have time to recover. Early in your working career, you have simple needs, and if you can satisfy your basic needs, maybe you can pull out ten or twenty thousand dollars and take a go at it. If you get into a position of being able to go for it and you make it work, then you will be very far ahead and can then afford to go with the more conventional approach. Because I have your attention with this unconventional approach, let's go for it. How many stocks should you buy? How about one! Many of the financial advisors in the world have been taught that you need a diversified portfolio with an asset allocation that reflects your age. In my opinion, one stock is an appropriate asset allocation for a young person. It is also appropriate for older people with risk capital. Diversification just kills the return on your aggressive and successful investments. Diversification is the bane of portfolio performance.

If you are under thirty, your asset allocation should be one stock. If it's possible and you are winning, put that stock on full margin. We just killed 30 percent of the world's financial advisors—even the mad man Jim Cramer just had heart failure. But when I am right, I want to capitalize and make a big run. If I am right, I want to go for all of the marbles right there and not hold back. I want to get it done at the exact moment of being right!

Lastly, if you have the money to try this strategy, but don't intend to use margin, then use your IRA or 401(k) if possible. Take that money in an IRA, and implement this strategy. IRA money is interesting money because you have no immediate tax considerations or consequences to worry about. I do not want the trading to be influenced by a long-term capital gain strategy so I like IRAs. Tons of high-tech geeks lost their proverbial shirts trying to take stock purchased with stock options and convert the stock into long-term capital gain status in the early 2000s. Pay your taxes when you have to! Just in case you have not noticed, the remaining financial advisors in the world just died. If they were so smart, they would be rich, so why should you pay attention to them anyway? If you have a little risk capital and are young, this is a must-try strategy.

However, you must control your losses. When you get concentrated and leveraged up, you cannot afford to take a serious loss or give back your gains. Further, you cannot afford to buy a stock that has a statistical probability of being a loser. So I would initiate this by buying the stock in the portfolio as it hits a new high. In every sense the conventional wisdom is that your risk profile is off the charts if you adopt this strategy. But do you think that the guy riding down the face of a sixty-foot wave has no risk? He is risking his life; you are risking a little money. You have the ability to set stop losses and cut your losses. You can set up your entire life in just a couple of trades. Do you think that there is no risk? Surf's up!

Why do I want a stock hitting a new high? There have been studies that show the most likely trend of a stock is its current direction, and that is the bet I want to make. If the stock is hitting a new high, its most probable course is to continue on up! Yes, this seems like a very dangerous strategy, but if we buy a breakout and are careful to contain our losses, we will have a high probability of success.

We will talk more about this subject in later sections, but remember that even a stopped clock is right twice a day. We only need to be right for a short period of time, and if we are right a couple of times, we can get it done. We can live the good life and have the big toys.

Paradigm Shifts

At points in time, it seems that all hell breaks loose in the technology business. At these points, there is some change in the basic paradigm under which business is done. It could be a new technology or the introduction of a far superior product into the product mix. You must be careful at the inflection points because to get maximum gain you cannot be too early or too late. You must catch the wave at the exact inflection point.

These points of inflection are difficult to judge and to catch because they tend to jump into the spotlight quickly. In many cases, these shifts are unseen, and by their very nature they are not predicted by any pundits or other luminaries.

It is the essence of the investment monies to be made in technology that you be able to spot and capitalize on these trends and changes in direction.

If you are in early, you will probably not leave money on the table. You may wait for a long time with dead money, and in fact, the technology may never come to fruition. Yet the greed factor says that you want or need to get in early when making your investment.

An old development joke is that it is a good thing that more products are conceived than developed and more products are developed than sold and that only a few thousand products actually make significant sales, or we would not be able to satisfy the demand for development talent. This is the too early problem. You want to get into a company from an investment strategy as early as possible, but you do not want to buy manure.

However, you do not want to be too late. You do not want to get into the investment strategy so late that you invest in a company at its peak stock price (top tick the company's stock price). You do not want to be too late once everyone else has gotten into the stock and you are the greater fool who buys the stock.

In terms of selling a technology or product that is new, this is also one of the sales conundrums. From a customer's viewpoint, you do not want to be too early or too late.

The rate of profit-margin gains and losses are the key to determining where you are in the cycle of too early or too late.

Paradigm shifts also occur in both start-up and existing companies. As we will see later in this chapter, margin shifts will be the key to sensing the time frame in investing.

Big financial firms have hundreds of analysts trying to figure out every nuance of the environment. How are you going to beat these highly capable professionals? Just remember that they have tons and tons of money to invest and the problem of keeping it in play and invested. You do not, as an individual investor, have that same problem. You are the master of your own destiny. You can sit on the sidelines until your conditions have been met.

Your challenge is to determine when the wave has started to form and if it is real enough to be a big wave. You could have millions of dollars and not even affect the investment world. The markets today are huge and liquid.

You just have to figure out the timing of the investment.

Synergy Strategy

One of the classic problems is synergy. The idea of synergy is pretty simple: Two parts, when put together, have a bigger combined value than the value of the parts if they were simply added together.

The idea is as old as investing itself. Can we take two similar or complementary companies, add them together, and get a new company that is more valuable than the sum of the values of the companies we are combining? For example, are there add-on sales that would result from having two products that we can combine into a package deal? In the consumer market, this is known as a product with product sale. If you buy item A, you get to buy item B at a reduced price. In the business of running companies, it is common to pursue a synergy strategy either by acquisition or partnering. Partnering has become the rage, particularly with large companies, but you need to be wary of the teaming agreement. Most teaming agreements contain a good faith negotiation clause that lets the other company off the hook if it chooses not to do business with you after the contract is won.

The synergy argument is a powerful argument in the technology business. The idea is that by combining two companies you get both product lines and the potential for product up-sells. Further, you can select the best of each company's staff as you pare down the workforce, which will obviously have duplications as it is combined into one cohesive, synergistic, focused vanguard of triumph. The basic idea is that you can increase sales while you reduce expenses. If things were really this easy, you would be able to juice the earnings and get the stock price up.

Periodically, in the technology business, this merger and acquisition process gets going. One of the dirty little secrets that no one talks about is that by combining, you also eliminate your competition and you can begin a process of trying to dominate a market. Further, if you are a large company, you can take technology off the street that might threaten your basic product position and keep competition from happening in your core markets. But you would never say such a thing for fear of hearing that the Justice Department wants to talk to you. Thus, synergy is the argument.

There are a few problems when you go into this type of

strategy. No matter what one says in the beginning, there will be one set of management that wins and one that loses. There is no such thing as a merger of equals. There is only one big wave surfer standing at the lectern. Further, synergy is never an easy, practical proposition because there are all of these little details like whose vacation policy we choose. By the time we get the answer, we have ended up with the most generous health policy of the two as well as the most generous vacation, sick leave, family leave, etc. Then all of those glorious synergistic savings have just gone up in flames and the merger is not performing well.

During the golden age of synergy when conglomerates were all the rage, they were putting everything imaginable together. Some things do not make sense, like putting together a pizza company and a software company, but in the next technology bubble, you should expect someone to try just that.

The promise of synergy is that two plus two will yield five.

Lean Companies

Sometimes we have a company that suffers from performance problems. The company gets bloated and has too many people in marketing and sales, production and product development are stagnant, and the place is generally a mess. The conventional solution to this problem is to go lean and mean and get the company back on track. There are a number of strategies to accomplish this feat. One often-used strategy is to look at the company and analyze its strategic business approaches. Get the company oriented toward its core competencies, and lean it down to get those profits down to the bottom line. The strategy is to make the company lean and mean by taking it apart.

Once the core business strategies are delineated, we can get down to brass tacks and jettison the businesses that are not essential to our well-being. Usually, going lean is a two-step process.

First, we will jettison any nonessential businesses, and then we will lean down the remaining strategic assets.

However it happens, it is difficult to stay focused upon the core business of the company. Inevitably peripheral stuff sneaks into the mix and chews up resources, and we need to get rid of this stuff. Throw out the nonessential businesses. At the very minimum, they take up management attention. Even when the business is pared down to its essential core, there are a lot of nonessential parts left that can become more productive and increase the profit of the company.

The issue is what to do with the assets and business parts. Usually, the nonessential parts are sold off and then the management gets rid of (fires and terminates) the excess employees.

The promise of lean and mean is that you can increase the margins and get strategic focus by shrinking the basic company so that it is refocused.

If you started with two companies and combined them to get synergy and in the process created a really profitable company, would you ever take them apart and get them lean and mean, thus further raising the profit? If you did this enough times, maybe you could get yourself a company with $30 or $40 billion of sales and only one employee. You need to really be wary of this synergy and lean and mean nonsense. Did AOL and Time Warner really generate any synergies when they combined? Did they really get any better when they eventually were taken apart?

The combining and spinning out of companies is an area of investing in which you really have to take the management's and Wall Street's words and pass them through a giant grain of salt. Actually, six-foot salt cubes may be too small.

This is not to say that all mergers or all spinouts are good or bad. It is to say that the investment landscape is littered with the corpses of companies that died on the assumption of lean and mean or synergy. No matter what the basic story, the road to success is littered with the bodies of dead companies that were involved in merger and acquisition strategies or leveraged buyouts.

Early Departure

One of the biggest problems I have had with my own investing is that I left the party too early. Once you get a technology stock that is moving and generating big earnings from product sales, you will be tempted to sell your stock. Don't! Set some stops, and hope that things continue to go your way.

If you are ahead, you are playing with other people's money and you can afford to let your winnings ride. You must remember that technology stocks are highly volatile, so you must be very careful not to mistake a loser stock for a normal correction. This is one of the toughest problems you will encounter. You are trying to judge whether a stock will really be another Cisco, Microsoft, Google, or Apple. If you get it right and get in early, you will make a ton of money. But eventually even these stocks will have their comeuppance.

One of my brokers once said to me, "They go up until they go down."

The naked truth of this is what kills investors. Your stock just hit a new high, or your stock just jumped 15 percent in one day. What should we do? Most people would sell. My advice is to think about what is going on here. If the trend is really your friend, then maybe you should exercise some restraint and stick with the stock you own and know. Dance with the girl who brought you to the dance! Why would you want to switch to another stock? Remember Google, Microsoft, Cisco, and other long-running technology stocks. All you really have to do is find one and control your risks.

Once we own one of these stocks, the big problem is when to sell. That is really the subject of this chapter. How do we find such a stock, and once we do, how do we know when to leave the party?

Finding such stocks is really quite simple. Leaving the party will also be quite easy. What will be difficult will be to stay for the time that we need to stay to get that part of the gain that is available to us.

The key issue is the purchase of your stock(s). If you buy it right, then selling is easy. Buying involves setting up the trade in a way that gets you into the stock so that if you're wrong, you can minimize your losses and get out in a hurry before you lose a lot of money. The key issue to understand is how to set stops. Unless you have the ability to constantly watch the market, you need to have stops in at all times. Another way to cut your losses is to use alerts. If you are in a business where you have the ability to respond if your stock sets off your preset alerts, then you do not need to have a preset alert in place. If I were to criticize my own trading, I would fault myself for not paying enough attention to the issue of stop losses. I can do quite well as long as I stay with the discipline of keeping my stops in place. Even when I get sloppy, I have been successful, but it is much easier if you have your stops set. The difficulty of setting or picking your stop point is the issue of how much money you are willing to give back to stay in the game.

Talking about the other end of the trade—the sell—we must figure out how to get out of our stock(s). This can be quite difficult because every stock is so different in the way it trades. When I talk about how to pick stock(s), I will give you a get-out strategy that is a hard and fast rule. But rather than use trend lines like professional traders do, I will suggest that we want to use semi-log high low close charts. I want to use semi-log charts as opposed to linear charts because semi-log charts allow me to see the slope of the chart and make a quick comparison to the growth rate of the company's earnings trend. I only care about simple daily movements of the stock, so I just use a simple high low close indicator for each day. On these charts, we will be working on setting up trend lines. In the semi-log environment, a trend line corresponds to a rate of growth, and we will correlate that rate to the trend line. The trend is your friend! If our stock breaks the trend line, I am out of there and you should be, too. Every time I failed to heed the breaking of the trend line I have gotten killed. You will also get killed, so when we get to trading the stocks and get our trend line set up, you must execute the trend line discipline. That trend line is the way to set up your stops so that you get taken out automatically.

Cap Rates

One of the key issues in evaluating investments is a concept that I call the cap rate. Various investments use versions of this concept.

Because we are talking about stocks, the variation is the price-to-earnings (PE) ratio. This is the ratio of the reported earnings of the company compared to the current price of the company. It is most useful when it is compared to the growth rate of the company in terms of the company's revenue growth or profit growth.

If we were bond investors, we would look at the yield of the bond in percentage terms. This yield is the amount of interest the bond pays. When the bond starts out, usually the yield equals the interest rate that the bond issue is sold with, but as interest rates go up and down, the bond price changes to provide an adjusted rate based upon the value of the bond if it is resold.

In commercial real estate, the real estate is said to have a capitalization rate, which is essentially the inverse of the yield of the real estate if you owned it free and clear. If the capitalization rate is 15, then the real estate investment effectively yields about 6.7 percent.

Cap rate (or the alternative specific to an investment class) is really a way to try to measure the amount of return that an investment will end up netting you.

For example, with a stock, the return of the stock would be the yearly dividend paid out by the stock plus an appreciation that you expect to get from the stock going up. If the stock goes up and you own it for a long enough time, you may be eligible for preferential tax treatment for long-term capital gains. If you own a municipal bond, the bond may be exempt from federal and state taxes. Thus, when you try to figure out how much an investment yields or its cap rate, you must factor in a lot of different variables.

There are numerous books on the subject of investing that deal with different asset classes and the types of yields and cap rates that you should expect or have been historically provided by the asset class.

But if we want to get up on that big wave and ride for our investment fortunes, we need to look at the specific asset class of stocks that would be owned by a big wave surfer and how you value these assets. This is the class of rapid growth stocks. Stocks where the rate of growth in the sales (revenues) of the stock is going up at an incredible pace are going to be the class of stock that will provide us with the opportunity to take a successful position. In many cases, these stocks may have little in the way of earnings even though they have a high-revenue growth rate.

In trying to find such stocks, we are looking for stocks that have very big revenue growth rates. Earnings (like actual profits) are a bonus. The problem with this type of investment is that in some cases, even though the stock may have increasing revenues, it may be losing money. Eventually, you hope that the company will be able to turn the corner and garner actual profits.

If an investment is truly unique and has a high-growth potential, you would expect that the investment would be expensive. If it has little or no earnings, it will be very expensive. But if the company is growing fast enough and can eventually start to convert the revenue growth into profit growth, then the company can actually be very cheap. This is the type of company we are looking for—a company with big revenue growth and the possibility to get to critical mass before the competition catches up. Therefore, it will be able to bring the profits down to the bottom line. It's like we are on the front edge of the big wave and we're hurtling down at a furious pace, hoping not to wipe out.

If we never achieve profitability, do not make it to our second product, fail to get the profits to the bottom line, or get overcome by events, we end up losing our money.

The return, yield, cap rate, or other measure of financial success says that we are looking for an investment that must by its very nature give us a very high return. Thus, we should not expect dividends, a lot of hard assets, or a low-risk profile.

It is incumbent on us to make informed and rational choices that allow us to manage our risk. Further, the type of company that we will be looking at is a company that is most probably in an area of technology that is not well understood or well developed, so the investment will be controversial.

Our real success will be how well we are able to understand and manage the risk associated with our investment. The higher the potential return, the greater the risk.

The higher the risk, the more return we should demand. In general, if we are going to pay a hundred times earnings for a stock, it had better be growing very fast.

If you think of a stock in terms of cap rate, we will be looking at the universe of stocks that seem expensive. We do not want cheap stocks if we are trying to get maximum gains. Low-cost stocks are not going to have the potential to get that rapid growth rate. Generally, all of the return we expect to get from our stock investment will be in terms of capital gains. If the stock pays a divided, then it does not know what to do with its extra cash other than to return it the shareholders as a dividend. We want to find stocks that have so much opportunity that they need every penny to continue their rapid growth rate.

Simple Game

We are looking for a stock that has a unique product. It also needs to have a market area that has the potential for growth and currently lacks competition. The stocks that we are looking for will always be on someone's list as too expensive. The stock will not be in a mundane business, and it will have a very high projected growth rate.

Only when a stock meets those criteria should we even consider investing in it if we are trying to surf the big wave. If we find one of these stocks, we can get enough money in one good trade to let us sit back and use more conventional strategies for the rest of our lives. Or we could try to compound our gains, but the strategy is to try to make at least one really big hit and lower our risk profile.

We do not want to risk the continual exposure of trying to ride on that big wave every time one comes by and begins to drive for the shore. We want to be selective in our choice of the time and the wave that we pick. We want one or two high-quality rides each time we head out into the ocean. In reality, we are looking to make enough money so that we will not have to constantly be exposed to the risks attendant in trying to make large amounts of money. There are times that no matter how good or smart you are, you will not make money. Further, it is quite often the case that if you have a stellar period of performance, then you will go into a period of underperformance due to the stress of your high-performance period.

If you look at the ocean and think about surfing on a big wave, the ride you take is both physically and mentally stressful. It tends to use up some of your strength. It is not realistic to expect that you can catch one big wave and then immediately go back and catch the next one. The period between consecutive waves is too short. Further, a large number of waves may have to go past before you can catch your second wave. Just go to one of the famous big wave surfing beaches and pick out a surfer. Watch that person for a day, and see how many rides that surfer gets. I assure you that the person will not ride every wave and, in fact, will probably only get in a few rides.

Investing is even worse. You have no idea of how frequent the waves will come or how big they will be. Further, you have no idea when the direction will change and thus you are realistically going to put in multiple, consecutive, high-level performance periods. There are some people who are able to do quite well for long periods of time, but the key is to find a trend and ride it big.

If you are primarily a long investor and the market is in a bear trend, you need to go on vacation because you will not find any reasonable stocks to buy. However, when times are right you will find a lot of opportunity and should go to a fully invested and highly leveraged position. You will know that the time is right if you pay attention to the news. If there is a financial meltdown of the U.S. and world economies, there is no investment that will work on the long side.

In these circumstances, you do have the option of the short side or the short-oriented funds, but being short is usually not something that people are comfortable or good at, and thus, it should be avoided if possible.

I have not known many successful short (bearish) investors. Most of the successful investors I have known buy stocks long, concentrate their positions, and use margin judiciously. This is known as being long and strong. There are times in which short selling works, but the better bet is long and strong.

Financial Futures

Now investment advisors are going to tell you about asset allocation and different classes of assets. They are right on. There are different classes of assets. Before we get into the actual discussion of asset classes, we need to discuss a more fundamental concept: cap rate. The great investors Benjamin Graham and David Dodd analyzed cap rates. However, different asset classes have different sets of terminology to describe what we are going to talk about. I will simplify the basic idea.

When your brokers or mutual fund managers talk stocks, they will talk about PE ratios and their related issues such as price/ earnings to growth (PEG) ratios and other measures like volatility. The PEG ratio is a ratio designed to measure a stock's value, taking into account earnings growth. I like to view things in a simpler fashion. I want to look at the PE ratio and the earnings growth rate and do it on a quarterly basis. The broker will say that a stock is expensive if it has a high PE ratio. However, a stock is only expensive if it has a high PE ratio and a slow growth rate. But do we really know what its growth rate is until the stock has already moved up? The high growth rate may be due to a fundamental change in the growth prospects of the company that has not yet been uncovered by the outsiders.

What that PE ratio tells you is what someone thinks the company's potential future is at any given moment. We are conditioned to think that a high PE ratio is dangerous or makes the stock too highly priced. Let's think about a stock with a PE ratio of 100. Outrageously priced would be the normal reaction of people in the investment game. But what if the stock had an earnings growth rate of 100 percent for the next year? We just bought a stock that will have a PE ratio of 50 in a year if the stock does not go up. What if it could double its earnings again for a second year? Then the stock could really be viewed as cheap.

I want to view all asset classes the same and figure out from there where to invest in the sense of what is cheap and what is overvalued.

Many people have complicated formulas to figure this stuff

out. I just look at the ten-year T-Bill. It has a yield that gives you a fixed rate of interest backed by the U.S. Treasury. Anything else should be compared to that basic investment. If I invest, I want to get a risk-adjusted reward compared to just lending my money to the U.S. government.

Now each asset class has its own language. Bonds have yields. Stocks have PE ratios. Commercial real estate has capitalization rates. But each general class of assets gives you either a potential for growth, an income stream, or both along with some type of tax treatment.

I view the cap rate of commercial real estate as the inverse of the interest rate that the real estate generates without leverage. A bond's interest rate can thus yield a cap rate because the interest rate can be measured as an income stream. A PE ratio can thus be similarly modeled.

Risk can then be compared. You can figure out what the yield or cap rate of an investment is and how it compares to the T-Bill. You can then decide if that rate of return allows for the risk you take on when you buy the investment. You need to adjust the risk you are willing to take as compared to keeping your money safe in your local T-Bill or money market–type account.

You should not invest if you do not get a premium over a safe government bond investment. There are some people and countries that have bonds that you never want to own, but that is another subject.

Entry Barriers

What do I want to see in a company? I want to see a company that for some reason has an unfair advantage. I want to see a barrier to entry. Typical barriers to entry are things like capital, facilities of a certain sort, or special classes of customers.

Some simple types of companies that exhibit the ability to

exploit the barrier to entry strategy are Intel (semiconductors are a capital-intensive business). Similarly, Boeing has facilities that act as a barrier to entry because the structure and facilities to build and certify aircraft are not easily duplicated. Companies such as Lockheed Martin that do massive amounts of classified business have special customers. However, the types of companies that have established barriers to entry are all big, slow, and lazy and will not grow at the rate we need to make big money as an investor.

We need a company that really understands the concept of going for the jugular. The only barrier to entry that it may have is the concept of hard work, fast turnaround, and great marketing.

The big companies will tout their barriers to entry strategy. Remind them of Apple, Microsoft, Cisco, and Dell. These are all companies that did not exist in any significant way in the early 1980s.

Seymour Cray used to say that the only way to protect your product position was to outrun the competition. Let them worry about barriers to entry; just run hard.

However, you must be mindful not to run over another company's intellectual property or you could be out of the game.

When evaluating a company, you need to really understand what they have as a barrier to entry. It is critical. Size and financing are not the solution to barriers of entry. If you are going to ride the big wave, you need a company that is setting up barriers to entry in its new market.

Smell Tests

In evaluating a company's progress and potential, you must be very careful to understand the reality of the situation. Some companies are just not growth companies—never were, never will be. No matter what fantasy they or you are trying to live out, there are just some situations that do not make a really fast-growing company.

Now we can force some companies into a growth mode. But be careful. The ability to force a company or an investment strategy into a growth mode is short lived and may not even be real.

The investment community wants to sell the sizzle. You need to figure out if there is really a steak on the grill when you hear the sizzle. You want to buy the steak, not the sizzle.

Does the concept pass the smell test? One classic example that I encountered early in my career was Equity Funding. Equity Funding was an insurance company that managed to become a growth company in the late 1960s. It had great earnings every quarter and was growing so fast that it became everyone's darling. The only problem was that it was a scam.

How can an insurance company be a growth company? Insurance companies are highly regulated. They must be conservative and not take risks. They are not the type of company to be a growth company. The same could be said of the banking industry in the early part of the twenty-first century. It just does not pass the smell test!

What Equity Funding was doing was creating fake people, insuring them, reinsuring the insurance policies, and then periodically killing off the fake people so that it could collect the reinsurance monies and then create more people. This was a classic version of a Ponzi scheme based on the death of a few fake people. However, the advantage of this scheme was that it could provide a growing and consistent set of earnings because the insiders controlled the death rate of the fake people.

Any time something grows with incredible consistency or grows much more rapidly than its peers, you need to watch out. Variations on schemes led to a string of fiascos: junk bonds, Madoff, Petters Group, Long-Term Capital, Datapoint, Flight Transportation, Micropolis, and Enron, just to name a few. In some cases, they are too far out to be real.

Consider Petters Group, a company local to the Twin Cities

of Minneapolis and St. Paul. It was periodically in the news as a great growth company. Once I had a number of people touting this company to me for the great returns you could get from the bonds, financial notes, and loans the company would provide in return for your capital. The Petters companies seemed to be in bizarre businesses if you were looking for growth and high profits. Companies included Sun Country airlines and Petters Group overstock retail sales outlets. Polaroid and Fingerhut were some of the other primary companies. I have said nasty things previously about the airline business. Overstock sales does not seem like a very profitable business. The camera and film business is lacking in growth. Lastly, Fingerhut just does not seem like a high-growth business. If these were the basic characteristics of the business, how could it generate incredible returns? I never found out because it seemed to be quite implausible, and I never bought into the scheme. In October of 2008, Petters Group Worldwide filed for Chapter 11 bankruptcy. In April 2010, founder and former CEO Thomas J. Petters was sentenced to fifty years in prison for running a Ponzi scheme.

Similarly, after Enron was on a major television show that explained how it made its money, some of my employees talked to me about how such a magnificent company could create such massive wealth. My response was pretty simple. If you do not understand the fundamentals of a business, you should not invest in the business. Petters Group and Enron were doing things I did not understand. But in the course of time, it seems that the principals behind the companies did not understand much either.

Dollar Relationships

Investing in high-technology companies is difficult. The stakes get to be very high, and you can win or lose a lot of money. Thus, I want to ignore the dollar value of investments. This can be very difficult because the amounts of money that we will be talking about can be very large. What if you are lucky and are suddenly playing with sums of money that are larger than your yearly income from other sources?

What if you are really lucky and manage to trade yourself into a position where the daily gain or loss on your portfolio is larger than your annual income from your other income sources? This is going to play with your brain because, unless you are really in the investment business, playing around with large sums of money is not what you have been trained to do. Further, if you have been taking my advice, you probably have a very concentrated position and are susceptible to large daily swings in the value of the investment position.

The solution for this situation is to think of money not in absolutes but in terms of percentages. This is a very difficult task but is about the only way that you can keep your senses. If you are lucky and latch onto a big-moving stock, you need to manage your risk and your fears. Thinking of the amounts will only compound your problems, but if you think of percentages, you can manage your fears when you are in the steep ascent or decline in your net worth.

If you end the day with a large percentage increase in your net worth, you will be pleased, but if you think of the amounts of money that are involved, you will quickly become distracted. Every successful, large individual investor that I am acquainted with uses this technique to control their fears. Stocks that move up fast can also move down fast, and it is when a stock declines that you need clear thinking and complete control of your mental faculties.

We are trying to manage the adrenaline rush and fear that you would experience if you were going down the face of a large wave. You must remain in control of your faculties to avoid disaster.

Additionally, you need the idea of percentages to control your risk. Because percentages are not linear (as previously discussed), you need to think in percentage terms to control your risk, and you do not want to allow large percentage losses to occur.

It is also advantageous to think in terms of percentages if you have any partners, because you do not want to have your partners going through wild emotional swings as the stock market swings wildly about in value and your stock(s) gyrates in value.

Options Curse

Options are a simple concept. The basic and important idea is that options in a start-up will reward the employees for the risks and efforts they are assuming as the company develops and grows. This is a laudable goal. And in many cases, the option strategy works as desired. However, in some cases, the use of options was an absolute disaster due to the tax implications and difference in tax treatment between long- and short-term capital gains.

The goal of the option is to encourage strategies where employees take a serious interest in the welfare of the company. The basic mechanism is that you, as a new employee, are granted an option to buy some number of shares at a fixed price for a fixed period of time. Usually the price is very low because the new company is not worth very much, and there is no good way to value a new company because there is usually no company to compare it to and no real market for the shares. Thus, getting a batch of shares at a low price is a clear advantage because the potential is all on the upside if the company does well.

Because you do not want the employees slacking off after getting their options or quitting shortly after getting their grant, usually the option grant also involves a vesting period. The vesting period allows the employee to vest or actually be able to own the option and be able to exercise it after meeting a time of employment. In many cases, the options vest over a period of five to seven years with one-fifth or one-seventh vesting each year at the option grant anniversary. An employee may receive more than one option grant and may also receive special grants for meeting special performance objectives.

After vesting, the employees can exercise the option and take possession of the company stock if they want. Usually, most employees let the options stay unexercised because they expect the company's stock to continue to get more valuable.

The curse of the options is that every option waters down the percentage of equity owned by the other shareholders. Although the amount of dilution may be small, if enough options are issued, it can be significant over time. But the real problem became visible when large numbers of people exercised options in dot-com companies around 2000 and then did not sell the shares because they had developed schemes whereby they would keep the shares until they had been owned long enough to qualify for long-term capital gains treatment. As the market began to tank, these shareholders ended up owing the IRS more money, based upon the exercised value of the shares, than the shares were worth. Thus, the companies ended up with a large number of employees who owed the IRS a ton of money, had no money, and had discovered the reality that the IRS does not screw around with you. It wants its money, and it wants its money now.

The IRS also has the ability to go in and take its monies out of your paycheck, giving you very little to live on. You can become nearly destitute instantly. Numerous articles in the press documented such cases in 2001 and 2002, but the IRS does not care about your problems. It simply wants its money. And you had better pay up.

Situations like this do not create the desired effect of motivating employees. It is counterproductive because numbers of employees can become more concerned about their personal financial problems than the company's progress. This is one of the curses of options.

Another curse is the problem of granting an option to an

employee who is a nimrod. When you are running a company where options have been granted, you need to make sure that each and every day every employee is focused and dedicated. Employees will be extremely critical of other employees' performance because the value of their options depends on everyone else's performance every day. This is just another curse of options— extreme daily pressure to perform at your peak. This, however, pales in comparison to the problem of the IRS chasing you.

In the debacle of 2000 to 2002, I had personal friends who managed to change millions of dollars of exercised value into zero dollars as they tried to avoid paying short-term capital gains. In the search for the elusive long-term capital gain, they lost everything. Sometimes you just need to pay your taxes.

Initial Public Offerings

The big dream of the big wave surfing entrepreneur, his angel investors, and his venture capitalists (VC) is an initial public offering (IPO). This is the point at which everyone becomes rich. This is what everyone has been looking and working for. If you believe the financial press and the conventional wisdom, this is an easy event. All you have to do is have a great idea, get your venture capital, grow the company, and suddenly you are incredibly wealthy. No! Let's look at reality.

I have had friends who have taken companies to the IPO stage and made a lot of money. But it was not easy and the guys who cooked up the idea were not really the guys who made the money.

Let's look at this process backward, starting from the market point of view. The conventional wisdom from the VC community is that it wants you to move forward, but if you do, you may not understand the process and the risk–reward situation you are looking at.

First, we have to have a market for the stock of the new

company, and we do not have access to the market unless we have an underwriter willing to take our company public. There are only a few companies that have access to the markets, so we will have to deal with one of the underwriting companies and meet whatever terms it wishes to impose. Typically, there are really few companies that actually become successful enough to go public.

Next, underwriters do not work for free. They have to put together all of the paperwork to take you public, and they run certain risks for doing this process. They could get sued if you are a fake company, so they must invest tons of money in due diligence. They may also have to support the market after the offering as the flippers try to get out with a quick and substantial hit. For this process, they will want huge amounts of money, although they will not get paid until the actual birth of the company occurs. It is possible that the investment bank underwriters could make more in fees than the founders make in the value of their equity holdings.

Before we can even get to the point of having a company that could get to a public offering, we need to develop and build a company that has successful product sales. To get the capital to build the company, we may need several rounds of capital financing. We could end up dealing with firms specializing in mezzanine financing, first- and second-round financing, seed capital, and angel investing. At each level of financing, the pie gets cut smaller and smaller in terms of your percentage.

Lastly, we have the employees, initial investors, and angle investors. By this time, we have actually traced our roots back to the guys who had the idea and took the initial risk. But their cut of the deal is so watered down that unless they make a huge fortune for all of the other investors, their share will be small.

In reality, you have as much chance of riding a big wave at Jaws on Maui or at the Banzai Pipe on the North Shore of Oahu as you have of making a fortune with an IPO.

Before you go out to ride the IPO dream wave, you should

look into the statistics. I have friends who have taken numerous companies public. In some cases, they have done well. In other cases, they have done okay, but the amount of money that is made and how it is distributed would make a grown man cry. In one case, a friend made over $3 billion in market capitalization in new start-up companies but he has personally realized only a couple of million in personal profit. Some of the big investors who made hundreds of millions of dollars off of his efforts did not even have the courtesy to return his phone calls to discuss his next idea. When you are dealing with money and Wall Street, you need to be cold hearted and vicious. They are and you need to be. You should have no illusions about the strategies and interest of your investors and the investment banks.

Keep your hands in your pocket and glued to your wallet. If you need capital, you will pay dearly, and you need to understand that in advance!

Directional Trends

There is a large number of days when nothing happens. Just like surfing, there are days when no significant waves break on the beach. Then a storm happens and all hell breaks loose. If you are running a company that is trying to go public, you will not go public unless a bunch of other companies are also in process. Investors tend to run and act like a pack of wolves.

Periodically, you have to be a complete loser not to make money in the markets. If the market is moving up, it will tend to keep going up. As investors become wealthier, they tend to put more money into the market, driving it even further up the value scale. This is human nature. You will know the market has topped when your barber talks about how much money he has made in the market. In some cases, it is easy to spot the top. In one case, a relative was discussing how much money he would be making off his new-found investment in an Internet start-up that had been public for a little time. Based upon suitability and his age, this was a grossly inappropriate investment. This really was a sign. It was the equivalent of your barber ringing the "time to head for the doors" bell to signal that the Internet investment bubble was about to burst.

This phenomenon is simply an observation that a rising tide lifts all boats. When a company is successful, everyone wants to have a similar company and money flows like booze to a drunken sailor who has just gone ashore after six months at sea.

This trend to follow each other over the cliff is observed numerous times in all kinds of manias. It will happen again and will always end badly for a large group of people.

When the storm starts blowing and the waves form, surfers come out of the woodwork and the game is afoot. There is no difference when you are building a new technology company. Once people figure out that a new technology is going to grow like Jack's bean stalk, everyone wants in.

Periodically, one of the companies involved in the mania will disappoint with its earnings or someone will decide that the companies have become overvalued. At this point, all hell will break loose. What everyone wanted just a little while ago is no longer wanted. Even good companies can get caught in this trap because the investment community cannot differentiate between good and bad companies. At the first sign of trouble, everyone will run for the exits.

Once, a particularly good company that I owned, and a similar company, reported earnings on the same day. The company where I owned stock killed the other company's earnings numbers by producing stellar results. The similar company lost market share and produced disastrous earnings. Both companies and lots of related companies got crushed in the market that day. When talking to the Weasel about the issue, he gave me some critically important advice. No matter how well your company does, when investors raid the whore house they take all the girls. And this fact is very important because it will explain a lot of bizarre behavior. The "professionals" begin to look at asset classes that are non-correlated. Then they try to set up portfolios that increase in value no matter what is happening. If they are successful, the word leaks out through the customer-satisfaction channel as customers talk about the results. Then, the competition tries to figure out what is happening, and quickly, there are a ton of other money managers using the same strategy. Then, the raid occurs and nothing works because they are all using the same model and it is like an explosion in a spaghetti factory. There is no way that you cannot be tarred with greasy, messy spaghetti. You can run, but you cannot hide. All of the girls get taken from the brothel at the same time.

You are at the mercy of sector analysis and a herd mentality. When the big waves are breaking, there are piles of money to be made, but when the game stops, there are no places to hide. You cannot make money when the market is going down in your favorite sector, and you need to take your money and go home until conditions improve. It does not matter how well your company does if its sector is not in favor.

You can do all of the fundamental analysis you want, but the reality is that you have no reason to be at risk with your capital unless things are going your way.

Channel Stuffing

A big problem for investors is gauging the realism of earnings. Stocks sell based on expectations, and the ability and proven acumen of the company and its management in meeting and exceeding earnings expectations. However, how they do that is really a black art. The end of a quarter is critical. The end of a year is critical.

A classic example of this reality is channel stuffing. Many times

you can go to a company's management or to its marketing department and ask, "Who buys your product?" In most cases, no one can
give you an answer. They will say the product is sold through our
distribution channels. The end user or purchaser then can register
(or not) the product and only then do we have any feel for the
actual customer who bought the product. This is really a disaster.
If the incentives are right, the salesperson can greatly manipulate
the system and come out way ahead and the company will get a
royal headache.

A classic example happened to a friend of mine. He worked
for Ma Bell before the breakup, and after the breakup, he went to
work for one of the Seven Sisters created by the breakup. After
a while, he got offered a job as the lead salesperson for a small
company that sold local area network products to one of the Seven
Sisters. He was excited as he moved to the headquarters location
of his big customer. This customer had bought a large amount of
his new company's product, and the sales were projected to more
than double in the next year. Yet with such a nice situation, the
salesperson had quit. My friend knew he could go in and, in the
next three months, get the orders necessary to reach that goal and
collect that great big bonus.

A couple of weeks later, we were talking and it was a disaster.
The previous year's sales were $3 million, and for this year (with
three months left), he needed to do over $7.5 million. Not a big
problem, except the customer had not moved any of the $3 million
product. It had not sold one unit. And in fact, it had no intention
of buying any new product under any circumstance until the $3
million was moved.

This was a real problem! My friend thought about this problem
over the weekend, and early in the next week he had a potential
solution. He got his boss to agree to give him about $70,000 in
extra incentive money. His big problem was to move that inven-
tory, get the next order, and then collect his bonus. The solution

was simple. It was based on the premise that it is better to ask forgiveness then ask permission.

The next weekend he went to an upscale jeweler and a Chevrolet dealer. At the Chevrolet dealer he located a red Corvette convertible. At the jeweler, he located four Rolex watches of appropriate value. Then he had flyers printed. The flyer simply said, "Who'll drive the Vette?" The flyer went on to say that the first salesperson who sold a certain amount by a certain date got the Vette as a gift. The next four salespeople who sold a certain amount within a certain time frame got the Rolex watches. On Monday morning when the salespeople came to work, flyers were on their desks. The Vette was parked by the entrance where everyone could see the big sign on it—Who'll drive the Vette? A couple of weeks earlier, none of the salespeople were interested in selling his product. Suddenly, they were interested. Within six weeks, the product was cleared out and he got the big order he was looking for.

The reality was that the product was not very good, and as soon as he got his bonus, he found another job. The only reason the product moved is that the sales force had incentive, or the embarrassment of not being one of the people with the Vette or the watches.

When he got his new job, he discovered that his predecessor had stuffed the channel and then ducked out. He solved the problem by figuring out how to move a bad product, stuff the channel, and move on himself.

What is the earnings reality behind this sale? Were these real sales, or were they simply a fiction of a clever salesperson? What was just described is commonplace, and it gets even more complex and bizarre.

What is the next step? Three million dollars got sold. The next salesperson escaped the $3 million trap but created a $7 million trap. What happens if the next salesperson escapes the $7 million trap? Does the goal go to $15 million? At some point, the stakes get so large that no salesperson will be able to get through the sales cycle. At least not with a position that is realistic, because the management wants larger sales each and every year and quarter. Eventually, the salesperson will miss a goal. This is not a big deal as long as the other salespeople make their goals, and this particular goal is not a big piece of the pie. But you will rue the day if this is an important goal and it is missed. The market will have no mercy.

Day Trading

In the late 1990s and early twenty-first century, the idea of being a day trader was all the rage. This is generally a losing bet. If you are trying to scalp a stock for a couple of points or a quarter of a dollar or fifty cents, you are going to lose over the long term. Not that you are not smart, but you are battling not only other smart guys, but also other smart guys' computers, as well as brokerage houses, hedge funds, and an assortment of other investors who have very sophisticated tools that dwarf the tools you get from your local discount broker. If you really want to try this strategy, just mail your money into Merrill Lynch or Morgan Stanley and save yourself a lot of frustration.

It is really not that bleak. If you have the fortitude to be chained to a computer screen each and every day for hours on end and can sustain long losing streaks (from an emotional as well as financial perspective), you can succeed. There are some really good day traders among my friends, but the emotional characteristics of their makeup are such that they are really unique characters. They are generally happy go lucky, and they have a devil-may-care attitude most of the time. At other times, they are extremely intense to a level of concentration that the work around them seems to go into slow motion as they see the significance of each and every trade that is going by on their screens.

For many days, their lives are very boring and then in a matter of seconds the world turns on and they are in play. It is those few seconds where they make big and large bets that determine what kind of day they will have and how much money they will walk away with.

This is the ultimate form of big wave surfing. You have caught the wave and you sail straight down the front of the wave at maximum velocity. These types of traders are a completely different breed, but if they are successful, they are really successful.

Over time, the stress will burn them out, and with luck, they will end up retired and riding that big ocean cruise boat or some other simple occupation.

How successful are they? I have known traders who had tens of millions of dollars in their IRAs. If they can do it, you might be able to also make your living this way, but you had really better be right each and every day for the rest of your life.

Order Flow

The concept of order flow like that of level-two quotes is the trader's edge. Once the realm of the specialist at the New York Stock Exchange, the concept may give the average investor an even chance to get a good trade and even scalp some points on a trade.

Order flow refers to the information detailing size, position, and execution of orders. At a trading platform, the people running it are really trying to match buy and sell orders. In some cases, they want to do this quickly, but in some cases, they want to destabilize the system so that they get a momentary advantage over the other investors. To do this, they may rely on a whole series of maneuvers.

The basic maneuver is to capture the difference between the bid and ask as many times as possible. All stocks have a bid and ask. If you can create a flow of orders coming into your trading system that are evenly matched, you should be able to capture the difference in price between the bid and the ask price. You will capture the difference between the bid and ask with little, if any, risk, if you can balance the buy and sell orders. Now your profits simply depend on the volume of orders. Further, you can use your knowledge of the flow of orders into your system to let you know when to sell or buy securities for your own account. If you later take the reverse side of the trade, your knowledge of order flow can enhance your profits over just taking the bid ask spread.

For example, if you are seeing a rash of incoming buy orders, you can buy up stock for your own account thus limiting the supply of a stock at a specific price, and when the price goes up, you can sell your stock back into the order flow at a higher price reaping the gains.

Discount brokers and the Internet trading system have taken this to a completely new level. In this case, your discount broker may get paid to provide order flow to a big market maker.

Here is one way this can work. I was short a particular mini-computer stock in the mid-1980s. It was getting pummeled. I was loving the result, the pummeling, not the stock. When, to my surprise, in the middle of the day, the thundering herd announced that the stock suddenly seemed to be a giant bargain even though the company had just announced poor earnings. How can this be? The effect was that the stock suddenly had an order imbalance and stopped trading. Based on the reopening price indication, I was now under water and not very happy. But the projected reopening price was at a level that was high enough that the thundering herd had previously called the stock overpriced. My only choice was to put in an order to short some more. The reason for this was order flow. The New York Stock Exchange specialist was not about to lose money, so he was going to set an opening price where he would not lose money. Further, he was probably going to short all of the losers who would be sucked in by the thundering herd's new recommendation. Last, with a huge trade going up and such a midday reversal of stock opinion, I felt that the thundering herd was clearly manipulating the stock. The herd really wanted to unload its position and its customers' positions. The stock reopened at the high level. It stayed for a little while. It closed up from the lows for the day and then started the inevitable drop back to where the herd viewed it as undervalued. Because it really did have earnings problems, it slowly ground away, settling lower until it eventually was acquired.

But all of the participants, the herd and its clients, the specialist, and the institutional players used knowledge of order flow to gain an advantage over the poor souls who did not have the inside track on what was happening or who did not have enough experience to take what could have been a large risk.

Order flow gives you the information to see where the market can go, and you do not have that information at the retail level. Thus, you need to be careful trading in and out of stocks because it is very difficult to get it right in the short term. You need to look beyond the short-term fluctuations. The key to your success depends on your ability to find situations where a company's stock prospects have a fundamentally high growth rate that may last for months, quarters, or years.

Incremental Margins

One of the great conundrums of my experience is the idea of overhead and general and administrative (G&A) expense. These are normal functions of the business and are the items that have the potential to make or break a technology business. If you set these expenses too low, you do not have enough money to sell your products or develop innovative new products. If you set these measures too high, you do not have enough room to make sure that your prices are competitive, and you attract rapid and vicious price competition even if you have a fortified market with a unique product.

Why are we discussing this topic in the investing chapter? The issue of expense is the key to investing—not in the sense you would normally think of, but in the sense of measuring a stock's growth potential.

Let's develop a perfect company. In this perfect company, we know with perfect knowledge how many products we will sell each and every day and, thus, we know what our quarterly sales will be. This is very nice because we can then develop a detailed financial model of our business and we can determine how much money we need for sales and medical benefits as well as other expenses. We can also set our profit margins and make sure that our competitors do not encroach on our little empire. We have a great company with magnificent predictability. This company is able to set its margins in a way that benefits the company each and every day. The people running the company have perfect insight into the processes and sales cycles.

In our perfect company, we have complete insight into all of the relevant factors that will affect the company.

But let's modify our expenses just a little. Then the dynamics in our company will change. But what will be the effect of these changes? Will they be to our advantage, or will they put us at a disadvantage?

Another type of modification is changes in sales. This can have a tremendous effect on the overall structure because this modification is at our top line and takes place before we apply our expense ratios.

It is these slight modifications of our expense or sales ratios that will make or break our company.

In reality, our company is perfect every morning, because we have a model of where the company is and where it is going each and every day. Sometime during the day, the expenses or sales differ from what we predicted, and that changes the dynamics of the company.

In reality, our margins change. But over a period of time as long as they meet our goals, everything works out. In the case of a public company, this period of measurement is a quarter. If we miss our targets, we will get shot. If we meet our targets, we have a bigger target to meet next quarter. After all, we are big wave surfers and that implies explosive growth and high expectations.

Margin Increase

Assume that our company is profitable.

Let's modify our perfect company. Let's get in a new sales guy—an aggressive, take no prisoners, motivated, big-time sales guy who wants to ride the big wave.

Let's say that the sales guy gets it done. During the current quarter, assume sales double from our projections. If by chance we can fulfill all of these orders, we have a substantially different set of financial results. Our profit margins will increase.

How are we going to fill all of our orders?

Let's make it easy and assume that we are a software company. In this case, fulfillment is easy. Just order up a set of CDs and some paper manuals, put them in a box, and call UPS, FedEx, or (even better these days) have the software downloaded directly from our site. In this case, almost all of that extra sales revenue will come down to our bottom line. When we report sales, two things will be true. First, sales will have basically doubled. Second, and more importantly, our profit margin should have gone up substantially. In fact, it probably went up much more than double. It might have gone up as much as a factor of five.

This is the type of company we want to find. A company that has profit leverage. That is, if sales accelerate, then profits accelerate even more.

I do not care what the PE ratio is. There are a lot of other measures to look at. Forget them all. I want you to find a company that has earnings growing much faster than sales. This is not hard to do. There are many companies that get into this situation. They are new companies or existing companies that have brought out new products. I do not care how they got there. What I care about is if their earnings are growing faster than their sales. If so, this is a company worth looking at.

Just because a company does not meet my criteria does not mean that it is not a good or worthy company with a great business, but if you want to be a big wave surfer, you need to go for growth and be aggressive. You will find this in a company that grows earnings faster than sales.

How can earnings grow faster than sales? In the software business, the cost of goods is about zero. Thus, such companies can meet this criterion. Even hardware companies can meet the criteria as they bring on new factories or more efficient processes. Even companies that do not have special cost factors going for them can sometimes grow earnings in an accelerated fashion. What if a company got a big order and to fulfill the order had to run its factory overtime? Such a company would possibly get itself into a situation where the overtime costs were less than the normal per-unit cost of its product because it did not actually add capacity, and thus had a profit margin increase. What if, for some reason, the cost of goods drops sharply, but the sales price does not drop significantly? Another possibility is that the company has implemented a new, more efficient process.

These are the types of companies that I like to look at.

The big question that you need to answer is, Are such earnings increases possible to continue into the future?

Margin Decreases

The type of company that I do not like is where margins are decreasing or have decreased. That is, I do not like companies whose earnings growth rate is less than the sales growth rate.

There are really two types of margin decreases: increasing overhead and price cutting.

Such companies have a fundamental problem. Whatever they are doing, they are not getting their earnings down to the bottom line and their profit margins are decreasing. I do not care what the problem is. I do not care what the management's explanation is. I do not like this type of company under any circumstances. It is on the road to a disaster. If the historical margins are decreasing or the unit costs to get the extra revenue of the sale are causing the financial issue, I do not care. I want out, and I want out now!

I am not implying that such a company cannot increase its stock price. If you are in a bull market, if some brokerage firm is pushing the stock, and if some guys get the right story out about new products or some big order coming in, even garbage can increase in price.

But I want out. I am married to my wife, not to any stock. Sell the stock and go home.

I have seen this again and again. I want out. As I noted, when you have rapid growth, you are not able to ramp up your fundamental services and, thus, can have a company where the profit increases faster than the revenue on a percentage basis. When you get a company that is having the opposite problem—the profit is increasing slower than the revenue, you have the beginning of margin problems. In such a case, you cannot get the overhead off fast enough and the profits can begin to decrease rapidly. Then you have to adjust the business, take charges for staff reductions, etc., and the company can go down very rapidly. I do not want to be in a position where this can happen. I do not want to get crushed.

Another situation that I dislike is when a company is growing rapidly but the product begins to have pricing pressures. Percentages are nonlinear and have many funny properties that people do not think about. Consider a rapidly growing company. Let's say it is growing revenues at a 50 percent annualized rate. Assume that its products are quite profitable and suddenly a competitor cuts its prices so that we are forced to introduce a new model that sells for half of the previous product's price, basically destroying our previous product. This is a disaster because we now must sell six times as many products to get our revenue increase. Let's do the math. Assume our product sells for $0.50 and we sell two products a year for a total revenue of one dollar. To keep up our growth rate, we need to sell $1.50 next year, or three products. But if the competition forces us to sell our product for $0.25, we now must sell six products to get that $1.50. This outcome is very improbable. The good news is that this will not happen instantly, and we should be able to spot the deterioration in margins.

Never ever buy a stock with deteriorating margins. We want to be on the big wave. We want the margins to be increasing. Deteriorating margins are a setup for the product(s) to go into the churn as the wave breaks on the beach.

Eternal Hope

I just gave you the first-order effect to screen your stock. Every value-oriented investor in the world just choked. Value investors have all kinds of stories about company turnarounds that will happen. They talk to management, and they seek out value. They believe they can find a stock that has a fundamentally undervalued characteristic because investors do not understand the stock.

I find this an interesting view. If the stock were really worth more than it is selling for on a per share basis, someone would buy the company and operate it as a business. Warren Buffet does just that. He buys companies he believes are good values in a business sense. But in general, a company sells for what it is worth.

What really changes that value is someone's perception of what change could be made to the company that would allow it to change its characteristics. In particular, is there something that can be done to correct its product mix or its overstaffing due to a change in the marketplace, etc.?

This is all fine and good, and there are successful value investors and turnaround stories that are the stuff of legends.

But I am lazy. Why would I want to risk my money trying to divine when a company will get its act together and get its products turned around?

It is easier to spot and profit from a new technology that is just entering the market and potentially will create a dominant market niche. Why do you want to play with a company that has acknowledged problems when there are hundreds of companies you can deal with that have a glowing future and are on the cutting edge of creating new products and innovations?

No matter how good I think I am at dissecting and understanding a business, I do not want to get involved in trying to decide when, if, or how a buggy whip manufacturer will begin to dominate its market. I want to find companies that are in new technology fields and are trying to ride that big wave. I want companies that are in positions of having the ability to create a new market and dominate that market for a number of years.

If we pick the right buggy whip manufacturer, we might get into position where we can make a nice percentage gain. I want to look for the next big wave that can create order of magnitude gains. Otherwise, if I am looking for those nice percentage gains, I have very little probability of beating the market and need to invest in a prudent fashion. Just buy the T-Bill. Why should you take risk?

The way to invest in technology is to understand that today's high-growth company is tomorrow's buggy whip manufacturer and constantly be looking for the next big wave. You need to understand that companies are not always breaking on the shore, and you need to do your homework and have patience. But the waves do come and you can identify and participate if you have patience.

In the sense that there will eventually be a new wave of technology, hope deserves to spring eternal.

Great Stocks

Stocks tend to be categorized into stock groups. These groups are amalgamations of stocks that are in similar areas. Yet, the stocks can have different characteristics. Some of the stocks can be well run. Others stocks might be unmitigated disasters. The conventional wisdom is that you should buy the best stock in a group that interests you. Some people call the stocks we want to invest in the best of breed.

Unfortunately, the environment is always changing and the best stock in a group may be at its apex and about to head into the tank.

The value of the best of breed is to find stock in a group of stocks that is really head and shoulders ahead of the rest of the stocks in the group in terms of growth and management.

Then, if you can identify the stock before others figure out that it is the best of breed, you can get a substantial advantage in terms of investment return.

Generally, you want to look for stocks that have the best new products and see if they are gaining acceptance. If you can find a stock or company with a superior product, you can figure that managers and salespeople will also find that company, and superior people will try to jump on board so that they can profit from the growth of the company. That is what you are looking for. We are looking for great products that generate a high rate of sales growth so that the company will grow rapidly.

If a new product category emerges, you want to see what companies can get traction. The company that gets traction with a completely new category of product may not be the company with the best product, but the company with the best marketing. Once the product category gets established, you will start to see the separation that provides you a view of the best of breed. You should assume that any company that becomes best of breed in a stock sector or in a product category will soon have competition. The investment community and the management of other companies are prone to follow success. Most people are not very innovative and like to jump on the trend. To be successful as an investor, it is incumbent on you to find the trend first.

If you are invested in a high-growth, best-of-breed company, you need to know that the party will not last. The more successful the company, the more competition will develop.

Eventually, another new product will crop up and your company will have to either move forward rapidly or no longer be the best of breed. Further, you cannot assume that companies stay in the area where they seem most competent. The iPhone is a classic example. Apple was not a phone company, and then one day it was, at least partially, a phone company.

Big brokerage houses and investment banks are constantly on the lookout for new technology that can create the next best-of-breed company in any category. There is an ocean of money chasing after what technology will end up being the next big thing. But like a big wave surfing event, it is difficult to figure out which wave will be the biggest and get aboard the wave in a timely fashion. Best-of-breed analysis is one way to get a handle on what may be the next big thing.

Bullshit Embellishment

One of the big issues when considering an investment is the bullshit factor. Everyone has the same story. They have the best widget. Their marketing strategy is the best. The marketing and sales department is incomparable and experienced.

There is no really good way to sort this out. How do you figure it out? One indicator is how well the people have done in the past. Another indicator is their current results and what the future looks like.

Baseball gives us a clue to cutting to the chase. When looking for a new manager to replace a fired or retiring manager, the choice tends to be a previous manager regardless of why that manager is currently unemployed. The theory is that any manager with experience and any reasonable previous results is better than any guy without experience. The problem with the technology business is that the previous experience may not be relevant. The experience might be outdated, and we need to figure out if the person actually learned anything in the previous position. In baseball, it is really more motivational than science. In technology, it is all about science. Just because the people you are dealing with are smooth and have a great presentation skill level does not mean that the company will actually be able to succeed. One of the most skilled engineers that I knew was a project leader. He was great as an engineer. He was great as a project manager, but when faced with actually having to deal with a customer, he folded.

He had the gift of gab around people he was familiar with, but when faced with people he didn't know and surroundings that weren't familiar, he folded because he was unable to face any form of conflict or rejection of his ideas. He could dazzle internally but was a complete external dud. A person's capabilities may not travel well.

Current results are another measure to see if you are dealing with charlatans trying to dazzle you or if the people and results are real. But no level of due diligence will ever detect fraud. How do you know if the results are real? You can check into a firm or a person's results as much as you want, but fundamentally you need a means of verifying results that is fool proof. There is no real way to do this. However, if the results seem too good, you are probably being dazzled. Very few people have a success rate above average over an extended period of time.

One trick I used when travelling around checking on companies I had invested in was to drive by their parking lots and count cars. Generally, the company would not want to hire extra staff to fill up the parking lot just to fool investors.

However, I knew a company that had well above normal revenue rates per employee. Knowing that the potential investors would not like seeing a very small company, when the investors came to visit, the company staffed up its facility with temporary employees so that it could look bigger than it actually was.

This form of gamesmanship pales in comparison to Ponzi schemes, but it may be just a small step away from bigger problems, as you have now set an expectation that is difficult to continue.

Presentation Sophistication

There are many investors who have no clue about their investments. That being said, they all like to look smart. One way they may compensate for their lack of knowledge is to employ knowledgeable money managers and technical staff.

The strategy is to have these professionals do the due diligence and run the investments. However, it is difficult to sort out reality in an investment pitch because the presenters will have made the pitch numerous times and have the advantage of knowing the facts.

At points, they may fall back onto, "We can't talk about that because it is proprietary." This may be true, but that means you cannot figure out reality.

Another area that is difficult to sort out, because it does not reveal flaws, is the demonstration. All demonstrations are carefully scripted.

A further issue is trying to sort out customer testimonials. The problem is that early customers who are very satisfied may not know they are receiving special treatment, so they have no way of telling you what the realities of the product are.

You would do well to make sure that your understanding of a possible investment tries to cover all bases of due diligence, but in the end, the only thing that counts is the result. Do not be fooled by slick presentations and fancy marketing strategies.

Overhead Shedding

One of the most curious problems that I have ever encountered or observed is the issue of corporate overhead. In the category of overhead, we will lump all costs that are not direct or material costs.

Consider the cost of the labor to put a product together in a factory. That is a direct cost. The costs of the materials that go into the product are also direct costs. Other costs such as marketing and sales costs as well as supervision of the labor costs are considered indirect costs. Indirect costs really consist of two components generally known as overhead and G&A costs. An example of an overhead cost is the cost of health care premiums. A typical G&A cost is sales commissions.

For our purposes, it will be enough to simply classify costs as direct or indirect. There is a third part of a corporate cost pool, and that is profit. In a simple model, the difference between sales income and the direct and indirect costs is profit.

Whether we view indirect costs as a percentage of direct costs or an absolute value, we know they are real.

Two interesting conundrums occur in the corporate world. One is extremes of optimism, and the other is an underestimation of the lag in terms of the effect of any actions that you take.

People seem to be pretty optimistic. My experience has been that the majority of people are more optimistic than pessimistic. Let's look at the effect of this optimism. If you are running a company, you need to build a sales forecast. This is done by periodically pulsing the sales force to get their input as to how much product we will sell this quarter or month and how much the plant will need to manufacture. Because most managers know that these forecasts are optimistic, they then apply a percentage factor to the forecast to normalize it based on their experience in the marketplace. In many cases, the salespeople may provide a factored sales forecast to the management. Based on this forecast, we set the budgets. The result was a disaster, as the salespeople's projections were completely wrong and our budgets were not close to reality.

You must be very careful in looking at and believing sales projections because by the time you figure out that the projections are wrong, you have no margin to get the overhead down to keep your profits up.

Quarter End

In the technology business, due to order-rate slow-downs that happened during the 1960s through the 1990s, the customers and buyers became very savvy about how to get the best bargains. In the early 1980s, the economy was so bad that Intel and other companies started shutting down their companies toward the end of the year to conserve cash. This presented an interesting problem for their suppliers because the accounts payable departments were shut down for up to two weeks and no money flowed in during that time period.

If you are inside the sales force of a high-growth technology company, you would find that generally the sales come in at the end of a quarter. In many cases, the majority of sales will occur in the last week of the quarter and the sales force will be trying to meet their street guidance if they are public. If the company is private and it is funded by venture capital, the management has unbelievable pressures to meet specific goals at the end of each quarter. In a private company, the very existence of the management will be at stake each and every quarter; whereas in a public company, you may have a couple of quarters to work out your kinks.

Customers know there are real pressures on the company at the end of the quarter, and they will try to take advantage of the sales department. The number of companies I have seen that make their sales goals at 4:30 p.m. on the last day of the quarter is astounding! The customers will wait until the last day and the last minute to commit to see how much the supplier will cut its price.

You will not believe the number of deals that will go off at an 80 percent to 85 percent markdown just so the company can make its quarter.

If you are the customer, you want to hold off to buy. If you can hold off until the last minute of the last day of the last quarter of the company's fiscal year, you can get some real bargains. Periodically, some management misses its numbers and the investment community cannot figure out how it missed. How come the investment community was not warned? The management did not know it had missed until the quarter was over because it wasn't until the last minute that the critical order failed to come in.

In general, the responsibility of the company is to warn when it has bad news, but it will not know if it has bad news until after the quarter is over. The company has no responsibility to reveal positive information as soon as it is known. But the stock price charts and the action of the stock will let you know if the company is likely to miss. A miss will kill the company's stock if it was a fast grower with a lot of expectations. The company will be dead money for a long time, and the management, if they are smart, will throw in the towel in terms of write-offs. A really smart management will throw in the kitchen sink, the toilet, and every paper clip that no longer functions to clean up current and future problems. If a stock misses, bottom fishing is counter-productive because the company has a serious problem. If the stock hits a new thirteen-week high after a disaster, you might consider it a potential investment. But only as a small-scale position until the stock proves itself as a profitable venture.

Dilution Effect

Dilution is one of the big secrets of the investing world. It is really a dirty little secret and strategy. It is the type of strategy that unless you have been through the drill, you would not really understand the potential effect.

Consider getting funding for your new enterprise. You have one of the greatest ideas of all time, and you know that it is an idea worthy of catching a big wave and you will soon be rich.

To fund the idea, you must get some capital. To help in this search, you have prepared a beautiful business plan. You have compiled all of the income and profit predictions. You know how the product will come to market. You are prepared for the great success that you will create, and everything is a go. You just need that little bit of funding to kick off the great surfing adventure.

Now all we have to do is get agreement with our selected set of venture investors so that we are on track.

There are a small set of problems that we now need to face and solve. First, we need to get a commitment from venture funds. This will be an unpleasant experience because they have difficulty making such decisions and we could starve before we actually get their decisions. But let's assume that we get past that point and we are now in the process of signing our papers.

The next hurdle we need to get past is the fact that to actually get the money, we need to give up at least 51 percent of the company. Now this is a little shock because we believe that we created a lot of value and deserve better. However, the venture people have a whole spiel that explains how and why they bring value and the very fact that they invest in us will create such a huge windfall and increase in our value that we are finally convinced that we should go ahead with the paperwork and close in on a deal.

Further, assume that we have gotten past the point where we have also ceded control of the board of directors to the venture capitalists.

Now there is actually a small clause in the contract for the money that should give you a huge pause. This is the dilution statement. This clause in the contract says that if we have to raise more money at an unattractive valuation, the venture capitalists' percentage position is not diluted. This means that if you have to raise more capital, then all of the dilution will fall on your shoulders. You will essentially be wiped out. The venture guys will keep their percentage, and the new money will come in at their agreed-upon percentage, and the founders and management team will be wiped out.

Everyone will say this is a standard clause. It is. Further, unless you agree to this clause, you will not get the deal done. However, this clause is the clause that wipes you out if and when you fail to meet any of the goals and milestones you have agreed upon.

Because the basic nature of human beings is to be optimistic, you probably set up your own demise. You built a business plan that is aggressive and optimistic. When negotiating with the money guys, you may have even priced the situation to perfection. If you miss and you have to go back to the money well, your shareholders who control the company are venture guys and they can make any deal for the new money that they want. Further, they are protected in any future deal and you take all of the dilution. But you say that you could not have gotten the money unless you had such an aggressive plan. You are correct, but you need to understand the ramifications.

If you have to go back to get any more money, you are wiped out, just like if you take a fall on the slope of a big wave.

Stock Strategy

Earlier in this chapter, I suggested that you could beat the professional investor and suggested that you run a concentrated portfolio. Why would I suggest that you do such a crazy thing? If you are or want to be a big wave surfer, but do not know how to do it in the marketing, product development, or company formation business, you can still do it in the stock market. But does it work? Yes, it really does work, and in this section, I will show you how to control the risks associated with this strategy and how to find the list of stocks to consider. Further, I will introduce you to a person who is probably the best at running such a strategy. Finally, I will tell you some results that support such an approach.

The basic strategy previously outlined is not crazy!

One way to play the game of finances is to just get a job and diversify your assets into a savings plan such as a 401(k) or IRA and let time work the problem for you. Conventional wisdom is to take that approach. I would not disagree that such an approach coupled with an asset allocation plan will probably get you a nice account value without a lot of heartache and effort.

But if you can build a substantial portfolio early in your life, your life may be a lot less stressful, more rewarding, and pleasurable. It is no surprise that a lot of people on Wall Street who are bringing down big bucks are young. If you adopt this strategy, you may need a stomach made of titanium to execute it, and the younger you are, the more you may be suited to stand the pressure and the risks associated with the strategy.

Previously, I have tried to shock you. I need you to think out-side the box because we are about to discuss concepts that are for-eign to the basic investment philosophy that is taught everywhere.

Concept one is that diversification is the bane of all portfolio success. Oh yeah! Asset classes are correlated or noncorrelated, and if you build a set of noncorrelated asset classes and diversify across them, you will get some smooth long-term return. There are three reasons you would take such a strategy. The first is that you have a large amount of money and diversification makes sense. The second is that you are bound to invest under the rules of the prudent man and need to build a diverse portfolio. The third, and most impor-tant, reason is that you cannot afford to be wrong. In reality, you do not know how to be right! You should go and collect some statistics. For the last ten years, how many stocks over $15 on the New York Stock Exchange or Nasdaq have doubled in each quarter? Make yourself a simple chart. You would be surprised at the number that doubled. In some years, the pickings may be slim, but I bet you are surprised at the numbers. One of my friends owned at least one stock on that list each quarter. Now he may not have gotten the full double for each quarter, but the feat of picking those stocks contin-ues as a classic effort on his part. Pick your stocks carefully, and you do not need to pick a lot of stocks or trade a lot.

Because of order-flow issues, I do not want to be a day trader. Even with the low commissions of discount brokers, I do not want to try to outsmart the professional and the computers. I want to build a big position in a stock and control my risk so as not to lose my gains.

Concept two is that because we are small we are nimble, and any trade that we make does not even cause a ripple in the world. Our trading is about as visible as a pimple on the ass of an ant. So we are seeking to be in a highly liquid market. Stay with stocks that have a certain volume. In particular, if a stock trades 300,000 shares a day, we will not want to own more than about 30,000 shares. When you are right, you need to get concentrated. Get long and get strong!

Concept three is correctness. I want to be right! However, I am seldom right. In my life, I have never made a good trade, and a near perfect or perfect trade is not in the cards.

It is impossible to buy a stock at the bottom and sell it at the top for any given period of time. Scale in and scale out. Get long and strong. Concentrate. You must manage your risk. When you are right, go to margin. Keep your stops close.

Because we are considering entering into a high-risk investment that we want to pay off in a very big fashion, we will eventually have to commit a lot of capital, at least in the sense of a lot of our investable capital. This means that we need to be aware of the cockroach theory. Whenever we see one cockroach, there is probably a bunch of cockroaches.

You cannot ignore this theory. Ignoring it is like getting into the water with sharks. Corollary to this theory is the idea that if it seems too good to be true, then it probably is. There are other variations on this theme, but the bottom line is that you do not make a lot of money by minimizing risk. When you try to make a lot of money in a short period of time, you are going to increase your risks by a large factor and you need to be aware of that fact and act accordingly. When a bad event occurs, you need to be prepared to take action and take it quickly. You have no time for indecision.

Dan Zanger (www.chartpattern.com) is a super big wave surfer investor. In eighteen months, Zanger turned $10,775 into $18 million. At one point in the early 2000s, he had a $42 million portfolio. His path to success was stock selection, technology stocks, and concentration of assets. This is the best documented result that I know of on an individual basis. And Dan's previous occupation was as a swimming pool contractor, so even if he was not well schooled in technology waves, he at least understood water.

Churn Entry

We are close to running out the wave. We must avoid entering the churn. If we get to an IPO, we have limited time left for exponential growth. But, we can still grow rapidly. Young, recently public companies have an opportunity to maintain high growth rates. We need to look for such companies as investments.

You can surf as an investor! The key strategy is to understand and manage your risks.

For over forty years, I have tried to make companies or products grow rapidly in technology businesses. The field I picked for a career has some of the worst business characteristics of any industry in history! The computer business has a very short technology half life. It has a pricing model that makes the airline industry look like it is filled with knowledgeable businessmen. In the computer industry, prices are continually falling. The product capabilities and quality increase dramatically. Yet, it is the most exciting and dynamic industry in the world.

You must embrace disruption. Disruption is a constant and will occur no matter what you desire. You cannot make a thirty- or forty-year career plan and expect to execute it. Change will occur! You must reinvent yourself. Management teams must reinvent their companies. The United States must reinvent its economy. Innovation is the key. Innovation allows you to reinvent yourself and your company. Leaders must incentivize industry to create disruption and its attendant innovative big waves.

I seek disruption. I advocate embracing disruption at the individual level. You can survive over an extended career. Companies and the United States should seek disruption as a way to encourage innovation. As manufacturing jobs flow to centers of low-cost labor, we will not employ large numbers of manufacturing workers! If goods flow to people who have money to consume, we can expect to import too many products. In this scenario, we will continually run a negative trade balance! The way to change the scenario is to shift to an economy (both personally and nationally) that is based on innovation. The key to innovation is creating big waves from technology disruption. Not everyone can be the creative person behind a technology disruption, but we need to create an environment where disruption and its attendant innovation are embraced and encouraged. We need to train and encourage big wave surfers. Big wave surfers must drive our economy!

Chapter Summary

This chapter provides an unconventional investment strategy that is designed to maximize your return. The strategy will dramatically raise your risk profile. If you can control your risks, it will provide outsized returns!

Today is a beautiful, sunny day. Somewhere, the waves are breaking on a beach. I encourage you to seek the beach where disruption has pushed the big waves. Good luck in your endeavors! Surf's up!

Index